A Very British Family

For Dad, with love

A VERY BRITISH FAMILY

The Trevelyans and Their World

Laura Trevelyan

BLOOMSBURY ACADEMIC
LONDON · NEW YORK · OXFORD · NEW DELHI · SYDNEY

BLOOMSBURY ACADEMIC
Bloomsbury Publishing Plc
50 Bedford Square, London, WC1B 3DP, UK
1385 Broadway, New York, NY 10018, USA

BLOOMSBURY, BLOOMSBURY ACADEMIC and the Diana logo
are trademarks of Bloomsbury Publishing Plc

First published in Great Britain by I.B. Tauris 2006
Paperback edition first published in Great Britain by I.B. Tauris 2012
Reprinted 2013, 2014, 2016, 2017
This edition published by Bloomsbury Academic 2019

A catalogue record for this book is available from the British Library.

A catalog record for this book is available from the Library of Congress.

ISBN: HB: 978-1-8606-4946-2
PB: 978-1-3501-5453-7
eISBN: 978-0-8577-3363-4
ePDF: 978-0-8577-2449-6

Typeset in New Baskerville by Dexter Haven Associates Ltd, London

To find out more about our authors and books visit
www.bloomsbury.com and sign up for our newsletters.

CONTENTS

LIST OF ILLUSTRATIONS

ACKNOWLEDGEMENTS

My profound thanks go to Elaine Thomas of the BBC, who is really the fairy godmother of this book. It was Elaine's idea for me to present a radio programme on the Trevelyans for the BBC World Service, a broadcast heard by Iradj Bagherzhade of I.B. Tauris, who thought it would translate into a good book. My thanks and apologies go to Iradj – sincere thanks for the opportunity, and many apologies for saying I was a journalist used to deadlines who could write the thing in six months. It actually took three and a half years, as babies, elections, and a move to New York intervened. I owe a debt of gratitude to my father, George, who has been unfailingly helpful and supportive throughout. My uncle Tom Trevelyan and my aunt Harriet Trevelyan have been generous with their recollections, as were Sir Geoffrey Trevelyan and his sister Patricia. Raleigh Trevelyan's books on the family proved invaluable, as was his initial guidance. Martin Bulmer has been endlessly encouraging, and provided much material for the chapter on his father, Charles Philips. My thanks go to David Cannadine for his insight and advice, and to Claire Tomalin who helpfully suggested extra reading. The staff of the Special Collections department of Newcastle University, keepers of the Trevelyan papers, have been patient and knowledgeable, and met my many requests for photocopies with equanimity. I am sorry that Lesley Gordon, former head of the department, did not live to see the book's publication. My cousin Robin Dower's tactful assistance has been much appreciated, as has the input of the trustees of the Trevelyan papers. Lester Crook and Liz Friend-Smith at I.B. Tauris have been patient and enthusiastic, while Gretchen Ladish at Dexter Haven has been cheerful and eagle-eyed.

For my husband and our children, a special thank you for bearing with me. Finally, to Sandra Doyle, our nanny, heartfelt thanks for keeping the boys occupied while I wrote.

THE TREVELYAN FAMILY

Owners of Wallington
are in CAPITALS

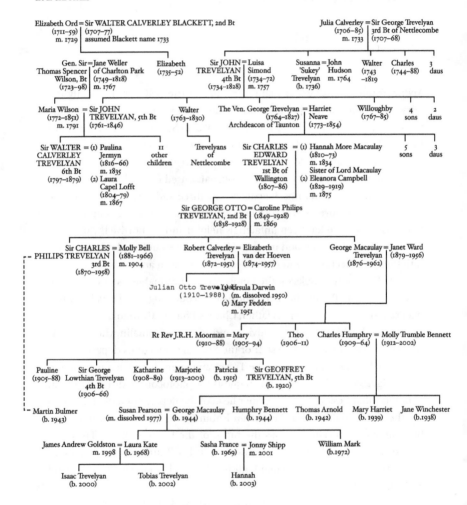

Elizabeth Ord = Sir WALTER CALVERLEY BLACKETT, 2nd Bt
(1711–59) (1707–77)
m. 1729 assumed Blackett name 1733

Julia Calverley = Sir George Trevelyan
(1706–85) 3rd Bt of Nettlecombe
m. 1733 (1707–68)

Gen. Sir = Jane Weller
Thomas Spencer | of Charlton Park
Wilson, Bt | (1749–1818)
(1723–98) | m. 1767

Elizabeth
(1735–52)

Sir JOHN = Luisa
TREVELYAN | Simond
4th Bt | (1734–72)
(1734–1828) | m. 1757

Susanna = John
'Sukey' | Hudson
Trevelyan | m. 1764
(b. 1736)

Walter
(1743
–1819)

Charles
(1744–88)

3
daus

Maria Wilson = Sir JOHN
(1772–1851) | TREVELYAN, 5th Bt
m. 1791 | (1761–1846)

Walter
(1763–1830)

The Ven. George Trevelyan = Harriet
Archdeacon of Taunton | Neave
(1764–1827) | (1773–1854)

Willoughby
(1767–85)

4
sons

2
daus

Sir WALTER = (1) Paulina
CALVERLEY | Jermyn
TREVELYAN | (1816–66)
6th Bt | m. 1835
(1797–1879) | (2) Laura
| Capel Lofft
| (1804–79)
| m. 1867

11
other
children

Trevelyans
of
Nettlecombe

Sir CHARLES = (1) Hannah More Macaulay
EDWARD | (1810–73)
TREVELYAN | m. 1834
1st Bt of | Sister of Lord Macaulay
Wallington | (2) Eleanora Campbell
(1807–86) | (1829–1919)
| m. 1875

5
sons

3
daus

Sir GEORGE OTTO = Caroline Philips
TREVELYAN, 2nd Bt | (1849–1928)
(1838–1928) | m. 1869

Sir CHARLES = Molly Bell
PHILIPS TREVELYAN | (1881–1966)
3rd Bt | m. 1904
(1870–1958)

Robert Calverley = Elizabeth
Trevelyan | van der Hoeven
(1872–1951) | (1874–1957)

George Macaulay = Janet Ward
Trevelyan | (1879–1956)
(1876–1962)

Julian Otto Trevelyan (1) Ursula Darwin
(1910–1988) (m. dissolved 1950)
(2) Mary Fedden
m. 1951

Rt Rev J.R.H. Moorman = Mary
(1910–88) | (1905–94)

Theo
(1906–11)

Charles Humphry = Molly Trumble Bennett
(1909–64) | (1912–2002)

Pauline
(1905–88)

Sir George
Lowthian Trevelyan
4th Bt
(1906–66)

Katharine
(1908–89)

Marjorie
(1913–2003)

Patricia
(b. 1915)

Sir GEOFFREY
TREVELYAN, 5th Bt
(b. 1920)

Martin Bulmer
(b. 1943)

Susan Pearson = George Macaulay
(m. dissolved 1977) | (b. 1944)

Humphry Bennett
(b. 1944)

Thomas Arnold
(b. 1942)

Mary Harriet
(b. 1939)

Jane Winchester
(b. 1938)

James Andrew Goldston = Laura Kate
m. 1998 | (b. 1968)

Sasha France = Jonny Shipp
(b. 1969) | m. 2001

William Mark
(b. 1972)

Isaac Trevelyan
(b. 2000)

Tobias Trevelyan
(b. 2002)

Hannah
(b. 2003)

THE TREVELYAN FAMILY

Owners of Wallington
are in CAPITALS

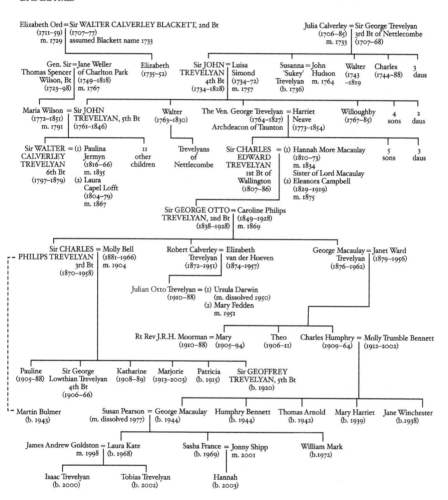

Elizabeth Ord = Sir WALTER CALVERLEY BLACKETT, 2nd Bt
(1711–59) (1707–77)
m. 1729 | assumed Blackett name 1733

Julia Calverley = Sir George Trevelyan
(1706–85) | 3rd Bt of Nettlecombe
m. 1733 | (1707–68)

Gen. Sir = Jane Weller
Thomas Spencer | of Charlton Park
Wilson, Bt | (1749–1818)
(1723–98) | m. 1767

Elizabeth
(1735–52)

Sir JOHN = Luisa
TREVELYAN | Simond
4th Bt | (1734–72)
(1734–1828) | m. 1757

Susanna = John
'Sukey' | Hudson
Trevelyan | m. 1764
(b. 1736)

Walter
(1743
–1819)

Charles
(1744–88)

3
daus

Maria Wilson = Sir JOHN
(1772–1851) | TREVELYAN, 5th Bt
m. 1791 | (1761–1846)

Walter
(1763–1830)

The Ven. George Trevelyan = Harriet
(1764–1827) | Neave
Archdeacon of Taunton | (1773–1854)

Willoughby
(1767–85)

4
sons

2
daus

Sir WALTER = (1) Paulina
CALVERLEY | Jermyn
TREVELYAN | (1816–66)
6th Bt | m. 1835
(1797–1879) | (2) Laura
Capel Lofft
(1804–79)
m. 1867

11
other
children

Trevelyans
of
Nettlecombe

Sir CHARLES = (1) Hannah More Macaulay
EDWARD | (1810–73)
TREVELYAN | m. 1834
1st Bt of | Sister of Lord Macaulay
Wallington | (2) Eleanora Campbell
(1807–86) | (1829–1919)
m. 1875

5
sons

3
daus

Sir GEORGE OTTO = Caroline Philips
TREVELYAN, 2nd Bt | (1849–1928)
(1838–1928) | m. 1869

Sir CHARLES = Molly Bell
PHILIPS TREVELYAN | (1881–1966)
3rd Bt | m. 1904
(1870–1958)

Robert Calverley = Elizabeth
Trevelyan | van der Hoeven
(1872–1951) | (1874–1957)

George Macaulay = Janet Ward
Trevelyan | (1879–1956)
(1876–1962)

Julian Otto Trevelyan = (1) Ursula Darwin
(1910–88) | (m. dissolved 1950)
(2) Mary Fedden
m. 1951

Rt Rev J.R.H. Moorman = Mary
(1910–88) | (1905–94)

Theo
(1906–11)

Charles Humphry = Molly Trumble Bennett
(1909–64) | (1912–2002)

Pauline
(1905–88)

Sir George
Lowthian Trevelyan
4th Bt
(1906–66)

Katharine
(1908–89)

Marjorie
(1913–2003)

Patricia
(b. 1915)

Sir GEOFFREY
TREVELYAN, 5th Bt
(b. 1920)

Martin Bulmer
(b. 1943)

Susan Pearson = George Macaulay
(m. dissolved 1977) | (b. 1944)

Humphry Bennett
(b. 1944)

Thomas Arnold
(b. 1942)

Mary Harriet
(b. 1939)

Jane Winchester
(b.1938)

James Andrew Goldston = Laura Kate
m. 1998 | (b. 1968)

Sasha France = Jonny Shipp
(b. 1969) | m. 2001

William Mark
(b.1972)

Isaac Trevelyan
(b. 2000)

Tobias Trevelyan
(b. 2002)

Hannah
(b. 2003)

INTRODUCTION

This is a book about my ancestors, the Trevelyan family, and the part they played in shaping the story of our nation. Some Trevelyans were famous and distinguished, others were also-rans, but for a hundred years family members from Lord Macaulay to G.M. Trevelyan contributed to both the writing and the making of our history. The Trevelyans were leading members of the intellectual aristocracy that influenced British public and cultural life from the mid-nineteenth century to the mid-twentieth. Privileged, wealthy, well-connected and motivated by a sense of civic duty, successive Trevelyans were public servants, politicians and distinguished historians, serving and chronicling in the age of Empire and beyond. In an era when Britain was a superpower, Trevelyans were at the centre of scholarship and politics.

Often eccentric, priggish, high-minded and utterly self-regarding, three generations of Trevelyans have nonetheless left their mark on our past. The family had a ringside seat in public life, at a time of enormous social and political change. This ancient lot could have simply exploited their position as landed gentry, enjoying the patronage their acres and money afforded them, yet instead, reflecting a radical tradition of their age, they became 'plain living and high thinking'. A.L. Rowse once summed up the family by ascribing these values to Trevelyans:

> Integrity to the point of eccentricity, honesty to the point of rudeness, tactless and rough handed but of an indubitably aristocratic distinction, devoted public spirit with an equal ability to carry it into action; a marked idiosyncrasy held in check by strong common sense; not much sense of humour. That distinguished family were apt to think there were Trevelyans – and then the rest of the human race.

Leonard Woolf, husband of Virginia, observed that the Trevelyans belonged to 'a class of society, an era of history, a world which has ceased to exist and can never return'.[1] That class, as Leonard Woolf was well placed to record, had its faults and absurdities but also much that was admirable, from the liberal tradition of public service to a belief in political principles and social obligations. Leonard Woolf found some of the Trevelyans he encountered faintly ridiculous, with their self-absorption and quite unconscious acceptance of their place in the governing classes. Yet he also found the family's zest, energy and passionate interest in history and politics quite bewitching. As did Michael Foot, the former Labour Party leader, who said: 'I can't think what my life would have been without the Trevelyans because the proper teaching of history, I think, is the most important question in the world. How else are we going to tell a new generation how we got here, and how we can deal with the world today?'[2]

My starting point will be the civil servant Charles Edward Trevelyan. This talented and obstinate man was responsible, along with Lord Northcote, for introducing competitive entry into the civil service during the Victorian age. Notoriously, he was also in charge of providing famine relief to Ireland. He has been demonised as a heartless providentialist who believed the Irish were responsible for their own demise. More charitably, he has been depicted as a product of his age and background, a nineteenth-century economic liberal with a laissez-faire approach. My intention is not to resolve this long-running argument, but to paint a picture of an important if flawed man.

Sir Charles inherited the family seat of Wallington in Northumberland, twenty miles from Newcastle. The imposing stately home stands alone in open country, before the moors and the sheep runs that sweep up the Scottish Border. Just beyond is Battle Hill, the site of Chevy Chase, where Hotspur and Douglas fought, the subject of one of the oldest Border ballards. Wallington, which gave Trevelyans the status of squires as well as intellectuals, is now owned by the National Trust. It is the setting for much of this book.

Sir Charles Edward married Hannah More Macaulay, sister of the historian Lord Macaulay, author of *A History of England*. That marriage produced one of the social networks so common in literary and scholarly circles at that time. Lord Macaulay was a regular visitor at the Clapham home of the Trevelyans, and a great influence on the elder son of Charles and Hannah, George Otto Trevelyan. There is a family joke that all history is relative – George Otto, to the delight of his distinguished uncle, became a historian of note as well as a Cabinet minister under Gladstone. This rather retiring figure, happiest when translating ancient Greek in his Wallington study, was hailed as a scholar and a statesman by the obituarists of the time.

George Otto and his wife Caroline, Lady Trevelyan, had three sons, Charles, Robert and George, a trio so close-knit that an acquaintance meeting the brothers at a party remarked, 'Are they a sect, these Trevelyans, like the Wesleyans?'[3]

That observer was not far off the mark. This particular generation of Trevelyans was imbued with a sense of its own history and significance. Leonard Woolf knew all three brothers, and found them 'tremendously English; in each one saw a family likeness to the other two and all had an immense energy and vitality of mind and body. Charles was very good looking, but Bob and George were physically large, craggy, looming, with a curious clumsiness of bod…Wobble was the one thing not tolerated by the Trevelyan brothers.'[4]

Leonard's wife Virginia was less tolerant of the brothers and their reverence for dead relatives. She poked fun at her fictional equivalent, the super-smug Alardyces. 'One finds them at the top of their professions, with letters after their name; they sit in luxurious public offices, with private secretaries attached to them; they write solid books, in dark covers, issued by the presses of the two great universities; and when one of them dies, the chances are that another of them writes his biography.'[5]

Charles Philips, the oldest brother, became a Labour politician and activist on the radical left. Robert was a poet and man of letters, a friend of E.M. Forster. The most famous of all was George Macaulay Trevelyan, the acclaimed historian whose engaging narrative sweep produced best-selling books still read to this day. In his writings and his civic-minded interventions, he was consciously echoing his forefathers, as observers more sympathetic than Virginia Woolf noted. 'All three generations have maintained that characteristic tradition of some of the greatest English writers – Chaucer, Bacon, Milton, Addison, Gibbon, to name only a few – who seem to have written all the better for being also public-spirited citizens and men of affairs.'[6]

With a reforming grandfather, Charles Edward, a historian for a great uncle, and a father, George Otto, who was both politician and historian, the three sons knew much was expected of them. G.M. offered his brother Charles Philips this code of conduct for the family. 'It is a rule that no Trevelyan ever sucks up either to the press, or the chiefs, or the "right people". The world has given us money enough to enable us to do what we think is right. We thank it for that and ask no more of it, but to be allowed to serve it.'[7]

There is a saying in the world of business that families who have made a fortune go from clogs to clogs in three generations. So it was with the

Trevelyans, whose chief currency was not money but intellectual clout backed up by a collection of stately homes. While there are still interesting and talented individual members of the family, that collective sense of achievement and status has gone, replaced by a vague aura of belonging to a once great dynasty. The times changed after the Second World War and so did the Trevelyans. The lofty, patrician intellectuals-cum-statesmen lost their money and their status and became members of the ordinary middle classes. This hasty re-entry into the world of mortals is best told by the story of my grandfather Humphry, son of G.M. Trevelyan.

Were he a member of any other family, Humphry would have done more than just pass muster. A German scholar and fellow of King's College, Cambridge, Humphry was recruited to work at Bletchley Park during the Second World War. There he translated the intercepted German messages cracked by the team who deciphered the famous Enigma code. Yet Humphry and his sister Mary lived in the shadow of their brilliant brother Theo, who died of appendicitis aged four. Mary went on to become a Wordsworth scholar of note. But nothing either Mary or Humphry achieved could match the lost promise of Theo, who, according to family legend, could recite Horatius not long after he could walk.

This book is primarily the tale of five men: Charles Edward, George Otto, Charles Philips, George Macaulay and Humphry Trevelyan. But it is also the story of the clever and formidable women they married, wives who in another age would have been high achievers in their own right. Charles Edward married Hannah Macaulay, the talented daughter of the anti-slavery campaigner Zachary Macaulay. George Otto's wife Caroline Philips had a political mind just as astute as her Cabinet minister husband's. Mary Bell longed to share Charles Philips's political career, and campaigned tirelessly for the Labour cause until her husband made it clear that that was his domain. Janet Ward was a writer and social campaigner, eclipsed by the shooting star that was her husband, George Macaulay Trevelyan. And Molly Bennett, the American wife of Humphry, was a meticulous and energetic correspondent, whose descriptive letters bring to life the mood of wartime Britain.

This book has its origins in a desire to overcome my own ignorance. As a BBC correspondent, I am always being asked by interested observers where I fit into the Trevelyan family. To my shame, I have not always been able to answer such questions in a convincing manner. In Northern Ireland, a place ever conscious of its own past, my lack of knowledge about the role of Charles Edward Trevelyan, my great-great-great-grandfather, in the Irish famine was only too apparent. As a 10-year-old, asked by an interested history teacher if I had ever galloped over the moors at Wallington, my only response was a blank one. So this is partly a personal journey through my family history, but it should be more than just a self-indulgent memoir of dim and distant relatives. I hope it can provide the reader with a genuine insight into the life and times of a family who helped shape and chronicle our history.

The Trevelyan dynasty at the end of the First World War. Photographed to mark the golden wedding of Sir George Trevelyan and his wife Caroline, Lady Trevelyan, 1919. Back row l-r – Robert Trevelyan and his wife Bessie, George Macaulay Trevelyan and his wife Janet, Molly Trevelyan and her husband Charles Philips. Middle row – Sir George Otto Trevelyan, Marjorie Trevelyan, Patricia Trevelyan and Caroline, Lady Trevelyan. Front row – the Trevelyan cousins – Mary, Kitty, Humphry, Julian, George Lowthian and Pauline.

I

A SHORT FAMILY HISTORY

The Trevelyan family's beginnings were inauspicious enough. A few miles above Fowey in Cornwall, in the parish of St Veep, there stood for many years a watermill. The ancient Celts called the spot Trevelyan, meaning 'the place of the mill', or so G.M. Trevelyan fancied. Others believe the more accurate gist of Trevelyan is Land of Milion, after the Celt who must once have lived there. Either way, the dwelling made it into the Domesday Book, which recorded that the farm had enough land for two ploughs – more than sufficient to scratch a living in the eleventh century. By the reign of Henry III, the farm was in the hands of people who took their name from it. And so the Trevelyans were at first Cornish farmers. Indeed, the correct but little-observed Cornish pronunciation of the name is 'Trevilian'. The journey from the wilds of the west of Cornwall to Whitehall and beyond took the family a leisurely seven hundred years. Land was acquired by a series of good marriages, but it was not until the high Victorian age, with its emphasis on work, duty and progress, that the Trevelyans became a significant force. Before then they just ambled along. A.N. Wilson has described the Victorian era as

> the period of the most radical transformation ever seen by the world. Before major industrialisation was confined to a few towns in Britain. After, the whole world was covered with railways and factories … Before them, the world was a small world of nation states … After them, the 'Dark Continent' had been penetrated by European powers: the destiny of Africa had changed; India … had become the linchpin of a huge British Empire.[1]

This new world, with its myriad possibilities, gave the Trevelyans the chance to come of age.

Despite the fact that the family made little impact before the nineteenth century, later Trevelyans were encouraged to believe that their own history went back almost as far as the history of the country. This is illustrated by the family coat of arms, which shows a white horse emerging from the sea with St Michael's Mount behind. 'Time Trieth Troth' is the motto. Family legend has it that upon the horse was a Trevelyan ancestor who escaped from Lyonesse, the mythical kingdom beyond Land's End, while the knights in King Arthur's court drowned. Doubts were cast on the legend of Lyonesse at the end of the nineteenth century, and it was somehow decided that this 'first' Trevelyan must have swum ashore on his horse for a wager. That is the version depicted in the needlework panel embroidered by Molly, Lady Trevelyan, to be found hanging in her parlour in Wallington. True or not, the legend had the effect of making the family feel they were authentically ancient.

The first family member to make any kind of impression was one John Trevelyan, a Member of Parliament during the War of the Roses. A staunch and wily Lancastrian, he was satirised as the 'Cornish Chough who oft with his train[2] hath made our Eagle[3] blind'.[4] As you might expect of an enterprising rouge of the period with the Cornish coastline at his disposal, John appears to have dabbled a little in piracy. His ship seized a Catalan galley full of treasures while it was anchored near Plymouth, an escapade for which he was arraigned while the House of York was in the ascendancy. As befits a West Country pirate, John had an eye for advantageous nuptials. Chaucer's granddaughter, the Duchess of Suffolk, arranged for his marriage to her cousin Elizabeth Whalesborough, a Raleigh heiress. Elizabeth's dowry included Nettlecombe in Somerset, which became the main seat of the Trevelyan family. As A.L. Rowse put it, 'Trevelyan had come a long way from that bare and windy spot of the name high above the banks of the river Fowey; but once he was entrenched in the royal household, he could marry an heiress, come by the desirable estate of Nettlecombe in Somerset and never look back.'[5]

And for almost half a millennium nothing much more was heard of the Trevelyans. The family was almost ruined for supporting the King against Cromwell during the Civil War. Two sons migrated to Virginia to escape the shame of their father's Royalist allegiance. Margaret Trevelyan, their mother, went to London in a cart drawn by bullocks to get a pardon from Oliver Cromwell, but died of smallpox at Hounslow on the way back. Charles II rewarded the family for their loyalty after the Restoration

with a baronetcy, but otherwise life was fairly uneventful. As G.M. Trevelyan
has written,

> Generation after generation went by, and neither the world of politics nor
> the world of letters heard talk of the Trevelyans. For five hundred years and
> more they went on, from father to son, pursuing the quiet life of country
> gentlemen in the remote south-west, farming, collecting rents and taking
> game, surviving in their middle station the storms that were sweeping away
> the great families, as the brushwood survives when the oak is rooted up.[6]

By the end of the eighteenth century, the Northumberland seat of
Wallington came into the family's hands. Once more, a fortuitous marriage
was behind the acquisition of property. As the diplomat Sir Humphrey
Trevelyan observed, marrying an heiress is 'the only way in which the
Trevelyans have ever succeeded in making money'.[7] Wallington's location is
unspectacular yet utterly beautiful. John Ruskin's description of 1852 holds
true today. 'In going over the Northumberland moors near Lady Trevelyan's,
if you stop and listen, you will hear nothing but the wind whistling – a
rattling brook perhaps among some stones, now and then the cry of a curlew,
now and then the bleat of a lamb; all plaintive and melancholy.'[8] In the
remote, wild country that is the border between England and Scotland, the
house has grown into the landscape so it now seems indivisible from it.

Sir George Trevelyan, the third baronet, married into the great riches of
the Blackett family. The Blacketts were shipping and mining magnates from
the North-east, who rebuilt Wallington in the 1680s. These merchant princes
of Newcastle bought the castle of Wallington from the ferocious Fenwicks.
Since around the time of the Norman Conquest, there has been a castle on
the site of the present house. In Chaucer's Reeve's Tale, about the two young
rascals who went out to 'Trompington, not fer fro Cantebrigge', one of the
duo is called 'Alein de strother'. Chaucer says he came 'Out of a town Far in
the North, I cannot tellen where'. This was Allan de Strother, who lived at
Wallington, and was a friend of Chaucer's at the court of Edward III.[9] The
Strother heiress then married a Fenwick. The formidable Fenwicks came to
Wallington Castle during the reign of Henry IV. It was the perfect spot for
this feisty border clan, who were perpetually poised to do battle against the
Scots. As a pun on their name, the Fenwicks adopted the phoenix as their
crest – lead waterpipes with their coat of arms crowned by a phoenix can
still be seen around the building. Sir John Fenwick, a staunch Jacobite, was
wildly extravagant, politically and personally. His mounting debts meant he

had to sell Wallington to Sir William Blackett for £4000. Fenwick persisted in plotting against William III, and was sent to the tower in 1689. Released that time, he was linked to another plot and eventually executed for high treason on Tower Hill in 1697.

Sir William Blackett, a Member of Parliament as well as a coal and ore man, was a political power in the North, with many followers to entertain. As James Lees-Milne observed, 'In the customary manner of new money he married his daughters into the aristocracy.'[10] One of the six daughters, Julia, became the wife of Sir Walter Calverley, a Yorkshire baronet, a significant marriage as we shall see. Sir William modified Sir John Fenwick's Wallington so it became a glorified shooting lodge – the grounds were perfect for entertaining his supporters during daylight hours, after which they could retire to the house and party all night after a successful shoot. A popular song of the time records his hospitality:

The wines of Wallington old songsters praise,
The Phoenix[11] from her ashes Blackett raise.[12]

The first Sir William was restrained in his entertaining, though, compared to his son, also named Sir William Blackett of Wallington. William Junior was a renowned reveller. His excesses passed into Wallington legend. Two hundred years later, George Otto Trevelyan related the antics of William and his crowd to Wallington's head gardener, Edward Keith.

Wallington was the scene of many of their orgies. It is said he kept half a dozen strong lackeys for the express purpose of picking up the fuddled ones when they rolled under the table, dragging them up the narrow staircases, and depositing them in rows on the strawbedded attics prepared for their reception. There they would lie until such time as they came to their senses. In the early morning they turned out to the horse-trough in the outer courtyard for a sobering cold douche, returning indoors for a change of linen, after which they would appear at the breakfast table ready for another day's outing and another night's eating and hard drinking. This would go on for a week together, after which time these honest Newcastle burghers, mostly Sir William's political supporters, would saddle up their mounts and ride back in orderly fashion to canny Newcastle to face business worries and domestic squabbles.[13]

Sir William was a closet Jacobite – he even toasted 'the King over the water'. But when it came to the rising in 1715, he went to ground. This undoubtedly saved his neck, but lost him the respect of his former conspirators in arms, and the friendship of his old-time neighbours. Still, William's wild lifestyle was resumed before too long. He married Lady Barbara Villiers, daughter of the Earl of Jersey, and there were rowdy scenes at Hexham, where hogsheads of wine and barrels of ale were cracked open to celebrate the union. It was quite a wedding. The great Fray Bell, weighing three tons, was cracked due to rough handling by the drunken guests. Bonfires were lit on the Shaftoe Crags, and the owner of East Shaftoe Hall got the local sculptor to enlarge the Devil's Punchbowl so even more punch could be ladled out to toast the newly-weds. William Robson of Cambo described the occasion in verse.

> The bottles stood all ranked in a line,
> The product of the barley and the vine.
> Healths to Sir William and his spouse did pass,
> And at each health they briskly broke a glass.
> And ev'ry time they drink a health they rise,
> And with huzzas they pierce the vaulted skies.[14]

When Sir William died, his sending off would not have disgraced the Krays, as George Otto Trevelyan related to Edward Keith. 'Sir William Blackett might not leave behind him a name in history but he certainly had the largest attended funeral ever seen in Newcastle in living memory. No less than 1086 black kid gloves were distributed to admirers who escorted him on his last journey to St Nicholas's church.'[15]

The departing Sir William left no natural heir – only an illegitimate daughter, Elizabeth Ord, of whom he was fond. In his will Sir William bequeathed Wallington to his sister Julia's son Sir Walter Calverley, on condition that he marry Elizabeth and add the Blackett name and coat of arms to his own. Walter accepted the conditions, and became Sir Walter Calverley Blackett. Walter was not a wastrel like his uncle. He inherited Wallington after years of partying and neglect in a poor state – the acres were little better than a wasteland, the workers were housed in hovels. Crippling debts of £77,000 were inherited by Walter too. But by 1777, when he died, it was one of the best-managed estates and one of the finest homes in the north of England.

Walter re-roofed the house, put in the sash windows, rebuilt the north side, and remodelled the interior. His architect, probably Daniel Garrett, one of the leading Palladian exponents in the North-east, employed the Italian Lafranchini brothers, who created the impressive rococo plasterwork of sphinxes, garlands and fruit on the ceilings and walls of the saloon and the dining room. Walter transformed the estate too. He drained the fells and the moors, put up bridges, created fields, built Cambo village, planted woods and constructed labourer's cottages. He created the park, which may or may not have been designed by Capability Brown. He commissioned a portrait of himself by Joshua Reynolds, the society portrait artist of the day, in which he stands with his faithful hound, looking impeccably decent, dependable and honest. Walter sat in parliament for forty years and delivered only one speech – a few words of apology for having voted for the Radical troublemaker John Wilkes. He entertained Butcher Cumberland upon his return from victory at Culloden in 1746 – presumably in a more restrained manner than his uncle would have.

Sir Walter's only child, a girl, died young, and so once again Wallington passed through the female line. The by now great house was inherited by the son of Walter's sister, another Julia, who had married into the Trevelyan family of Nettlecombe. Sir George Trevelyan, Julia's swain, was far from a model husband, surely causing his brother-in-law Sir Walter Blackett to

'Where the wind whistles, and the brook rattles.' Wallington, the Trevelyan family home in Northumberland, circa 1900. Courtesy of the Trustees of the Trevelyan family papers.

regret the union. Wicked Sir George, as he was known, indulged in fisticuffs and was rumoured to have sired a bastard child. Nor was he the last Trevelyan to do so. Sir George's father was shocked by his offspring's 'vanity, folly, vice, extravagance and ill nature'. The black sheep of the family even made it into verse.

Sir Richard de Neville rode to the Devil,
All in a coach and four,
Sir George Trevelyan (Trevillian), the Devil's Postilion,
Handed him in at the door.[16]

What Sir Richard had done is unknown, but Sir George was seen as villainous enough to escort him to Hell. Fond as he was of scuffling, Sir George had a fight with one of his neighbours, Sir Thomas Acland. Sir Thomas, whom he accused of knocking him down, replied, 'No. On my making a blow at you, you ran to the other end of the room, fell down of your own accord, turned upon your back and cried out "Murder".'[17] Eventually the roguish Sir George did his family a favour by deserting them – leaving his son John to be brought up by the Calverley family in Yorkshire. Educated at Eton and New College, Oxford, John became altogether more respectable than his disgraced father. Indeed, influenced by the Calverleys, John is the first Trevelyan who shows signs of having a hinterland beyond the narrow existence of a comfortable member of the landowning classes. Humphrey Trevelyan wrote,

The literature about the Trevelyans of Wallington sometimes gives the impression that they emerged by a special procreative act of Providence from the evangelical families known as the Clapham sect. They were, in fact, by Nettlecombe out of Clapham and their remarkable qualities were the endowment as much of one as the other.[18]

The life of Sir John at Nettlecombe helps us understand how the squires began to develop scholarly interests.

Sir John inherited Wallington in 1777 when Sir Walter Blackett died. Now the baronetcy carried with it two estates at opposite ends of the country, Nettlecombe and Wallington. They were very different – the late-Elizabethan Nettlecombe, in a romantic valley below the Quantocks; and the Georgian Wallington, with rather more austere views and architecture. Where Nettlecombe was cosy and drowsy in its setting, Wallington was bracing and exhilarating. Sir John struggled with the burden of managing the two properties, and opted eventually for Nettlecombe. There, inspired by

Wallington and perhaps too by his travels in Europe after Oxford, he redecorated the new wing with marble fireplaces, Ionic columns and furniture designed by Robert Adam.

Although a portrait of Sir John by Romney shows a portly English squire, this Trevelyan was interested in more than just traditional country pursuits. Humphrey Trevelyan credits him with 'being elected to Parliament without bribery, which was an improvement on family habits; he was a keen ornithologist who earned the respect of Thomas Bewick and was regarded as a good judge of painting'.[19] A friend of Josiah Wedgwood the potter, Sir John was also knowledgeable about natural history, creating a museum, or cabinet of curiosities as the Victorians liked to call them, at Nettlecombe. A lover of food and wine, he had a winch installed at Nettlecombe in his later years so his vast bulk could be hoisted up to bed. There Sir John died aged 94 in 1828.

Sir John the younger, son of the gouty squire-cum-natural historian, carried on his father's interest in agriculture and ornithology. He was a founder member of the Royal Horticultural Society, set up by John Wedgwood, son of Josiah. This Sir John also undertook the Grand Tour of Europe, so fashionable for monied young men of the day, travelling in France and Italy and collecting Dutch pictures. Ideological too when he heard of the fall of the Bastille in 1789 he rushed to Paris in his enthusiasm. This idealism had vanished by 1798 when Britain and France were at war – then John prepared to see off the threatened French invasion, with himself in command of a scratch unit at Wallington.

Idealistic John married the wealthy Maria Wilson, sister-in-law of the Prime Minister Spencer Perceval, who was assassinated in the lobby of the House of Commons in 1812. Legend has it that on the day of the attack Perceval told his wife, Maria's sister, he had been dreaming of being gunned down. Maria's marriage was considerably less eventful than her sister's. Her dowry included not only money but a fine collection of porcelain, much of which can be seen at Wallington today. Maria was rather formidable, aware of the power of her riches and status. Maria's mother, Dame Jane Wilson, was, just like the older Sir John, fascinated by natural history – in fact, Dame Jane is still known as a pioneer beetle expert, as well as an observer of the habits of snails. The thought of the prospective in-laws comparing their collections of dried insects is quite irresistible – and Dame Jane and the elder Sir John of Nettlecombe did become friends, so perhaps they swapped tips on keeping their fossils and stuffed birds looking their very best.

Maria and John had twelve children, nearly all born at Wallington, and a stormy marriage. At one point, when John took over the management of Nettlecombe and Maria stayed at Wallington, they met only in transit when one was travelling north and the other south. There, through the windows of their coaches, they would bark family news at one another. This behaviour unsurprisingly distressed their children, who eventually forced their parents to live under the same roof. As to the cause of the rift, Raleigh Trevelyan has observed that it may have been Sir John's fondness for the singer Clara Novello. Notoriously stingy when it came to managing his twin estates, Sir John thought nothing of showering Clara with presents and flowers after her opening nights, whether at Covent Garden or St Petersburg.

The eldest son of Maria and John was Walter Calverley Trevelyan. He was a true Victorian, with an inquiring mind and a relentless interest in progress of all kinds, be it scientific or literary. His reign 'witnessed Wallington's first intellectual heyday'.[20] Walter married Pauline Jermyn, after they met at a Cambridge conference of the British Association for the Advancement of Science. An unlikely setting for the flowering of love, one might think, but Walter, fascinated by the new science of phrenology, was impressed by Pauline's 'anterior development'.[21] The tall and lanky Walter was 36, the small and bright Pauline just 17. He had chosen well.

Walter was a well-known geologist – and that was only the beginning of his talents. His studies were eclectic – he was an authority on oxygen, urine and the parasites of starfish. As James Lees Milne says, 'he was an intellectual of a dry professional order'.[22] But Pauline was a polymath – she straddled the worlds of science and literature. In the world of art, she was a player in her own right, both a critic and an intimate friend of the painter John Ruskin. Her circle grew to include the pre-Raphaelites – a tale well documented by Raleigh Trevelyan in his book about Pauline and those artists. Ford Madox Brown, Holman Hunt, Arthur Hughes, Thomas Woolner, William Michael and his sister Christina Rossetti were all part of Pauline's set. She is credited with first recognising the talent of the poet Algernon Swinburne and encouraging him to write. Popular and sociable, George Otto Trevelyan wrote of her:

> Pauline, Lady Trevelyan was a woman of singular and unique charm; quiet and quaint in manner, nobly emotional, ingrainedly artistic, very wise and sensible, with an ever-flowing spring of most delicious humour. No friend of hers, man or woman, could ever have enough of her company; and those friends were many, and included the first people of the day in every province of distinction.[23]

Sir Walter and Pauline, Lady Trevelyan are pivotal in this tale of how country squires became scholars. They were the quintessential Victorian couple, concerned with self-improvement, social reform and progress. Concepts of thought and duty weighed heavily with Sir Walter. Smug and dull he could be, but in his rigorous quest for modernity he was a man of his times. The 1851 Preface to G.R. Porter's *Progress of the Nation* sums up the prevailing mood of Victorian Britain in the year of the Great Exhibition celebrating the achievements of the industrial age: 'It must at all times be a matter of great interest and utility to ascertain the means by which any community has attained to eminence among nations. To inquire into the progress of circumstances which has given pre-eminence to one's own nation would almost seem to be a duty.'

Such inquiries were the stuff of Sir Walter and Pauline, Lady Trevelyan's life. Wallington was their test tube. The couple brought many changes to life on the Northumberland estate. Sir Walter explored modern farming methods, built hygienic cottages for his workers and won prizes for his shorthorn cattle. Wallington was like a well-run government department, noted the estate's heir, Charles Edward Trevelyan, approvingly. A pacifist who opposed capital punishment, for good measure Sir Walter was a campaigning teetotaller who emptied much of the contents of his father's cellar into the lake. The rather earnest trait so evident in later Trevelyans was writ large in Walter Calverley – guests at a Newcastle banquet hissed when he asked them not to raise their glasses for the toast.

But then with so much to learn and explore, Sir Walter must have seen alcohol as the enemy of his beloved progress. All of which made Wallington rather a trial for guests. Here is Augustus Hare's description of staying there in the early 1860s when he was writing a scientific paper. He found

> endless suites of huge rooms only partly carpeted and thinly furnished with ugly, last century furniture…if Sir Walter found the place papered and furnished like those of other people he would certainly pine away from excess of luxury. His hostess seemed hardly concerned with her guests' comfort, feeding them solely on artichokes and cauliflower.[24]

Wallington's head gardener, Edward Keith, also recorded Sir Walter's famously frugal ways.

> After breakfast, he saw to it that the leavings in the coffee-pot were not wasted. Personally he heated up the brew on the dining-room fire to wash down his American tinned beef, his favourite luncheon meal. Meanwhile

his full staff of servants did themselves well in the servants' hall…if economy was practised under his roof-tree, it was not so out of doors. His prize cattle were in a sense eating their heads off.[25]

The pickings may have been a bit thin when it came to food for humans, but intellectually Sir Walter and Pauline did not leave their guests wanting. As John Ruskin wrote to his father in 1853,

> Lady T. kept us laughing all day long…The pleasantness of these people consists in their very different qualities: in Lady Trevelyan in her wit and playfulness, together with very profound feeling; in Sir Walter in general kindness, accurate information on most every subject, and the tone of mind resulting from a steady effort to do as much good as he can to the people on a large estate, I suppose not less than twenty square miles of field and moor.[26]

Augustus Hare depicts them a little differently – Sir Walter he found 'gruffly kind and grumpily available', while 'as to information he is a perfect mine and knows every book and every ballard that was ever written, every story of local interest that is ever told, and every flower and fossil that was ever formed'. Pauline he described as 'a pleasant bright little woman…who paints beautifully', but she too was 'abrupt to a degree, and contradicts everything'.[27]

The couple's most enduring legacy at Wallington is the central hall. George Otto Trevelyan, when showing it off to the visiting Steve Runciman in 1918, declared, 'My boy, man has not achieved anything more beautiful than this.'[28] A little over the top, but it is quite something. Sir Walter and Pauline, Lady Trevelyan decided to roof over the central courtyard, creating a huge room for sociable family gatherings. John Dobson, the leading architect in the North-east, was called in, and William Bell Scott, Pauline's pre-Raphaelite friend, painted eight historical scenes reflecting Northumbrian subjects to decorate the hall. 'Illuminate the history and worthies of Northumbria' was Scott's brief. Pauline wanted these paintings to echo the pre-Raphaelite Brotherhood principles she so admired – and Scott, poet and friend of Dante Gabriel Rossetti, was well chosen for the task. Ruskin contributed too – he suggested that the balustrade around the upper gallery should be copied from the one at Murano Cathedral, illustrated in Ruskin's own *Stones of Venice*.

So a visitor to Wallington today can admire the result of all this talented collaboration. William Bell Scott's cycle of scenes range from the building

The Victorian scholar. Sir Walter Calverley Trevelyan by William Bell Scott. Courtesy of the National Trust.

of Hadrian's Wall to the industrial prowess of Newcastle in the 1860s. I can imagine Sir Walter nodding his approval at the completed room, particularly the final painting, which celebrates the achievement of local firms who secured their place in the Industrial Revolution by making guns and railway engines. Progress, progress. Sir Walter's love of detail and precision may have won the day over Pauline and Scott's pre-Raphaelite leanings, but it is a fine achievement still – the total effect is, as the historian Robin Ironside has said, not without an 'illogical unity'.[29]

The marriage of Sir Walter and Pauline, creative as it was, did not produce children. William Bell Scott regarded Pauline as 'a true woman, but without vanity, and very likely without the passion of love'.[30] A childless union meant Nettlecombe and Wallington should automatically be left to the next heir of the baronetcy, Alfred Trevelyan. But Walter considered it wrong for one man to own two estates. So he decided not to leave Wallington to Alfred.

Typically interested in the young and their promise, Pauline and Sir Walter were very taken with the teenage George Otto Trevelyan, son of Sir Charles Edward and nephew of Macaulay. George Otto, bright, boisterous, scholarly, yet also worldly-wise, was a great favourite of Lady Trevelyan's. William Bell Scott records how '[t]his young fellow George Trevelyan says he wonders how anybody can be moping and dull. There are so many things to interest one, and so many books to read, and Lady T. with the sparkle in her eye calls out, "Oh yes, I can't bear people who

'No friend of hers, man or woman, could ever have enough of her company.' Pauline, Lady Trevelyan, by William Bell Scott. Courtesy of the National Trust.

don't enjoy life and moon about."'[31] George Otto later told his head gardener at Wallington, Edward Keith, how he came to learn that the great house would one day come to him. The young George had journeyed from London to Northumberland for a weekend with his agreeable cousins.

On arriving at the stone stile at the east end of the terrace, I found Sir Walter Trevelyan awaiting me, a fine personality, dressed faultlessly in mid-Victorian style. He had noticed his expected visitor climbing the hill and had come forward to grasp me by the hand and bid me a hearty welcome. Lady Trevelyan was seated by the hawthorn, sketch-book in hand. By her I was most graciously received. I was a young man then and honours had been falling thick upon me … We found Pauline … awaiting us with a tea urn and a bounteous spread on a spotless linen cloth covered table. There under the old hawthorn tree we talked about many things, and it was there with no-one to pry on us I was made to understand that, with certain reservations, I might in the course of time be the owner of Wallington.[32]

George Otto's sparkle caused Sir Walter to change his will in 1852, leaving Wallington not to Alfred but to George's father, Sir Charles Edward Trevelyan. This decision was kept secret – Sir Charles only learnt in 1863 that he was to inherit Wallington. The momentous news came as a postscript to a lengthy letter – Sir Walter was, characteristically, opining about the evils of alcohol throughout. Alfred was most annoyed at losing Wallington, and unsuccessfully tried to challenge Walter's will, a costly course of action. Sir Charles Edward's inheritance of Wallington was another defining moment in the family's history – the radical civil service reformer was elevated from his Clapham townhouse to an aristocratic stately home. As David Cannadine puts it, such a dwelling was 'a citadel from which a landed family superintended its economic affairs, organized its political activities, and proclaimed its social position. The country house was a going concern, from which confidence, leadership and authority radiated outwards.'[33] Charles Edward, his son and grandsons now had a suitable backdrop for their ambitions.

Not that Charles Edward was able to make money from the estate – the retired civil servant spent much money improving Wallington, and George Otto inherited the place with sizeable debts. But by 1889 the historian and politician had paid off all the mortgages, some dating back to the seventeenth century, thanks to his *Life and Letters of Lord Macaulay*. George Otto's eldest son Charles Philips, the Labour Cabinet minister, announced in 1936 that he would leave Wallington to the National Trust. 'As a socialist,' said Charles in a broadcast, 'I am not hampered by any sentiment of ownership. I am prompted to act as I am doing by satisfaction at knowing the place I love will be held in perpetuity for the people of my country.'[34] It was a decision of which Sir Walter Calverley, who thought it was bad for a man to own too much property, would undoubtedly have approved.

The question of why the Trevelyans did not simply defend the aristocratic, landed tradition to which they now belonged, but rather became zealous and public-spirited, is an interesting one. Why were the Trevelyans different from the Devonshires, the Salisburys and the Cecils? In part, the family was less established and therefore had less to lose from challenging the status quo. Attitudes had not become entrenched over hundreds of years. Then there was the impact of what David Cannadine calls the separate but overlapping aristocracies of late-nineteenth-century Britain: the aristocracy of privileged birth, and the aristocracy of exceptional talent. Charles Edward, a talent, married Macaulay's sister Hannah, who was both talented and privileged. She was the daughter of Zachary Macaulay of the anti-slavery Clapham Sect, and brought an atmosphere of middle-class piety and liberalism to the

'Man has not achieved anything more beautiful than this.' The Central Hall at Wallington, with scenes painted by William Bell Scott, circa 1900. Courtesy of the Trustees of the Trevelyan family papers.

family. When Charles Edward's son George Otto married Caroline Philips, daughter of a Manchester free-trader who was a friend of Cobden and Gladstone, the ties with liberalism were further strengthened. G.M. Trevelyan married Janet Ward, daughter of the novelist Mrs Humphry Ward and great-granddaughter of Dr Arnold of Rugby School, who was immortalised in the novel *Tom Brown's Schooldays*. Janet's aunt Julia married the writer and editor Leonard Huxley, father of novelist Aldous Huxley and the Nobel-Prize-winning physiologist Sir Andrew Huxley. Trevelyans, Huxleys, Darwins, Wedgewoods, Wilberforces, Butlers, Keyneses, Thorntons, Stephens and Haldanes were all related by marriage – an example, said the historian Noel Annan, of 'the way in which a great intellectual connection attracts to it in each generation distinguished brains from other families'. These serious-minded families created the intellectual climate in Victorian Britain. As Noel Annan says:

> They became school inspectors or took posts in museums or were appointed secretaries of philanthropic societies; or they edited or wrote for the periodicals or entered publishing houses; or, as journalists ceased to be hacks scribbling in Grub Street, they joined the staff of *The Times*. Thus they gradually spread over the length and breadth of English intellectual life, criticising the assumptions of the ruling class above them and forming the opinions of the upper middle class to which they belonged.[35]

David Cannadine says that these extensive family connections produced a disproportionately large number of eminent men and women, who collectively formed a stable and influential intelligentsia.

> They moved easily between the worlds of learning, literature and public affairs. They were a formidable presence in Cambridge (in Oxford rather less so), and in the home and Indian civil services, and they provided the backbone of the great Victorian and Edwardian periodicals. They believed in hard work, academic excellence, public duty, competitive examination, intellectual integrity and unostentatious living. They had little time for London society or conventional high politics, but exerted influence indirectly through their writings and their public works. From the days of the Clapham Sect, they had no doubt of their right to mould intelligent public opinion.[36]

The timing of the family's elevation into this freemasonry is also important. Sir Walter Calverley Trevelyan was an early Victorian, Charles Edward a late one – these two indefatigable campaigners embraced the spirit and zeal of their age, finding it invigorating. Others found Victorian Britain narrow-minded and oppressive. In Leslie Stephen's judgement, 'One thing is pretty certain, and in its way comforting, that however far the rage for revivalism may be pushed, nobody will ever want to revive the nineteenth century.' H.G. Wells was even more damning. 'Will anyone,' his anti-hero Remington asked in *The New Machiavelli*, published in 1911, 'a hundred years from now, consent to live in the houses the Victorians built, travel by their roads or railways, value the furnishings they made to live among or esteem, except for curious or historical reasons, their prevalent art and the clipped and limited literature that satisfied their souls?'[37]

Yet nearly a hundred years after Wells's book was published we are still living in their houses, reclining on their furniture, using their railways, and benefiting from their sewage system, while the Victorian novel has only grown in popularity. As A.N. Wilson has written:

> The Victorians are still with us. This is not a whimsical statement, intended to suggest that the shades of the Prince Consort or Elizabeth Barrett Browning or Dan Leno are still to be discovered floating in the night air if we empathize sufficiently with their memory or purpose. Rather, the Victorians are still with us because the world they created is still here, though changed.[38]

When Walter Calverley Trevelyan died, in March 1879, that world was being forged. Our Cornish squires had acquired property, the beginnings of intellectual pretensions, and an interest in social reform. The trait of marrying well had been established. Trevelyans were beginning to move in literary and scientific circles, but they were not yet household names. For that we must turn to the iconoclastic reformer Sir Charles Edward Trevelyan.

2

THE CIVIL SERVICE PHARISEE

As a young lad, Charles roamed the woods by Nettlecombe armed with an old flintlock, trying to shoot woodcocks, and nearly crying with vexation when the elderly weapon refused to fire. His grandson G.M. Trevelyan remembers him 'sixty years later, on his Northumbrian estate, carrying his modern breech-loader in an old fashioned and rather alarming manner, grasped with both hands behind his back'.[1] Charles spent his life taking aim and firing at orthodoxies – from corruption in imperial India, to inefficiency in the civil service, to famine relief in Ireland, this awkward but brilliant man was forever seeking out controversy. His lasting legacy is the Northcote–Trevelyan reform of the civil service, which prised open the gates of Whitehall to the middle classes. The novelist Anthony Trollope satirised Charles as Gregory Hardlines, chief clerk of the imaginary Whitehall Department of Weights and Measures.

> To be widely different from others was Mr Hardlines' glory. He was, perhaps, something of a Civil Service Pharisee…Great ideas opened themselves to his mind as he walked to and from his office daily. What if the Civil Service, through his instrumentality, should become the nucleus of the best intellectual diligence in the country, instead of being a byword for sloth and ignorance![2]

And Charles spent his life rooting out what he saw as sloth and ignorance in public life. The Whitehall historian Peter Hennessy has credited Charles with creating 'the DNA of the modern civil service' by recommending, with

Lord Northcote, recruitment by competitive entry. To this day the civil service is based on the Northcote–Trevelyan principles of impartiality, open competition and a career service.[3] Charles's legacy in Ireland is altogether murkier. Between 1845 and 1849, he was officially responsible for the administration of relief during the Irish famine. He carried out this appallingly difficult task meticulously, but, as his many detractors would have it, without much obvious sympathy or compassion for the suffering of the Irish. His name is infamous in certain circles in Ireland even today, as I learnt while working as a journalist on both sides of the border. The name Trevelyan retains a potency more than a hundred and sixty years later. To those inclined to believe it, Trevelyan is shorthand for the genocide of the Irish at the hands of the English.

Before turning to how and why Charles behaved as he did, let us begin with the small boy charging through the Nettlecombe woods with his flintlock. Charles was born in 1807, one of nine children. He later described his background as 'belonging to the class of Reformed Cornish Celts, who by long habits of intercourse with the Anglo Saxons have learned at last to be practical men'. His grandfather, portly Sir John of Nettlecombe from the previous chapter, encouraged the young boy's enthusiasm for field sports, probably providing him with the beloved flintlock. Charles's father George was the vicar of Nettlecombe, Harriet the dutiful parish wife, and together they brought up this large family in the secluded rectory just a mile or so from the family seat. George later became Archdeacon of Taunton – so that Protestant upbringing provided the foundations for Charles's subsequent evangelism. Indeed, four of his brothers entered the Church.

In 1820 Charles went to Charterhouse, and from there to the East India Company's college at Haileybury, where eventually a dormitory was named after this famous pupil. At school Charles was impatient and energetic, learning Oriental languages at record speed. Home for the holidays, he would insist on walking the 18 miles from Bridgwater to Nettlecombe, in order to spare the family's horses. The normal pace of life was not for him, full as he was of 'uncoordinated zeal'.[4] Simon Schama observes that while at Haileybury Charles was taught economics by the Reverend Thomas Malthus. Broadly, Malthusian economics teaches that the world can only support a population of a certain number – after that death by starvation is the inevitable outcome. Schama says the experience of being taught by Malthus was to have 'a profound and terrible influence' on Charles's later career in Ireland.[5] Yet Malthus was not the only influence on Charles at Haileybury. Scotland's

eminent eighteenth-century philosopher William Robertson was widely read
there – he argued for the harmonised progression of humanity towards
civilisation, inevitable once divine will was accepted into the worldly sphere.
Robin Haines, a historian more sympathetic to Charles than Simon Schama,
writes, 'His lifelong belief that there were enduring intellectual and
commercial benefits for less developed countries who adopted the higher
learning of an advanced society, appears to have been acquired directly from
Robertson.'[6] Adam Smith's *Wealth of Nations* was also a set text, and Charles
was clearly influenced by Smith's views on the benefits of universal free trade.
A star pupil in classics and Sanskrit, as well as a budding political economist,
Charles passed out top of the list for the Bengal Civil Service. Charles's foes
have depicted him as a moral crusader who learnt all his dastardly theories
at Haileybury, but in fact he was as much a creature of the eighteenth-
century Enlightenment as of Malthus.

Now the 19-year-old was equipped for Empire, with the ideals of
utilitarianism and laissez-faire uppermost in his overactive mind. Christianity
provided him with yet more moral backbone. He prepared to travel to
India, to serve the interests of Britannia abroad. The East India Company
vetoed Charles's preferred method of travel – on horseback, through Persia
and the mountains of Baluchistan. So this eager teenager had to be content
with the usual six-month voyage round the Cape. He did, though, manage
to ride from Bombay to Calcutta. From there he was sent to Delhi as First
Assistant to the English Resident, Sir Charles Theophilus Metcalfe, and almost
immediately began to make a name for himself.

In Delhi, Charles discovered that the chief magistrate, Sir Edward
Colebrooke, had been taking gifts, or as he saw it bribes, from Indians. This
was theoretically against the policy of the East India Company. Yet, told that
everyone did it, Charles was shocked. Everyone shouldn't, according to his
view of the world. Was Charles a prig, unable to see that refusing these gifts
would cause offence, or a radical reformer, for whom only the very highest
standard of behaviour was acceptable? I prefer the reformer tag to that of
prig, although Charles could be unbearably smug. He was not the man to
'make allowances for human frailty or old bad habits'.[7] His own letters record
how he 'determined to denounce this vile mass of corruption'.[8] And so,
courageously, he reported Colebrooke to his superiors in Calcutta, knowing
that the whole weight of the British community was against him. As Charles
wrote, 'If I was known at all, it was as a boy who had been little more than two
years in the country, and had never filled any situation in which his character

and views could be developed.'[9] Lady Colebrooke had a fit of the vapours whenever Charles was within spitting distance. She circulated this round robin to officers and officials in Delhi:

> Lady Colebrooke begs to take this mode of appealing to the public and of leaving them to form their opinion of the base and dishonourable conduct of Mr Trevelyan, who is found to have been plotting and fabricating falsehoods against her, and clandestinely transmitting them to the Government for several months past, during which he was partaking of Sir Edward's hospitality. Lady Colebrooke cannot but think that liar and villain are the mildest terms which can be applied to such an act of depravity in so young a man.[10]

Charles was a snitch, in the view of Lady Colebrooke and many others. 'A perfect storm' swirled[11] around the youthful accuser. Fortunately for Charles, the Governor General of India, William Bentinck, was a kindred spirit. An evangelist known as the Pennsylvanian Quaker, because of the plainness of his appearance and his modest lifestyle, Bentinck's explicit goal was to bring Western liberal and enlightened principles to bear upon India. His aim, as Macaulay's inscription on his monument in Calcutta puts it, was to infuse 'the spirit of British freedom into Oriental despotism'.[12] His favourite motto was one Charles could cheerfully subscribe to: 'The happiness and improvement of the condition of the people'. Bentinck abolished suttee, the custom of widows burning themselves to death upon their husband's funeral pyres, and encouraged freedom of assembly and the press. He never tired in his attempts to 'elevate the intellectual and moral character of the nations committed to his charge', as Macaulay's inscription says. Bentinck and Charles were at one in their patronising view of their Indian charges. Both were reformers with an abundance of moral fervour.

Bentinck took a dim view of Colebrooke's activities and sent him home in disgrace, declaring him unfit for office. Charles had claimed his first scalp, at the tender age of 21. He was lavishly praised by Bentinck.

> The Governor General avails himself of this opportunity of recording his high opinion of the character and conduct of Mr Trevelyan who has ably, honourably and manfully discharged his duty as a public servant and by his zealous and unremitting exertions in the performance of a most painful and invidious task, has justly entitled himself to the warm approbation of government.[13]

Charles summed up the episode in his pious way: 'God befriended me and supported my conscience.'

This early success may not have been an entirely good thing for the arrogant Charles. Henceforth, as Sir Humphrey Trevelyan has written, 'he was the triumphant reformer with a strong sense of mission but with no disposition to see anyone else's point of view'.[14] Even Bentinck, Charles's supporter in chief, told Macaulay, 'That man is almost always on the right side in every question; and it is well that he is so, for he gives a most confounded deal of trouble when he happens to take the wrong one.'[15]

Moved from the scene of his triumph in Delhi to Calcutta, Charles was soon engaged in a new battle, this time over Indian education. Should the Company be spreading the English language throughout India or teaching in the traditional languages? Charles argued fiercely that the colleges in Delhi should teach English, saying India's middle classes would then be in a position to oversee the country's commercial transactions with what he predicted would be an English-speaking outside world. English was the language of progress in Charles's book. Asked if this would hasten Indian independence, Charles replied, that whatever the consequences, it was England's duty. Ranged against him were the Orientalists, leading Anglo-Indians who argued equally powerfully that it was right to cherish and respect the Indian culture rather than impose an alien culture. It is here, into this raging row, that Thomas Babington Macaulay enters our story and the lives of the Trevelyans.

The glittering Whig socialite, brilliant *Edinburgh Review* essayist and future historian, acclaimed orator and MP for Leeds, Thomas Macaulay was enthused by the English vision for India. Son of Zachary and Selina Macaulay, members of the Clapham Sect, evangelicals and campaigners for the abolition of slavery, Macaulay had been raised truly to believe that he could make a difference. Zachary Macaulay, a wealthy shipowner and merchant, was a friend of the Wilberforces, the Grants and the Thorntons, like-minded families who joined with him in the battle to abolish slavery in the early nineteenth century. 'Clever Tom' could read at the age of three, and by six was at work on a history of the world. Tom the prodigy saw India as a canvas upon which he could imprint his ideals. Inert India was to be revitalised by the dynamic values of progress, industrialisation, social reform and good government. Liberalism could be spread from Birmingham to Bombay to the mutual benefit of both countries. In the House of Commons in July 1833, Macaulay outlined his view of the British responsibility to India:

It may be that the public mind of India may expand under our system till it has outgrown that system; that by good government we may educate our subjects into a capacity for better government; that, having been instructed in European knowledge, they may, in some future age, demand European institutions. Whether such a day will ever come I know not. But never will I attempt to avert or retard it. Whenever it comes, it will be the proudest day in English history. To have found a great people sunk in the lowest depths of slavery and superstition, to have so ruled them as to have made them desirous and capable of all the privileges of citizens, would indeed be a title to glory all our own... there are triumphs which are followed by no reverse. There is an empire exempt from all natural causes of decay. Those triumphs are the pacific triumphs of reason over barbarism; that empire is the imperishable empire of our arts and our morals, our literature and our laws.[16]

Having outlined his liberal manifesto for India, the 34-year-old Macaulay packed his trunk and set sail for the Near East. There he took up his position as first law member of the Governor General's supreme council. Like Bentinck and Charles Trevelyan, Macaulay was a zealous reformer – but as John Clive, his biographer, observed, he possessed something the other two lacked. Macaulay had a firm conviction that European history was the history of progress, and a profound knowledge and love of the highest achievements of Western literature. 'This he combined with a belief that this history and those achievements gave convincing proof of a superior civilization, and, as such, warranted the introduction of the values they represented to a benighted continent so evidently in need of improvement and enlightenment.'[17]

Macaulay, then, was just the ally Charles was looking for. Should higher education be carried out in the ancient languages of Arabic, Persian and Sanskrit? Or should English be introduced at elementary as well as university levels, replacing the Indian vernacular languages as well as the classical ones? Macaulay was on Charles's side of the argument. The long-held idea that the English in India should immerse themselves in the language and culture of the country so they could assimilate was challenged by Charles and Macaulay. Instead, their theory that Indians should become acquainted with English language and culture so they could assimilate themselves to their rulers gained weight. Charles argued in a letter to Bentinck that it was Britain's moral responsibility to bring not only the English language but Christianity to India. If Persian was abolished in the courts and in the government offices, that would firmly establish 'our language, our learning and ultimately our religion in India'.[18] Charles went on to outline his grand vision, of India as a mere staging post to the rest of Asia. Providence, he argued, 'was evidently concentrating her means of improvement here in order that setting out from India as a base of operation, these may afterwards be applied with greater effect to the surrounding nations'.[19] Charles suggested to Bentinck that only the practical part of the scheme be disclosed to the public – he had no desire to have his world domination scheme aired for all to see.

Macaulay did not elaborate on that aspect of Charles's views in his famous Minute on Indian Education. The Minute was, according to John Clive, less an attempt to persuade William Bentinck, the like-minded Governor General, of the reformers' case. It was more an effort to justify a policy already made. Macaulay employed his soaring rhetoric to argue that whoever knew English had access to 'all the vast intellectual wealth, which all the wisest nations of the earth have created and hoarded in the course of ninety generations. It may safely be said that the literature now extant in that language is of far greater value than all the literature which three hundred years ago was extant in all the languages of the world together.'[20] The most infamous passage of Macaulay's Minute is this attack on the Orientalists, in which he remarked that he had never found one among them 'who could deny that a single shelf of a good European library was worth the whole native literature of India and Arabia'.[21]

Charles thought along much the same lines. He may have been a brilliant student of Indian languages but, as we have seen, he was a firm and unabashed believer in the cultural superiority of English. In a letter to Macaulay written the previous year, he argued, 'What is it that keeps India in a state of moral and intellectual debasement except the false religion, false morals and false science contained in the sacred and learned books of the Mohammadens and Hindus... by getting rid of these books we shall stop the polluted stream at its source.'[22]

In one of his habitual pamphlets, also published in 1834, Charles wrote about the supposedly superior values of the West, expressed less eloquently than Macaulay but with equal vigour. 'The countries of the east have for centuries past, been gradually relapsing into a state of barbarism, while the nations of Europe have simultaneously advanced to a height of civilisation which has never been attained before in any age of the world.'[23]

And of course, as Charles and Macaulay saw it, giving the Indians the opportunity to learn English was to provide them with the route map to the dizzy heights of civilisation. The argument between the reformers, led by Macaulay and Charles, and the Orientalists, who were utterly opposed to enforced English instruction, was a bitter one. The Professor of Sanskrit at Oxford University, H.H. Wilson, a leading Orientalist, was not won over by Macaulay and Trevelyan. Wilson spoke of 'individuals of undoubted talent but of undeniable inexperience … who set themselves up to undo all that was effected by men at least their equals in ability and their betters in experience and who can never be surpassed in an ardent desire to accelerate the moral and religious amelioration of the natives of India'.[24]

Inexperienced they may have been, but Macaulay and Charles were persuasive – if not positively hectoring. The Governor General of India, already sympathetic, was swayed, particularly by their claim that much of the demand for learning English was coming from the Indians themselves. Armed with Macaulay's Minute, Lord Bentinck declared that 'the great object of the British Government ought to be the promotion of European literature and science among the natives of India'. Persian was dropped as the official language of British India.

The ever-ardent Charles was somewhat distracted during this controversy by the significant matter of a love affair with Macaulay's sister Hannah, who had travelled to India with him. Macaulay was unusually dependent upon two of his sisters, Hannah and Margaret. His buttoned-up father Zachary had pushed the gifted Macaulay into premature adulthood, wanting the boy genius to use his gifts as an instrument for the greater glory of God and humanity.[25] Consequently Tom was playful, silly and loving with his adoring sisters – in their company, at least, he could be a child. When Margaret married, Tom was distraught. When the opportunity of going to India presented itself, one he wished to take up not least because it would prop up the ailing finances of the Macaulay family, he pressurised Hannah into coming too. Later in life, she recalled that Macaulay would not have gone out unless she agreed to accompany him.[26] He claimed he was willing to accept the Indian position on her account.

> It is that I may have a home for my Nancy [his nickname for Hannah], that I may surround her with comforts, and be assured of leaving her safe from poverty, that I am ready to leave a country which I love and a sister who is dearer to me than anything save one in this world.[27]

Poor Hannah, who dreaded not only the long journey to India but what she might find once she arrived, gave in to his emotional blackmail. The

six-month voyage in the *Asia* began just as she had feared. Separated from her
dear family, in a horrid dank cabin, she was miserable.

She wrote to her sister Fanny, 'I have sealed my destiny for the next six
years and after that what will be left.'[28] But life aboard soon picked up, with
other girls bound for Calcutta to gossip with, and a charming young
Frenchman who gave dancing lessons. India was regarded as a marriage
market for a young girl in Hannah's position, something Margaret tried to
warn her about.

There is one thing my dear Hannah I would gladly impress upon you
which is the old-fashioned lesson 'beware of men'. You must remember
that to a man whose prospects are Indian you are as great a catch as you
would (be) in England had you been an heiress…Remember how very
pleasant a flirtation you may have with a man who has no quality that
will make you really happy, and how much a man of any quickness and
knowledge of the world can affect as to his sentiments, feelings, and
tastes according to what he sees of the mind of the woman he wishes to
win. Above all do not become a flirt. I have no doubt that is your tendency
and therefore I honestly warn you against.[29]

Hannah, responding to her sister's entreaties, did not engage in any on-board
romances. She liked the look of the first mate, one Mr Wolfe, 'for he is really
a pleasant looking young gallant frank young sailor'.[30] But that was about it.
Within six months of arriving in Calcutta, though, she had fallen for a young
officer in the East India Company, none other than Charles Edward Trevelyan.
As Charles was rather stiff and strait-laced, this was no champagne and flowers
romance. Macaulay found his future brother-in-law to be a stormy reformer,
with few of the conventional social graces.

His reading has been very confined. He has very little English literature
and, which surprises me greatly, does not know a word of French…he
has no small talk. His mind is full of schemes of moral and political
improvement, and his zeal boils over in all his talk. His topics even
in courtship are steam navigation, the education of the natives, the
equalization of the sugar duties, the substitution of the Roman for the
Arabic alphabet in the oriental languages.[31]

So Hannah More Macaulay was wooed not with perfume and gifts, but
lengthy descriptions of Charles's policy passions. Macaulay knew all was lost
when he found Hannah studying some lengthy minutes written by Charles.

I knew it, I believe, before she knew it herself; and I could most easily have prevented it by treating Trevelyan with a little coldness, for he is a man whom the smallest rebuff would completely discourage. But you will believe, my dearest Margaret, that no thought of such base selfishness ever passed through my mind. I would as soon have locked my dear Nancy up in a nunnery as have put the smallest obstacle in the way of her having a good husband.[32]

Birth, Macaulay claimed, was a thing he cared nothing about. He then flatly contradicted himself, by observing that Charles's family was one of the oldest and best in England. However, lineage was no guarantor of social graces. His future brother-in-law's lack of finish was conspicuous to the more gregarious Macaulay, although, as he observed in another letter home,

under Nancy's[33] tuition he is improving fast; his voice, his face and all his gestures express a softness quite new to him. There is nothing vulgar about him. He has as yet no great tact or knowledge of the world; but these drawbacks, were they six times more serious, would be trifling when compared with the excellencies of his character. He is a man of genius, a man of honour, a man of rigid integrity and of a very kind heart.[34]

Hannah was under no illusions about her suitor. She even described him as ugly. But Charles was clearly a man going places. If not handsome, he did at least look good on a horse, and was a master in the art of spearing wild boars, which perhaps appealed to Hannah. Naturally, she had faith in the transforming power of her love. In a letter to her mother shortly after their wedding, she quoted Bentinck, the Governor General of India, as saying Charles's wife would give him the only quality he needed, discretion. A loving and dedicated wife as Hannah was, she never achieved the impossible task of teaching Charles the value of discretion.

Although Macaulay approved of Charles, he found the thought of Hannah's marriage and what it would mean for him quite intolerable. He wrote to his other dear sister, Margaret, as though he had lost a lover, not a sibling.

Everything is dark. The world is a desert before me. I have nothing to love, nothing to live for. I have been prodigal of my love, and I have had the fate of other prodigals. My tenderness would have been more highly prized if it had been less lavishly given. This bitter lesson, which comes too late to be of any use, is all that I have got in exchange for the blighted hopes and squandered affections of a life.[35]

G.M. Trevelyan, Macaulay's great-nephew, intriguingly wrote that his relative had 'imprudently lavished his affections' upon Hannah, 'without whose company he did not expect to be able to live with happiness'.[36] G.M., who inherited Macaulay's letters and journals, refrained from using what he called 'the more intimate sentences in which Macaulay poured out his heart'. G.M. initially decided against giving permission for Macaulay's journals to be extensively published. 'Papa with great skill extracted the best part,' he wrote to his brother Bob. 'The rest is interesting, much of it, if one really cares about Macaulay, but was never meant by him for publication but only for his own amusement in re-reading it.'[37] When S.C. Roberts suggested the full text ought to be published, he was surprised by the vehemence of G.M.'s

'Uncle Tom'. A marble bust of Lord Macaulay at Wallington, by Patrick Park. Courtesy of the National Trust.

outburst. 'Over my dead body,' he said. 'I'm not going to have those Bloomsbury people laughing at my great-uncle.'[38] Eventually John Clive persuaded the protective great-nephew that he was a serious scholar, not a mocking Lytton Strachey type, who could be entrusted with Macaulay's papers. One can only speculate on what G.M. was trying to protect from Bloomsbury and co. Macaulay never married, so perhaps G.M. feared the Bloomsbury set would construe his devotion as 'evidence' either of homosexuality or incest. But Macaulay was once infatuated by a young woman – so perhaps G.M. simply feared that his revered relative would be given the Eminent Victorians treatment by a Strachey imitator.

Hannah knew just how anxious her brother was about her forthcoming marriage to Charles. The couple's engagement was broken off, presumably because Hannah was so worried about her brother, and only resumed once it was settled that all three could live together afterwards. This, Macaulay reported, Charles and Hannah made a condition of their marriage. Macaulay arranged for the newly-weds to share his house in Calcutta. But his sense of loss was profound, as he confided to Margaret.

> At thirty four I am alone in the world. I have lost everything and I have only myself to blame. The work of more than twenty years has vanished in a single month. She was always most dear to me. Since you left me she was everything to me. I loved her, I adored her. For her sake more than my own, I valued wealth, station, political and literary fame. For her sake far more than my own I became an exile from my own country. For her society and affection I found an ample compensation for all that brilliant society which I had left. She was everything to me, and I am to be henceforth nothing to her...

Then Macaulay, overcome with self-pity, quoted from an old nursery rhyme.

> There were two birds that sat on a stone,
> One flew away and then there was but one.
> The other flew away and then there was none.
> And the poor stone was left all alone.[39]

Margaret never read this confessional letter – she had died of scarlet fever by the time it reached England. Macaulay's misery deepened, and he apparently resolved never to be parted from Hannah, his surviving sister. Many years later, Hannah recalled that her brother became mentally disturbed by her engagement to such an extent that Lord William Bentnick was actually 'frightened' about him.[40] This devotion to Margaret and Hannah is the subject of considered discussion in John Clive's Macaulay biography. Clive wonders whether Tom was aware that his attachment to his female relatives might have been less than perfectly innocent – after all, rumours of Lord Byron's incestuous relationship with his half-sister Augusta were widespread when Macaulay was a teenager. Clive points out that intense feeling between brothers and sisters was not unknown in a society where early marriage was uncommon, and sex before nuptials frowned upon. He concludes thus:

> Macaulay's imagination, that powerful instrument, often so beneficial to the orator and the historian, had tragically misled him in his personal life, where just as in his view of the past, the concrete and the imagined were indissolubly linked. It was quite true that Margaret and Hannah both adored him. It was quite true that for a time he was at the very centre of their existence. But youthful and inexperienced as they were, they knew that idyll they lived with their brother was bound to be but a stage in their own lives, that it could not and should not last. This was an insight that Macaulay, in spite of all his learning, did not attain until it was brought home to him in India. Then his eyes, like those of the hero in one of his beloved Greek tragedies, were indeed opened. He had built his castle in the air; and now it lay in ruins about him. He was never able to rebuild it.[41]

Macaulay could not let go of Hannah, though, for all that his castle was ruined. He didn't want her to stay on in India while he returned to London alone. It was probably Macaulay's intervention that secured Charles an important Whitehall job in 1840, and began a significant new chapter in his life. Charles became the top civil servant at the Treasury, the Assistant Secretary, at the age of only 32. James Stephen, a Whitehall mandarin, almost certainly engineered this appointment, at Macaulay's behest. Macaulay later told his sister Frances to remember how much the family owed Stephen. 'But for him, Hannah and her children would now be fifteen thousand miles from us, if indeed they had escaped the tropical maladies.'[42] Whatever Macaulay's motivation, Charles felt his virtuous conduct in India had been recognised and rewarded. He returned to London with his already sizeable self-belief enhanced still further.

Home life for the Charles Edward Trevelyans was Clapham, in South London. There lived Charles, Hannah and their children George Otto, Margaret and Alice, with the now cheerier Macaulay a frequent house guest. Although he officially lodged at the Albany, Macaulay was often in

Clapham, seeing his beloved sister, Charles, whom despite everything he regarded as an adopted younger brother, and his nephew and nieces. The intellectual competition in that household is revealed by a letter George Otto wrote many years later to Lord Rosebery. 'When my father was a young man in high office, keeping common house with Macaulay, he used to bring Macaulay printed matter...and at first he was rather piqued by his brother-in-law casting his eyes down the pages more rapidly; but he soon found that he had mastered, and for a time remembered, the actual words and sentences.'

The Zachary Macaulays, Hannah and Tom's parents, lived nearby, as did Marianne Thornton, Hannah's lifelong friend, also from a prominent Clapham Sect family. The aura of evangelical Christianity pervaded the house of Hannah and Charles and the upbringing of their children, making George Otto, the subject of the next chapter, rather uninclined to take up organised religion. But this was not just a house of God. G.M. Trevelyan fondly writes that

> a happier, a more affectionate, a more book loving, talk loving, laughter loving house there was not in Britain, especially whenever 'Uncle Tom' came round to make up the number. If in some societies Macaulay was sometimes 'overpowering', there was never any such feeling in the household at Clapham – nor indeed are Trevelyans at any age very easily overpowered.[43]

Charles was never knowingly overpowered, but he was about to be tested severely. As he rode on horseback from Clapham to the Treasury each morning in the summer of 1845, across the Irish Sea a tragedy was unfolding. The potato blight or *Phytophthora infestans* struck Irish crops that summer, with devastating results. Between 1846 and 1850 Ireland lost a quarter of its population – one million perished, another million emigrated to survive. In County Mayo, one of the worst-hit areas, a third of the men, women and children died. Charles at the Treasury was responsible for directing relief operations in Ireland. The legacy of the way he and others in London handled the famine relief casts a shadow over Anglo-Irish relations even to this day, as I discovered for myself. The Irish historian Austin Bourke has written: 'When what was done was done, more than six million people came out alive from an unprecedented catastrophe, and the number of survivors amongst those who lived wholly or largely on the potato was substantially greater than the number of victims.' But the folk history of the famine places the blame squarely upon the British Government and its chief agent, the fiendish Charles Trevelyan.

The conventional wisdom on Charles's role in the famine was shaped by an article written by Jennifer Hart over forty years ago.

Trevelyan believed the Irish famine was the judgement of God on an indolent and unselfreliant people, and as God had sent the calamity to teach the Irish a lesson, that calamity must not be too much mitigated: the selfish and indolent must learn their lesson so that a new and improved state of affairs would arise. However as the distress was aggravated by ignorance, efforts should be made by individuals (not by the hand of government if possible) to relieve it; but they must not distribute relief with such a liberal hand that what was meant for a blessing was turned into a curse.[44]

Cecil Woodham-Smith, author of that influential work *The Great Hunger*, published in 1962, put the boot into Charles just as powerfully. Mrs Woodham-Smith attributed the attitude of the British Government during the famine to

obtuseness [that] sprang from the fanatical faith of mid nineteenth century British politicians in the economic doctrine of laissez-faire, no meddling with the operation of natural causes. Adherence to laissez-faire was carried to such a length that in the midst of one of the major famines of history, the government was perpetually nervous of being too good to Ireland and of corrupting the Irish people by kindness, and so stifling the virtues of self reliance and industry. In addition hearts were hardened by the antagonism then felt by the English towards the Irish … It is impossible to read the letters of … Charles Wood and Trevelyan … without astonishment at the influence exerted by antagonism and irritation on government policy.[45]

A caricature of Charles emerged from the work of Hart and Woodham-Smith – the heartless, callous British administrator who believed it was God's will for the Irish to die. Robert Kee's monumental television series *Ireland: A History* compounded this unsympathetic view. Simon Schama's 2002 BBC television series *A History of Britain* portrayed Charles in much the same light. Kee acknowledged that historical liberties had been taken in order to make a television programme that would not lose the attention of the viewer. He wrote, 'No academic historian could regard the treatment here of the British Treasury official, Charles Trevelyan, as sufficiently fair, but from the point of view of the television programme there were more important considerations than being wholly fair to Trevelyan.'[46] As Robin Haines, author of a sympathetic, revisionist book about Charles and the famine, says,

'Trevelyan has generally been characterised as the omnipotent dictator of relief policy, a parsimonious egotist determined to exploit the devastation wrought by the Famine to impose a social and economic revolution upon the survivors.'[47]

Haines argues forcefully that 'an intriguing fusion of half-truth, innuendo and careless repetition' has made its way into the secondary literature about Charles, when a careful reading of his archive reveals a more nuanced portrait of his role in famine relief. This more balanced interpretation, she points out, does not fit the role assigned to him 'by those for whom the demonic picture is fundamental to their understanding of the Famine in all its horror'.

My own experience of the potency of the famine legacy and Charles's pivotal part began in 1994, shortly after the Irish Republican Army declared an historic ceasefire. In Dublin to interview Irish officials about the peace process, I was attempting, somewhat ineptly, to park my car. A passer-by kindly offered a few handy hints, and after I had successfully manoeuvred into the space he asked my name. Laura Trevelyan, I told him. He dropped theatrically to his knees, and began to sing a ballad called 'The Fields of Athenry'. Amused and then alarmed, I listened with a growing sense of disquiet to the song, which tells of a young woman outside a prison, knowing her lover is to be sent to Botany Bay in a convict ship.

By a lonely prison wall
I heard a young girl calling
Michael they are taking you away
For you stole Trevelyan's corn
So the young might see the morn
Now the prison ship lies waiting in the bay

What, I wondered to myself, is Trevelyan's corn? Only later did I learn that the 'The Fields of Athenry', which sounds like a traditional Irish ballad, was actually written in the late 1970s. Which might explain why it has been sung to me so many times – it's not an ancient song passed down through the generations, despite appearances to the contrary.

Entering the Irish Department of Foreign Affairs a few moments later, the official I was meeting immediately enquired if I was related to Sir Charles Trevelyan. 'I'm his great-great-great-granddaughter,' I replied. At which point I was shown off round the department as a piece of living history, to general interest and amazement. Gerry Adams and Martin McGuinness, the leaders of Sinn Fein, the IRA's political wing, found my name a source of wry amusement when I interviewed them. Martin McGuinness, always keen on influencing opinion within what he called 'the British Establishment', regarded the programme I reported for, BBC1's *On The Record*, as a good outlet for getting the Republican message across to that constituency. That I was the correspondent perhaps only confirmed his view. In South Armagh, known then as republican bandit country in Northern Ireland, I was interviewing a member of Republican Sinn Fein. She too asked about my name, and I confessed to the relationship. 'To think you're driving round South Armagh, as casual as can be, while the hills of Ireland are drenched in the blood of Charles Trevelyan,' was her reaction. And this was a hundred and fifty years after the famine.

If we rewind from a windy hillside in South Armagh to Charles Edward's spacious office in the Treasury in Whitehall, the tale of his role in Irish affairs begins in 1843, when he made a private visit across the water. Cecil Woodham-Smith in *The Great Hunger* claims Charles disapproved of the Irish, and that some slight family difficulties may have intensified his feelings. His cousin Alfred Trevelyan married the daughter of a Limerick solicitor, but she was soon widowed, leaving a baby son in whose welfare Charles took a great interest. The boy was brought up in Limerick, but unsuitably, thought Charles, who typically tried to interfere by telling the mother she should educate the child in England. Robin Haines, who has meticulously challenged the assumptions of Woodham-Smith and Hart, says that in fact his relations with Alfred's mother remained genial.

So Charles visited Ireland on family business in 1843, two years before potato blight was to turn crops across Ireland into a sickening purple-and-black mush. There he witnessed the gatherings of the O'Connellites in Dublin, who were agitating against British rule. Being a man who refused to keep his opinions to himself, Charles returned from Ireland and told the Prime Minister, Sir Robert Peel, about the condition he found the country in. Not content with having the ear of the Prime Minister, he then sent two lengthy letters to the *Morning Chronicle* signed Philalethes ('lover of truth'). The letters predicted an early uprising in Ireland, which he accused Catholic priests of fomenting. Charles also recounted his hair-raising encounters with Irish labourers. Peel knew full well the identity of Philalethes, and was indignant. 'How a man after his confidential interview with us could think it consistent with common decency to reveal to the editor of the *Morning Chronicle*, and to all the world, all he told us, is passing strange. He must be a consummate fool. Surely he might have asked us what we thought of his intended proceedings?'[48] wrote an infuriated Prime Minister.

Fool Charles Edward was not, convinced of his own rectitude he most certainly was. What drove this civil servant to write letters to the newspapers? Charles was the master of the strategic leak throughout his working life, until at the very end this bad habit caught him out. He was, as Peter Hennessy has written, a whizz-kid, and like many whizz-kids he was also abnormal. A combination of missionary and revolutionary,[49] normal rules of behaviour did not apply to him. Chapman and Greenway, historians of administrative reform in Britain, described Charles as the very reverse of the conventional mandarin. 'Energetic, incisive and intensely self-confident he was also impulsive, tactless and insensitive to the difficulties of others. Life for him was a battleground where the forces of enlightened, altruistic moral progress were to triumph over the dead weight of obscurantism and self interest.'[50] Those traits are more often found in politicians than civil servants, and Charles was a highly political animal. A back-room Sir Humphrey he was emphatically not – Sir Gregory Hardlines was anything but publicity-shy. His high profile during the famine was due to this love of the limelight. He could have simply kept his head down, but instead he persisted in writing pamphlets and penning letters to the papers in addition to his administrative work.

Robert Peel's reaction to the events in Ireland was to create a Relief Commission, and to buy in Indian corn to be sold cheaply to those in need. And he repealed the Corn Laws – all the protectionist duties on grain imported into the UK and Ireland were removed, in order to lower the price of bread. This highly political act, which deprived English farmers of their protectionist measures, split Peel's Tory party, between those in favour of free trade and the protectionists. Peel, who had long believed in free trade and wanted to repeal the Corn Laws anyway, was accused of exaggerating the extent of the famine in order to justify his actions. Charles was frustrated both by the protectionist critics, who didn't seem to want any public money spent in Ireland, and by *The Times* newspaper, which refused to accept the situation as desperate.

In February 1846 the Relief Commission for Ireland was reorganised, and Charles was in charge of drawing up its remit. This was an influential position, leaving him responsible for the detailed policy work of the Commission. Robert Peel then introduced public works boards to try to increase employment in Ireland – they were under the overall control of the Irish Board of Works, which was answerable to the Treasury. Or, more precisely,

Charles was now in charge of not only the Relief Commission but also the administration of public works.

In May 1846, Charles was trying to apply market forces to the sale of Indian corn. Told that the corn available in Ireland could not possibly keep the people fed until the new potato crop was expected in September, Charles was resolute. If the corn was selling out, the price was too low. Too much government intervention would only crowd out the voluntary sector. His concern was that the cheap Indian corn was going to people suffering from the distress normal in Ireland at that time of year, and not just to those going hungry because of the potato famine. 'Indiscriminate sales,' wrote Charles, 'have brought the whole country on the depots, and, without denying the existence of real and extensive distress, the numbers are beyond the power of the depots to cope with. They must therefore be closed down as soon as possible.'[51] The poor were supposed to earn what they could from the public works, buy what was left, and await the fresh crop of potatoes. Charles believed the new crop would be a good one, leading to the end of the relief effort in Ireland.

In June 1846 the tottering government of Robert Peel, wracked by the decision to repeal the Corn Laws, finally fell. The ever-resourceful Disraeli devised a way of defeating Peel over the Irish Coercion Bill, and in came a new Whig Government under Lord John Russell. Here was a man Charles could work with. 'I think we shall have much reason to be satisfied with our new masters,'[52] wrote Charles. The new Chancellor of the Exchequer, Charles Wood, was also much to the liking of the top Treasury official. Another adherent of laissez-faire economics, he, like Charles, was scrupulous and hard-working. This meeting of minds gave Charles yet more sway over famine policy, allege his critics. In Woodham-Smith's judgement, 'Charles Wood...came increasingly under Trevelyan's influence. The two men were alike in outlook, conscientiousness and industry, and Charles Wood brought Trevelyan a further access of power in the administration of Irish relief.'[53]

In July of 1846 reports reached London of the disease reappearing in the new potato crops. It is here that Charles's reputation for heartlessness begins in earnest. His reaction to news of a further diseased crop was to argue for winding up the relief scheme. If Government relief was still available when the people became aware of another crop failure, they would expect to be fed. 'The only way to prevent people from becoming habitually dependent on government is to bring operations to a close. The uncertainty about the new crop only makes it more necessary,'[54] wrote Charles to Sir Randolph

Routh of the Relief Commission on 17 July. He went even further in a subsequent letter. 'Whatever may be done hereafter, these things should be stopped now, or you run the risk of paralysing all private enterprise and having this country on you for an indefinite number of years. The Chancellor of the Exchequer supports this strongly.'[55]

Unfortunately, the crop failure of 1846 was far worse than Charles, sitting in London, could possibly realise. Diligent as he was, seizing reports from Ireland and on occasion spending all night at his desk awaiting news, the true picture eluded him at first. The awful extent of the potato blight was such that people in the West of Ireland were beginning to starve. In a private letter, Charles admitted he was frightened by what was happening in Ireland. He also acknowledged that his outspokenness was impolitic, cautioning his colleague not to reveal how frustrated he was with the landlords' constant requests for special treatment.

> ... unless every person of property in Ireland will heartily exert himself in his private capacity, famine and rapine and general confusion must ensue. And the existing race of proprietors will deservedly come to ruin and disgrace. They even do worse than nothing, they avail themselves of the danger and distress of the people, and the embarrassing situation of Govt. to press upon the Lord Lieutenant schemes for improving their private Estates, and relieving themselves from their encumbrances out of the Consolidated Fund... But all have the same end in view to shirk making any sacrifices and to reap a rich harvest from the public calamities. I have written you my whole mind in the entire confidence of friendship, and intimate official cooperation, but although it is of much importance that we should understand each other, it is of still greater consequence that my unreserved feelings and expressions should not be seen by other persons... Without departing from my principles, my language must be translated before it will be fit to be produced to the public.[56]

In Skibbereen workhouse more than half the children admitted after 1 October 1846 died – due to 'diarrhoea acting on an exhausted constitution',[57] said the workhouse physician. The terrible winter of 1846–47 only made matters worse. The snow prevented the now hungry labourers from being able to cultivate their land in preparation for the next season. Reports of starvation in the West persuaded Charles to give permission for the corn depots there to be opened in December 1846. He was finding the administration of the relief effort hard going, often going into the office at 3 a.m. He wrote to his officials, telling them not to bother him with trivial concerns.

> I am so pressed by having to provide for several millions of people in Ireland and Scotland who are in serious danger of starving, in addition to the current Treasury business which is heavy enough – that it has become an indispensable duty to avoid any claims upon my time which are not absolutely necessary, in order that I may give myself up entirely to my task – and for this purpose I have relinquished my holiday and left my family in the country and am living in Lodgings that I may work early and late.[58]

Meanwhile an organisation Charles thoroughly approved of was stepping into the breach, in line with his expectations of how political economy should operate. In January 1847 the British Association for the Relief of the Extreme Distress in the Remote Parishes of Ireland and Scotland, or the British Association, was formed. Charles had done more than just will the British Association into being. As he wrote to a colleague a month earlier,

> the calamity is extensive enough for all the assistance that can be given in relieving it, private as well as public, and in fact there are numerous cases which our public assistce. cannot easily reach ... Once started I am satisfied that a good deal of money would be raised, & when it is considered that if God were to deal with us all on the principle of benefiting only those who behave well we should all of us be badly off & that it wd be disgraceful to us to have it recorded in History that we allowed our Countrymen to die of famine without making every possible effort to save them, I am convinced that private, as well as public benevolence ought to be called upon to aid; the ... Famine will be remembered long after the abuses are forgotten.[59]

The great, the good and the wealthy of the day, the Rothschilds, the Barings and the Kinnairds, duly banded together to relieve the suffering of those 'who are beyond the reach of Government'. Food, clothing and fuel were to be provided, 'but in no case shall money be given to the parties relieved'. Charles gave the Association £25, Queen Victoria herself gave £2000. Nearly half a million pounds was raised by this powerful grouping. The heartless image of Charles does not sit entirely comfortably with his donation – in his single-minded way, he was convinced that government alone could not be responsible for alleviating the condition of the Irish, believing private enterprise too should play a role.

By now, January 1847, Charles knew the extent of the calamity in Ireland. 'This is a real famine, in which thousands and thousands of people are likely to die,'[60] he told Henry Kingscote of the British Association Committee. But caution was still his watchword. 'If the Irish find out there are any circumstances in which they can get free government grants...we shall have a system of mendicancy such as the world never saw,'[61] he wrote. Yet this on-your-bike mentality did not preclude him from being moved by the horror of the famine – Charles was capable of being both laissez-faire political economist and man of compassion. In February 1847 he wrote this to a relief inspector: 'We deeply sympathise with you and other officers who daily have to witness heart rending scenes of misery without being able to give effectual relief but, as justly observed by you, we must do all we can and leave the rest to God.'[62]

Leaving the rest to God has been used as evidence that Charles was a callous providentialist, who believed it was God's will that the feckless Irish should die. The letter most often quoted in support of that view is this one, written by Charles to Lord Monteagle, a leading Irish landowner, after the crop failure of 1846.

> I think I see a bright light shining in the distance thro' the dark cloud which at present hangs over Ireland. A remedy has been already applied to that portion of the maladies of Ireland which was traceable to political causes; & the morbid habits wh. still, to a certain extent, survive, are gradually giving way to a more healthy action. The deep & inveterate root of social evil remained, & I hope I am not guilty of irreverence in thinking that this being altogether beyond the power of man, the cure has been applied by the direct stroke of an all-wise Providence in a manner as unexpected and unthought of as it is likely to be effectual. God grant that we may rightly perform our part & not turn into a curse what was intended for a blessing.[63]

Cecil Woodham-Smith and those who have shared her views have used this letter to prove definitively that Charles disliked the Irish poor, and saw the famine as a God-given chance for a fresh start. Robin Haines, Charles's supporter, says he actually saw the emergency as a God-given opportunity for the landlords and the gentry to save the poor from starvation. Haines quotes further from the letter, to show that it is the proprietors of the land who are Charles's target, not the poor. Charles told Monteagle he could see no indication that

> the Landed Proprietors have even taken the first step by preparing for the conversion to grain cultivation of the land now laid down to Potatoes,

I do not despair of seeing this class in society still taking the lead wh. their position requires of them & preventing the social revolution from being so extensive as it must otherwise become.[64]

As Haines points out, Charles repeatedly wrote to his officials, telling them 'the People cannot under any circumstances be allowed to starve'.[65] It is easy to see where the caricature of Charles has sprung from – but, as always, the reality is more complex. A believer in the free market and the proper role of private charity, Charles was not inclined to spend government money without restraint. He believed in doing all he could within the intellectual limits he set himself. He saw the famine as an opportunity for land reform in Ireland – admittedly one sent by God – but that is not the same as believing it was God's will that the Irish should die.

Still, there is no disguising the fact that in the summer of 1847, Charles was anxious to be rid of famine relief. Reports of good crops delighted him – the fact they were insufficient he glossed over. Now at last perhaps the operation could be wound up. 'After two years of such continuous hard work as I have never had in my life', he decided to take a holiday, and went with Hannah and the children to France for a fortnight, visiting the chateaux of the Loire and the valleys of the Seine. Even Woodham-Smith acknowledges that Charles's exertions had been superhuman,[66] and it was hardly surprising that he was exhausted.

But, far from being over, the famine was to intensify. The yield of the potato crop might be superb, but the amount planted was woefully inadequate. Another harsh winter for the starving of Ireland was followed by a crop failure in 1848 as complete as in 1846. The government's response was to offer only the Poor Law as support to the Irish people. No relief commissions, no grain depots – just the minimal assistance of the Poor Law. Ireland was left to Charles's 'operation of natural causes'[67] doctrine. It is the behaviour of the British Government from 1847 onwards that has so outraged many. As Robin Haines says, 'It is universally agreed that the premature termination of the most successful relief operation in 1847 – distribution of cooked food by soup kitchens – was a disastrous and inhumane move which compounded the distress...'[68]

Charles encouraged the passing of the Poor Law Extension Act in 1847, which gave the Treasury greater influence over the use of poor-law funds. He was determined that relief should be financed by the raising of local rates rather than through grants from the Treasury. This involved him in a prolonged dispute with Edward Twistleton of the poor-law commissioners, and only furthered his reputation for brutal complacency. The lawyer and journalist John Mitchel, who endured the famine and was transported to Tasmania, cast Charles as the villain of the piece. Mitchel depicted Charles as the slaughterer of future generations. 'I saw Trevelyan's red claw in the vitals of those children…His red tape would draw them to death.'[69]

The rational, but unpalatable, explanation for the hated policy is the grip of laissez-faire upon Charles and the Chancellor, Charles Wood. As A.N. Wilson has written, 'The tendency of modern historians is not so much to single out individuals for blame, such as Charles Edward Trevelyan, as to point to the whole attitude of mind of the governing class, and the, by modern standards, gross inequalities which were taken for granted.' Both Charles, the Chancellor and Lord John Russell were ideologically convinced that the virtues of self-reliance and industry would be undermined by too much aid to Ireland. Short-sighted and unkind as that appears a hundred and fifty years later, it is the mindset that prevailed among political economists then, as Cormac O'Grada and others have pointed out. Simon Schama argues that it is possible to be 'over-eager to acquit as well as over-eager to prosecute' Charles and the government, adding, 'If Trevelyan did not actually want to kill and dispossess large numbers of the Irish, neither was he excessively distraught about their disappearance. If he can be acquitted of villainy, he can be accused of obtuseness…'[70]

Robin Haines's painstakingly researched book convincingly challenges the view that Charles was a heartless monster. Haines, who has studied Charles's letterbooks thoroughly, argues convincingly that Hart and Woodham-Smith quoted selectively from the vast archive of Charles's papers. Lazy repetition of their work by subsequent historians compounded the original error. Haines says

> Rather than a harsh disciplinarian, a policy maker bent on punishing Ireland, Trevelyan was the visible and audible point at which pressure was transmitted downward from the Treasury boardroom to officials in the field…He felt compassion for the Irish poor whose suffering he pitied; he did not loathe them as his critics aver. It would be perverse to see him as anything other than a friend to Ireland and the Irish poor, determined to take his place in establishing a permanent infrastructure capable of contributing to the welfare and prosperity of Ireland and its people whom he saw as his fellow countrymen.[71]

As the famine petered out, leaving a legacy of bitter resentment between Ireland and England, Charles was feted for his efforts. In April 1848 he was made Sir Charles Trevelyan KCB. Lord John Russell expressed gratitude for his civil servant's 'constant attention and indefatigable exertions'[72] in Ireland, and awarded Charles £2500 from the civil contingencies fund, the equivalent of a year's salary. There was uproar in parliament at this, however. Charles's subsequent letter to the Prime Minister gives some indication of the personal strain he was under.

> Considering all the anxiety, the responsibility and the labour I had undergone during the two preceding seasons of relief in Ireland...I gratefully accepted the donation...because I felt conscious of having undergone labours...much exceeding what could have been contemplated when I was placed in my present situation in the public service...I now perceive from the report of yesterday's report in the House of Commons that the propriety and regularity of the donation are called into question, and as it could under the circumstances be inconsistent with my sense of what is due to the public service and myself to retain it, I shall repay the amount.[73]

The David who had slain the Goliath of Lord Colebrooke in India 16 years earlier knew allegations of impropriety should be neutralised instantly. Useful as the money would have been, and much as he felt he deserved it, it had to be forgone for the sake of his reputation. The ever-restless Charles had much he wanted to achieve – next on his list was civil service reform.

In an age where reform and progress were held up as shining principles, Charles had identified an area of slothfulness and incompetence. The civil service, he felt, was resting on its laurels, excluding the talented yet unconnected lower-middle classes from its hallowed inner sanctums. Once more, Charles took pen to paper to make his case, this time to the Lord Chief Justice, Sir J.T. Coleman.

> It will not do to rest on traditions or on ancient privileges; if we will lead, we must make ourselves fit to be leaders; if even we will float with the current, and not be overwhelmed by it, we must, by discipline and training, learn to throw out our intellectual powers with the strongest and best trained...While all around us, the underwood of the forest is making vigorous shoots, our own growth must not stand still, lest we should be overgrown and stifled.[74]

In 1848, Charles tried to make the case for clearing out the undergrowth to parliament. The Commons Select Committee on Miscellaneous Expenditure was treated to his views on the merits of competitive entry by examination, and the benefits of dividing work into routine and intellectual categories. The MPs were not won over, but Charles was not discouraged. The Whitehall historian Peter Hennessy has called him 'a monster, but a monster in the public interest'.[75] Charles busily monstered all the permanent secretaries and ministers across SW1, persuading them to set up efficiency reviews into their own departments. Resistance was great – not even Charles's great ally from the days of famine relief, Sir Charles Wood, could be won over. No real progress was made until Charles gained a political master in his own mould. When William Ewart Gladstone was appointed Chancellor in 1852, the minds of two reformers met.

Gladstone brought in Sir Stafford Northcote, a politician who was formerly a civil servant at the Board of Trade, and together he and Charles Trevelyan planned their overhaul of the civil service. With Gladstone as their patron, the two men worked fast. They began in April 1853, and by November Charles had written the first draft. The historian Henry Roseveare saw him as 'a bureaucratic hound of the Baskervilles…born to do violence to all that was idle, wasteful and ungodly'.[76] Scenting victory at last, Charles was wasting no time – in February 1854 the influential 20-page report was published. Roseveare judges the Northcote–Trevelyan report 'a remarkable piece of propaganda, a brilliant manifesto for views by no means wholly based on an objective appraisal of facts'.[77] For Peter Hennessy, it is Whitehall's equivalent of Lincoln's 'Gettysburg Address'.[78] This was Charles's central argument for reform.

> It would be natural to expect that so important a profession would attract into its ranks the ablest and most ambitious of the youth of the country; that the keenest emulation would prevail among those who had entered it; and that such as were endowed with superior qualifications would rapidly rise to distinction and eminence. Such, however, is by no means the case. Admission into the Civil Service is eagerly sought after, but it is for the unambitious, and the indolent or incapable that it is chiefly desired. Those whose abilities do not warrant an expectation that they will succeed in the open professions…and those for whom indolence of temperament, or physical infirmities unfit for active exertions, are placed in the Civil Service, where they may obtain an honourable livelihood with little labour, and with no risk…[79]

The backlash was instant. Macaulay reported an 'open-mouthed'[80] reaction in Brooks', the gentleman's club in Piccadilly. Surely 'John Bull would not be

'The people cannot under any circumstances be allowed to starve.' The recently knighted
Charles Edward Trevelyan, with his Treasury Box and Famine papers at his feet, by Eden
Eddis. Presented to Lady Trevelyan in 1851. Courtesy of the National Trust.

so insane as to set up an Austrianised bureaucracy in Downing Street',[81] asked an appalled critic. A leader written in the *Morning Post* claimed Charles wanted to set questions to candidates such as 'Compare Lord Clive with Julius Caesar and contrast the reigns of King Stephen and Queen Victoria'.[82] Lord John Russell, the Prime Minister, was outraged, fearing republicanism was now on the rampage. 'In future the Board of Examiners will be in place of the Queen,' Russell wrote to Gladstone. 'Our institutions will become as harshly republican as possible…I cannot say how seriously I feel all this.'[83] The novelist Trollope had tremendous fun at Charles's expense with his satirical civil servant Gregory Hardlines, overlord of the Department of Weights and Measures:

> He was thinking of higher things than the Weights and Measures, and at last he published a pamphlet…Mr Hardlines had many enemies, all in the Civil Service…they were down on Mr Hardlines with reviews, counter pamphlets, official statements and indignant contradiction; but Mr Hardlines lived through this storm of missiles, and got his book to be feted and made much of by some Government pundits, who were very bigwigs indeed.[84]

Tno call him Sir Gregory in the family,' Hannah Trevelyan told Trollope.[85] And Trollope wrote in his autobiography, 'I never learned to love competitive examination, but I became, and am, very fond of Sir Charles Trevelyan.' It was to be 16 years before the radical ideas of the real Sir Gregory were fully accepted. The very idea of competitive entrance threatened the upper orders, who saw it as a direct attack on their privileges. Gladstone, wily old bird that he was, chose to emphasise the other part of the reform, separating work into routine and intellectual categories, in a persuasive letter designed to appeal to the aristocratically inclined Prime Minister Lord John Russell.

> One of the great recommendations of the change in my eyes…would be its tendency to strengthen and multiply the ties between the higher classes and the possession of administrative power. I have a strong impression that the aristocracy of this country are even superior in their natural gifts, on the average to the mass…it must be remembered that an essential part of any such plan as is now under discussion is the separation of work, wherever it can be made, into mechanical and intellectual, a separation which will open to the highly educated class a career and give them a command over all the higher parts of the Civil Service, which up to this time they have never enjoyed.[86]

As Peter Hennessy has observed, it is clear from Gladstone's letter that the purest democratic principle was not fuelling the reform.[87] Peter Gowan has portrayed the Northcote–Trevelyan report as a 'means of providing a bulwark in the context of rising democratic and labour strength'.[88] But, from the frenzied reaction of Upper England, one would never have thought it. By May 1854 even Gladstone had to admit that legislation was not in prospect. He had to ask the frustrated Charles to refrain from his favourite trick of writing to the press without first consulting him. Then the Crimean War intervened and the machinery of government was otherwise occupied.

War in the Crimea meant the British Army needed equipping. Charles was in charge of the Commissariat, the supply organisation for the Crimea. Unfortunately for the radical reformer, it all went terribly wrong. Just as Charles was assuring Lord Raglan that he would have 'as efficient a department as ever accompanied a British Army into the field',[89] the poor soldiers were without sufficient boots or food. The first war correspondent of modern times, William Howard Russell of *The Times*, exposed the short-comings of the Commissariat – typically dismissed by Charles at first. Jennifer Hart has written that Charles's only remedy 'was to write more and more hectic letters, and to dissipate his energies on eccentric schemes such as getting pamphlets about Eastern Languages prepared for the troops, and in sending commissariat officers New Testaments in Bulgarian and Serbian … '.[90]

Ironically enough, the incompetence over which Charles presided was seized upon by another nascent movement for bureaucratic change – the Administrative Reform Association, formed in 1855. Generally self-made men who wanted government to adopt more businesslike methods, they included among their number the novelists Charles Dickens and William Makepeace Thackeray. An ARA supporter in parliament, Henry Layard, moved a motion blaming the Crimean supply debacle on 'the manner in which merit and efficiency have been sacrificed, in public appointments, to party and family influences, and a blind adherence to routine'.[91] How excruciating for Charles, who wished to reform the civil service of such tendencies, to be accused of propagating them.

But, with pressure for reform growing, in 1855 the first Civil Service Commission was created by an Order in Council. Not quite Charles's Board of Examiners, but the Commission was supposed to give candidates a certificate of fitness. Gladstone continued to press for full implementation of the Northcote–Trevelyan report, to Charles's delight. 'Friday's debate,' wrote Charles to Gladstone in 1858, 'and especially your speech, gratified me extremely. It seemed to me as if that which I had been labouring for so many years in obscurity and discomfort was all at once realised.'[92]

Charles's dream was not fully realised until 1870 – then, finally, the Northcote–Trevelyan report was engraved across the heart of Whitehall. In that year Gladstone was Prime Minister and another impatient reformer, Robert Lowe, was Chancellor of the Exchequer. Lowe and his supportive permanent secretary Sir Ralph Lingen drafted a new Civil Service Order in Council, which gave the Treasury influence over recruitment in all departments. Only the Foreign Office and the Home Office resisted, arguing that as their departments dealt with confidential material the first requirement of their officials was not intellect but character, a quality no exam could test. That self-serving justification held sway, but the rest of Whitehall rapidly fell into line.

Charles was not in England to witness his ultimate triumph. In 1859 he returned to his old stamping ground of India, becoming Governor of Madras. India had never been far from his thoughts. Indeed, just as Charles was proceeding with reform of the civil service in England, so his brother-in-law Macaulay was asked by the government to report on recruitment to the Indian civil service. The two men were working in tandem once more, just as they had over Indian education twenty years earlier. Imagine the conversations over breakfast in Clapham – the cult of meritocracy, the discussions over whose reform project was most likely to succeed. Macaulay called for the monopoly of Haileybury, alma mater to Charles, to be broken up so there could be other recruiting grounds for service in India. Just as the Northcote–Trevelyan report began to gather dust in Whitehall back offices, Macaulay's proposals were adopted for the Indian civil service.

In evidence to a House of Lords select committee at the time of the renewal of the East India Company's charter in 1853, Charles developed the ideas that had guided him in India as a young man. The imperialism of free trade, as John Clive called it, was still very much on display. Charles argued for the education of the elite Indians in English to continue, although he was in favour of vernacular schools to educate everyone else and give them the means of learning the elements of English. The tie between the two countries could not be permanent, he pointed out, and independence was bound to come. With education, India would be left a highly improved country, one it would be profitable for Britain to trade with afterwards, just like the United States. Aping Macaulay, Charles predicted that 'we shall exchange profitable subjects for still more profitable allies'.[93]

But Charles was not merely concerned with the economic opportunities India afforded Britain. In front of their lordships, he pressed for the employment of Indians in positions of trust and responsibility. The British Government should observe religious neutrality, he argued, calling for the missionaries to work on their own without the patronage of a conquering government. He attacked the use of legal sanctions that enabled plantation bosses to oppress their workers. And, presciently, he warned that the social prejudices of the white, Christian British would arouse a dangerous spirit of religious patriotism in the ranks of the Indian Army. The Mutiny of 1857 proved how right he was. One of the ostensible causes of the mutiny was the British insistence that the Indians grease their cartridges with fat the men believed to be made of animals. Charles, writing to *The Times* after the Mutiny, this time with the pseudonym 'Indophilus', observed that 'to bite a cartridge greased with cow's or pig's fat was more to the Hindus, and the Indian Mohammedans, than eating Pork to a Jew, spitting on the Host to the Roman Catholic, or trampling on the Cross to a Protestant'.[94]

Charles's relative and mine, the diplomat Humphrey Trevelyan, points out that in both India and Ireland he applied a rigid general premise. In Ireland, Charles believed the famine was an act of God that must be seen to be for the general good. In India, he believed Britain was there for the good of the Indians. Against this principle, all his decisions in both countries can be judged. His views were simple, based on the cultural superiority as he saw it of the English, and he didn't believe in keeping quiet about them. As he told the House of Lords select committee, 'It is a plain moral duty to govern India as well as we possibly can for the benefit of the Natives; and Providence has so arranged, that the performance of duty shall always be found to be conducive to the best interests of mankind. Honesty in this, as in everything else, is the best policy.'[95]

When Charles was offered the Madras governorship, Macaulay was, again, horrified at the very thought of losing his darling sister Hannah. And he feared, with unerring accuracy, that Charles's rashness would be his downfall. Macaulay wrote that all Charles's virtues and faults were brought out strongly and that, between ambition and public spirit, he was as much excited and as unfit to be reasoned with as if he had drunk three bottles of champagne. A reaction would come and he would have very much to suffer.[96] Macaulay was nearing the end of his life, and Hannah could not leave him in his final illness – had Hannah been able to accompany her impetuous husband to Madras, the outcome might have been different. Charles's son George Otto recalled later, 'I remember going down with my father to Southampton in the early months of 1859, when he was leaving England for India, and watching the P. and O. liner getting dim in the distance. Ah me! What an avoidable catastrophe it was. People should always beware the governing impulse in their character.'[97]

Charles started off in fine form, his governing impulse sufficiently under control. For the voyage he had a Hindustani bible, a book of hymns from Hannah and a set of parliamentary blue books. Florence Nightingale, with whom he had corresponded over Crimea, sent him a pleasing farewell letter: 'You are going to Madras but all India is what you are going for…I could not let you leave England without saying God bless you for all you have done for us.' From his cabin aboard the *Ceylon*, Charles wrote to Hannah: 'Do not feel anxiety. I feel sure God will have me in His holy keeping. I have committed myself to Him, believing that I have been prepared and called for what is before me, and I do not doubt that strength and grace will be given me.'[98]

And initially Charles did well. The whole tenor of his second term in India is marked by its instinctive sympathy towards the Indians. The dismissive young ideologue of thirty years ago seemed to have modified his patronising views. Immediately, he invited the Indian elite to Government House durbars in Madras. Previously only British officials had attended such occasions. He abolished the exclusion of Indians from public balls given for special celebrations such as the Queen's birthday. Charles took on an Indian aide. In a letter home to Hannah, he wrote:

> The high minded insolence of a dominant race is the greatest danger to which a power like ours in India is liable. I shall take immediate and decisive action in any case of personal abuse or ill treatment of Natives by Europeans, and I shall hold such conduct as an offence and shall punish it as such.[99]

True to his word, Charles abolished the bad practice of impressment of labour in the army. Land reforms were instituted. He improved the drainage and the drinking-water supplies of Madras. Furious when one James Smith was acquitted, against the weight of evidence, of murdering an Indian, Charles insisted there should be more Indian jurors. And, of course, Sir Gregory Hardlines could not resist reorganising every department. Not for the first time in his career, Charles's brusqueness made him enemies. Lord Canning, the Governor General of India, took a dim view of the new boy in Madras. Then Mr Wilson was appointed finance minister. Macaulay instantly predicted trouble between the two. Wilson, he told Hannah, would not rest until he had procured Charles's recall, since he knew Charles was the only man in India who could act as a check on him.[100] And there was bad blood between Charles and Wilson, from when the latter was financial secretary to the Treasury. Wilson wanted to impose an income tax, and Charles could not have disagreed more. Charles's essential case was that Wilson had come to India with some English ideas that did not suit the country. As usual, Charles was not content to be overruled. He went over Wilson's head to the Governor General in Calcutta – a tactic that had served him well during the Colebrooke affair. But Canning was away and Wilson managed to keep Charles's dissenting views quiet.

At this juncture, *The Economist* magazine, edited by Walter Bagehot, future constitutionalist and son-in-law of Wilson, reported on this 'monstrous act of misjudgement and insubordination on the part of Sir Charles Trevelyan'.[101] Charles was being not so subtly undermined in London, and knowing this he went for the extreme option – writing to the Indian press. This time it went badly awry. Charles published in the Indian-language papers in Madras not only the Madras Government's objection to the income tax, but also – and herein lay the fatal mistake – the assenting minutes of the members of his council, whom he had neglected to consult. As G.M. Trevelyan noted, 'This was a breach of administrative custom and propriety astonishing in so experienced a civil servant.' *The Times* in London said it was like a secretary of state who had been overruled by the Cabinet sitting down to write a letter to the paper quoting secret documents.[102] A paper at Lucknow prophesied bloodshed, and ladies there who had endured the siege were said to be in a panic. Hannah begged Charles to resign, but he refused, saying to do so would be mean and cowardly, a betrayal of the people of Madras.

Inevitably, Charles was recalled from India in disgrace. The deed was done by his old friend Charles Wood, once again at the India Office as President of the Board of Control. Wood expressed his great personal sorrow in having to take this humiliating course, but then Charles had acted indefensibly. Wood told the Commons,

> A more honest, zealous, upright, and independent servant could not be. He was a loss to India, but there would be danger if he were allowed to remain, after having adopted a course so subversive of all authority, so fearfully tending to endanger our rule, and so likely to provoke the people to insurrection against the central and responsible authority.[103]

Hannah had arrived in Madras in 1860, having just buried Macaulay, to find she could barely unpack her bags. The family used to say that if Hannah had been there at the time, the minutes would never have been published – but this time there was no saving Charles from himself. Macaulay would not have been surprised. Hannah wrote to Charles Wood, 'When I arrived here, the mischief was done … it was exactly my brother's prophecy put into practice.'[104]

However, Charles and Hannah were heartened by the reaction from the Madras community. Eight and a half thousand people signed an address from the general public of Madras, beginning 'Our belief is that your departure is a public calamity'.[105] Mr B.G. Baliqa of the Madras Records Office, writing ninety years after Charles was recalled, assessed him as the most popular Governor since the days of Bentinck or Munro.[106] The awkward character had mellowed in late middle age. Cecil Woodham-Smith, his arch-critic, concedes that in India this time, he 'conducted himself with a fearless sense of justice, instituted land reforms and won the esteem and confidence of the local population, who through his administration became reconciled to government by the British'. The last sentiment is a bit sweeping but the point is that even his detractors recognised his achievements in India.

But, for now, Charles had to leave India – it was back to London in a cramped and cockroach-ridden steamer for the family. From his armchair in Clapham, Charles was able to read in Hansard the debate triggered by his recall. Lord Palmerston, the Prime Minister, summed him up rather astutely:

> I am quite sure that no one will impute to Sir Charles Trevelyan anything but an exaggerated belief in his own opinions, and a recklessness of consequences which I feel was a great fault … but a fault which, nevertheless, does not detract in any degree from those eminent qualities which anyone who knows Sir Charles Trevelyan must acknowledge he possesses.[107]

Hubris was to befall Charles's arch-foe, Wilson the finance minister of India. He died in office, his taxation plans unpopular. Charles brightened up – he had been right all along, as usual! After some debate, Charles Wood at the India Office decided to give his old ally the vacant post – after all, as Wood rationalised it, Charles had been almost right in the taxation row, and he would not risk such insubordination again. Wood lectured Charles on the need to stick to his job, and for once he did indeed exercise self-restraint. Charles was delighted to be given the chance to redeem himself. As he wrote to his cousin, 'As a mark of confidence, nothing could be more complete, for it involves the management of the entire finance of India…income tax included.'[108] Once more Charles sailed to India, accompanied this time by the watchful Hannah and the children, including George Otto, who was to be the finance minister's private secretary in Calcutta. The author of the Northcote–Trevelyan report was indulging in a little nepotism in his old age – though doubtless Charles would have argued that his brilliant son was the best person for the job.

Just as the family was leaving, Charles received a letter from his wealthy, childless cousin Sir Walter Calverley Trevelyan. A brief postscript left Charles choking over his coffee. Sir Walter had made a will leaving Wallington and its thirteen thousand acre estate to Charles, and therefore ultimately to George Otto. Charles was overwhelmed, but decided against telling his heir, fearing the news would unsettle him.

Returning to India in 1863, Charles and the family were greeted at Madras by a crowd and flags with the words 'Welcome Trevelyan'.[109] It was a triumphant arrival for the man who had been banished with his reputation tarnished. Charles allowed himself only six hours to savour the atmosphere at Madras – no time to waste, Calcutta beckoned. Immediately he was embroiled in worries about currency reform and a storm over the salt monopoly. Charles Wood at the India Office in London received many missives from his friend and colleague. Charles was particularly concerned by an ill-planned adventure on the north-west frontier from which the army had been lucky to escape unscathed. As usual Charles's less able colleagues were dismissed in his letters with complete contempt. Hannah, though, was keeping a close eye on her unpredictable husband, trying to ensure that such thoughts never made it into the public domain. As she recorded,

> I really have a great deal of occupation working with Charles. You see entre nous it is very important for me to keep the threads of everything he does in my hands, or else I should not know enough to be able to interpose a word of caution or opposition at the right time…I read all the dispatches, negotiations, instructions sent, and I assure you I know a great deal more about it [finance] than anyone here but C…and he is far more willing to hear reason that he used to be.[110]

Hannah's letters also provide an insight into the petty but bitter rivalries of Empire life. The entire Government of India moved to the hills of Simla every summer, to escape the heat of Calcutta. The entertainment programme for 1864 provoked much disagreement, as Hannah noted.

There is another great quarrel going on with which we have nothing to do. She Stoops To Conquer is going to be acted, and Mrs Strachey and Mrs Innes are fighting for the part of the heroine. I do really think the part suits Mrs Innes best, though Mrs Strachey is the best actress, but her despotic and violent behaviour has set the whole corps dramatique up in arms…I do not think anything seems to stir up more bad blood than theatricals.[111]

The Trevelyans and the Stracheys had much in common. West Country landed families both, they had acquired titles, administered India, and were to become members of the intellectual aristocracy. But just as Hannah was irritated by Mrs Strachey, so G.M. Trevelyan was to be riled by her son Lytton's attitudes in later life. While the ladies of Simla waged war by the means of amateur dramatics, little knowing that their feuding would be honoured by future generations, Charles was becoming frail. His varicose veins flared up, made worse by the descent from Simla to Calcutta. A return to London was inevitable, but the dogged finance minister wanted to deliver his budget in April 1865. Charles wanted to abolish the income tax that his enemy Wilson had introduced, but his political masters in London were not keen. Charles pressed on with his agenda of social reform, advocating the abolition of the whipping of criminals and calling for an improved prison system. The enormous cost of this scheme was hardly consistent with Charles's usual cheese-paring approach, as his enemies in newspapers such as the *Friend of India* wasted no time in pointing out. Charles was changing though, and the man who refused to open the corn depots in the West of Ireland because of the cost was now all in favour of expensive public works. Florence Nightingale urged him to build new sanitary barracks for the troops, a plan Charles greatly approved of.

Charles delivered his budget in 1865, and abolished the hated income tax. It was reimposed in 1867, but he departed from Calcutta feeling he had left the finances of India in an 'excellent state'.[112] Hannah was most relieved, as she oversaw the interminable packing for the long trip home. 'I am sure nothing will bring me here again, or Charles either. We leave at daybreak Sunday morning. Che giorno felice!'[113] Not that it was for Hannah, who caught measles on the way home.

A baronetcy was awarded to the doughty reformer in 1874, and in 1879 he inherited Wallington. Charles kept busy upon his return. He became involved in the question of army purchase – he wanted to abolish the practice whereby commissions could be bought, another example of bad practice in

British public life. This was a campaign his son George Otto carried on. He became interested in a number of social matters, such as charities and pauperism, on which he published – naturally – yet more pamphlets. Hannah died in 1873, and he married again soon after, Eleanora Campbell, who kept him company for the last few years. Never one to sit still, he launched himself into improving the Wallington estate. G.M. Trevelyan remembered his grandfather in his new role as squire:

> with his tall, wiry frame, his snow-white hair, his face as rugged as a sea-worn rock, its deep lines instinct with energy and power, the eyes alive for every happening. Though always talking or brooding over some scheme of improvement, he was kind and uncensorious in the ordinary ways of life. His evangelicalism had by that time become an attitude of the soul rather than a dogmatic creed; at least it was tempered by reason and good sense, and by wide reading conducted on plans originally suggested to him by Macaulay.[114]

Charles became a familiar sight, galloping at top speed on his cob Peter before breakfast with his coat-tails flying, off to give instructions to the workmen. The dedicated commitment he had bought to administrative reform was now applied to estate management. Edward Keith, formerly the head gardener at Wallington, recorded the reaction of the locals to this whirling deverish of a baronet.

> The steady-going Northumbrian squires of the 'eighties marvelled at the energy shown by this white-haired septuagenarian in the last decade of a strenuous life. The range and amount of work attempted and the results achieved in such a small space of time by his by no means big staff of workmen was amazing.[115]

Ever one for high moral standards, Charles was mortified when he committed an error of shooting etiquette. When rabbit shooting at Wallington one afternoon Charles saw his prey, but it was out of gunshot range. Instead a hen pheasant sprang up in front of him. It was a week before the pheasant-shooting season began, but Charles shot the bird anyway. Edward Keith was looking on, and judged this incident to be typical of the man.

> Turning to me without comment his face took on that drawn horrified appearance as if he had broken the whole of The Commandments and smashed up The Stones as well. For the once I deliberately lied to save the situation. 'I, too, Sir Charles, mistook it to be a rock pigeon, it rose so

rapidly.' His face brightened for a moment, he never suspected my duplicity... today I see him as real as I looked upon him fifty-four years ago, dressed in his loose-fitting, light-coloured soft Otterburn tweeds, the seals dangling at his chain-watch, a big, tall, loose figure, head bent forward, the rugged manly countenance, the strong jaw, the white wisps of hair showing underneath his straw panama hat ruffled with the wind, the merry twinkle in his eye, his boyish bursts of laughter when the brighter side of life appealed to him, and at other times his periods of dejection and pose of resignation and quiet dignity, all come back to me as I think of him on that day too upright in character, too consistently honest to pretend for one moment that anything had happened but what had occurred, viz. he had shot his bird simply because he couldn't help himself. As he walked away I knew he had made his peace with his conscience and cared not one whit what the world might say.[116]

Charles built two schools and improved the church at Cambo, building the tower on the hilltop. He told his friends, 'I have reared this tower to the glory of God, so that all men may look at it from afar and think of the giver of all good things. In a way,' he added, 'I have made certain of my own memorial, for I am sure nobody will erect one to me.'[117] There he was wrong – he was commemorated in a window in his beloved church tower, by the saying of St Paul that sums up his life: 'I have fought a good fight, I have finished my course.'

From his vantage point in Northumberland he could look back on his lifelong struggle. He must, I think, have been a difficult man to know – he was not a comfortable individual. Humour was one tool he rarely deployed – energy, single-mindedness and relentless logic were his hallmarks, leading to rigorous but inflexible conclusions. Yet those traits enabled him to leave his mark on British public life. His enduring legacy is civil service reform, his most controversial one is famine relief, and in his later years in India Charles championed the cause of social reform for Indians. By acquiring Macaulay as a brother-in-law, Charles introduced the tradition of literary history into the family, one that was to inspire future generations, beginning with his only son.

3

THE RADICAL ARISTOCRAT

I f anyone was born with a silver spoon wedged firmly into his mouth, it
was surely George Otto Trevelyan. His circumstances could hardly have
been more advantageous. Adored nephew of the Whig historian Lord
Macaulay, son of the zealous reformer Charles Edward Trevelyan, he had
ability, connections and, unlike most of his Trevelyan relatives, social poise too.
Born into the Victorian era at the zenith of its power, George Otto embodied
the values of his age. He was to become a literary historian and a liberal
politician, a man of powerful intellect shot through with the reforming
instincts of his father, heavily influenced by his brilliant uncle. And his
marriage to Caroline was a great love match. However, just like his eldest son,
he was erratic and impatient, a footnote to history rather than one of its
great volumes.

George Otto was born on 20 July 1838, at Rothley Temple in Leicestershire,
where his uncle and future mentor, Thomas Babington Macaulay, had been
born 38 years earlier. Macaulay had great ambitions for his nephew from the
very beginning. The Clapham terrace in which George grew up was a high-
octane household, as we have seen. Macaulay was a house guest for much
of the time, and the combination of Charles, Hannah and 'Uncle Tom', as
Macaulay was affectionately known, made for a senior-common-room
atmosphere. History was in the very air. Macaulay's conversation was peppered
with jokes and references to Rome, Greece and England past – all of which the
young George absorbed readily. Charles wasn't much of a one for literature
– he banged on as usual about public affairs and administrative reform.

Hannah and Tom, despite being children of those earnest social reformers Zachary and Selina Macaulay, nonetheless combined bookishness with laughter. As George was to write in his *Life of Macaulay*,

> When Lady Trevelyan married, her husband whose reading had lain anywhere rather than among the circulating libraries, used at first to wonder who the extraordinary people could be with whom his wife and brother in law had lived. This style of thought and conversation had for young minds a singular and a not unhealthy fascination. Lady Trevelyan's children were brought up among books as a stable boy among horses. The shelves of the library, instead of frowning on us as we played and talked, seemed alive with kindly and familiar faces.[1]

Macaulay was the crossover figure here, the man who was a master of literature and a public servant too. As Macaulay and Charles plotted together to push forward their reform agenda for the civil service in India and England, George was sitting by the hearth, next to his sisters Margaret and Alice, absorbing it all. One of George's earliest memories was of Macaulay telling him he was going to spend five more years collecting material to write a history of England. Little George thought that meant his uncle was spending five years buying the very best pens and plenty of blue and white foolscap paper. Macaulay, whose emotional life was channelled through his family, adored his nephew and nieces. As Hannah wrote, 'Many people are very fond of children, but he was the only person I ever knew who never tired of being with them. Often he has come to our house, at Clapham or in Westbourne Terrace, and finding me out, has dawdled away the whole morning with the children.'[2]

Macaulay, who was easily bored in general company, found the unconditional love of his little companions endlessly rewarding. George wrote later,

> It is impossible to exaggerate the pleasure which Macaulay took in children, or the delight which he gave them. He was beyond all comparison the best of playfellows; unrivalled in the invention of games, and never wearied of repeating them. He had an inexhaustible repertory of small dramas for the benefit of his nieces, in which he sustained an endless variety of parts that at any rate was sufficient for his audience.[3]

When not dreaming up plays for George, Margaret and Alice, Macaulay would take the children on epic trips to see the sights of London. These were red-letter days for the little Trevs – they would take the horse and carriage into town, eat a sumptuous midday meal including oysters, caviar and olives, and tour London, until, in Macaulay's favourite expression, they 'could not drag one leg after the other'.[4] In summer, the quartet would see the bears and lions at the Zoo, and in winter they would head for the Panorama of Waterloo, the Colosseum on Regent's Park, or Madame Tussaud's gruesome Chamber of Horrors. If it was raining, the British Museum was a favoured destination, where Macaulay was an inspired guide. George recalls him 'making the statues live and the busts speak by the spirit and colour of his innumerable anecdotes paraphrased offhand from the pages of Plutarch and Suetonius'.[5] The precocious children were not always delightful companions, as Macaulay wrote to Hannah after he entertained them at his home in the Albany, Piccadilly. 'I gave them some dinner; fowl, ham, marrow-bones, tart, ice, olives, and champagne. I found it difficult to think of any sights for the children: however, I took them to the National Gallery, and was excessively amused with the airs of connoisseurship which Charley[6] and Margaret gave themselves, and with Georgy's honestly avowed weariness. "Let us go. There is nothing here that I care for at all." When I put him into the carriage, he said, half-sulkily: "I do not call this seeing sights. I have seen no sights to-day."'[7]

Religion was the other dominant topic in that Clapham household. Charles, evangelist that he was, loved to read the Bible and hold family prayers. Macaulay and Hannah, children of Zachary Macaulay, were also well versed in evangelism, although Macaulay was not quite as enthusiastic as his sister and brother-in-law. George observed all this tub-thumping for God, and was left unmoved. As his son G.M. Trevelyan has written, 'Since he did not understand Christianity, he left it alone with little remark. He recognised it as a great fact in the history of England, and in human nature...The battle for religious equality which was fought in his early manhood interested him a great deal more than religion...'[8] The head gardener at Wallington, Edward Keith, remembers George telling him, 'My mother was reared in a household steeped in Evangelicism. It affected her outlook on life, or rather I should say narrowed it. It certainly had no such belittling effect on her brother, Lord Macaulay.'[9]

The little boy who grew up with this narrative of religion, history and public affairs ringing in his ears went to Harrow in 1851, the year of the Great Exhibition at Crystal Palace, the high point of Victorian self-confidence. The Christmas holidays in 1852 gave George the chance to witness history in the making. His father, the top civil servant at the Treasury, took him into the House of Commons to watch Disraeli's epic speech on his budget. This was one of the parliamentary set-piece occasions of the age, a pitched battle between Disraeli and Gladstone, and the 14-year-old George saw it all. Years later, he described Disraeli's performance as

> an inconceivable masterpiece. Bristling with points, blazing with fierce and fiery outbursts of rhetoric, and all alive with an inexhaustible profusion of epigrams and sarcasms, it was intelligible and comprehensible to the multitude of hearers who listened to it eagerly for two, or three, hours after midnight had sounded, and who were sorry when the speech was over…at three in the morning…Mr Disraeli resumed his seat, and Mr Gladstone, looking singularly lithe, active, young and handsome, bounded onto the floor…[10]

George, much moved by the sight of the duel, was destined to become a member of Gladstone's Cabinet in later years. That was all to come – for now, he returned to Harrow, where he swept up school prizes, much to the delight of his ambitious uncle, Macaulay, who proudly noted his achievements in a letter to his friend Ellis in 1857.

> George is buried under laurels – first in the examination, Gregory medal, Peel Medal, every prize that he has contended for without exception. And really he is a good modest boy, not at all boastful or self confident. His home indeed is not one in which a young fellow would be likely to become a coxcomb.[11]

Harrow Speech Day in 1856 merited this glowing entry in Macaulay's private journal: 'George was the hero of the day. All his exercises had merit. I was much pleased with the Latin verse. The English heroics too were good, and very well recited. I hope and believe that he will turn out a distinguished man.'[12]

George's golden progress continued. In 1857, his triumphant Harrow time at an end, George celebrated with a walking tour of the Tyrol. He was accompanied by another budding member of the great and the good, Montagu Butler, future headmaster of Harrow. George records how their trip ended in Paris.

> We were to meet Macaulay at Paris; and we knew, from the experience of a golden week in the near past, what meeting Macaulay in Paris meant. He received us in a large and comfortable Salon in the old hotel Wagram,

which looked across the Rue de Rivoli on to the massive gilt railings of the Tuileries garden. He was in joyous spirits, brimming over with welcome, and with a piece of news which he insisted on our guessing. His old friend Palmerston had offered him a Peerage, and he accepted it amidst what may fairly be described as rejoicing on the part of his countrymen. Henceforth we should have to address him in our letters, after the fashion prevailing in the seventeenth century, as 'Right Honourable my Singular Good Lord'.[13]

Homage paid to Uncle Tom in Paris, George began another journey of homage to Macaulay, this time to Cambridge. Macaulay had attended Trinity College, and for George no other academic institution could compare. As G.M. Trevelyan records in his biography of his father,

> In October 1857 my father went up to Cambridge, like a man entering into an inheritance. Never was anyone more eager or better fitted to make the most of University life of his day. Ever since he was a child, his uncle had been talking to him about Trinity, as the wide open field of friendship, freedom, work and youthful laurels...All his life long he felt towards Trinity as an Athenian towards Athens.[14]

The ever-watchful Macaulay was worried that George would not live up to these Olympian expectations. During his nephew's first term, Macaulay expressed those fears in his private journal. 'I am anxious about George. He has spoken at the Union with éclat. He is feted and asked to parties and is wild with spirits. I am afraid that he may neglect solid achievements for showy trifles. I shall see him on Monday and give him some advice.'[15]

Such was Macaulay's anxiety that he broke his own rule and placed two French words in two successive English sentences in that entry. And George was indeed having far too good a time by the standards of his high-achieving father and uncle. He was busy writing 'The Cambridge Dionysia', and 'Horace at the University of Athens', satirical plays based on Athenian comedies. High-minded Hannah, his mother, was also worried about her irreverent son. George, who unlike his father possessed a keen sense of humour, wrote an article making fun of Harriet Beecher Stowe's *Dred, a Tale of the Dreadful Swamp*, an anti-slavery novel of the time. Hannah, daughter of an abolitionist, was unamused.

> My dearest George,
>
> It is very seldom I have to find fault with you, but I really have been very much vexed by your article on Dred. I do not mean whether it is a good

book or not, but it was written by a woman burning with a holy zeal for a cause which is really a very noble one; tho' I do not think she acts wisely, yet it is the cause of God…Then it is particularly ungrateful in anyone of your grandfather's descendants to speak disrespectfully of any Antislavery exertions…Then there is another objection which I should not have felt so strongly but that Tom pointed it out. No man should ever write of a woman but with a tone of respect and gentleness…[16]

Uncle Tom was being somewhat disingenuous with his sister. For while he might not be rude about women in print, he was capable of poking fun at them in private – and the sober Harriet Beecher Stowe was just the kind of target he would have loved. Such double standards aside, Macaulay continued to monitor his nephew's progress avidly. George was preparing for the classical and mathematical triposes, the academic ordeal when 'the man is weighed as in a balance'.[17] Candidates were placed in individual order of merit, so there was no disguising a less than world-beating performance. Macaulay, in April 1859, was fretting. 'His neglect of Mathematics is to be ascribed to the bad example which I set him. It is owing to me too, I must say on the other side, that he lives in an atmosphere reeking with Carlylism, Ruskinism, Browningism, and other equally noxious isms, without the slightest taint of the morbific virus.'[18]

Once Macaulay was dead, George embraced those noxious isms with enthusiasm, which suggests the famous uncle acted as something of a brake on the impressionable nephew. However, Macaulay's passion for the classics was passed on to George. The uncle wrote many pedantic yet instructive letters to his nephew on this topic.

Dear George,

I take the liberty to point out to you a false spelling of which you are guilty, a false spelling too, particularly censurable in a scholar – 'to pander to the insatiable love of rhetoric'. Now you are surely aware that the word pandar is simply the proper name of the warrior whom Homer calls Pandarus, and who is prompted by Minerva to break the treaty between the Greeks and the Trojans…Thence the name Pandarus or Pandar was given to pimps. When Falstaff wishes Pistol to carry a love letter to a married woman, Pistol exclaims 'Shall I Sir Pandarus of Troy become?' It is therefore most incorrect to spell the word pander. In fact this spelling…raises a strong presumption that the person who is guilty of it does not know the Greek…

I am glad that you are properly interested about the siege of Syracuse. The Seventh Book of Thucydides is the finest piece of history in the world. Livy, Tacitus, Sallust, Xenophon vanish before it. It is absolutely perfect ... [19]

The last letter Macaulay received from George was found on his writing table at his death. The nephew had taken his uncle's advice to heart, although the national volunteer movement inspired by the fear of Napoleon III was also preoccupying him.

> Dearest Uncle,
>
> Amongst all the wars and rumours of wars it is not very easy to keep one's head empty for the reception of Latin and Greek. I must do my best to enlist your sympathies in the cause of our wretched rifle-corps...
>
> You must not think, however, that the misfortunes of our rifle-corps distract my attention to any great extent from Cicero and Plato. The Athenian philosophers were disputing poker and tongs while the Spartan army was ravaging Attica ... [20]

Macaulay died in the closing days of 1859, at his London home. George called in at Holly Lodge, hoping to be asked for dinner. As he entered the library, he found Macaulay in the final hours of his life. 'My uncle was sitting, with his head bent forward on his chest, in a languid and drowsy reverie. The first number of the *Cornhill Magazine* lay unheeded before him, open at the first page of Thackeray's story of Lovel the Widower.' [21] George sent for help, and rushed back with his mother Hannah.

> We found him in the library, seated in his easy chair, and dressed as usual; with the books on the table beside him, still open at the same page...He died as he had wished to die; without pain; without any formal farewell; preceding to the grave all whom he loved; and leaving behind him a great and honourable name, and the memory of a life every action of which was as clear and transparent as one of his own sentences. [22]

Macaulay, author of *A Shortened History of England* and *Lays of Ancient Rome*, was gone, and George was finally free from the burden of his expectations. As G.M. Trevelyan wrote perceptively, 'I cannot help feeling that Macaulay's death ... was not an unmixed catastrophe to his nephew. It set him free from the burden of his own too loyal heart.' [23]

Macaulay's influence on George was critical – he instilled in him a love of literature and history, combined with an unerring belief that one could make a difference not just in the world of letters but of politics too. But upon his death, George was released to do more than merely imitate his uncle. The lasting impact of their relationship could be seen in the books George was to write. The historian H.A.L. Fisher summed up the character of their work.

> The histories of Macaulay and his nephew could not have been produced by University chairs. There is something unacademic in their impetuous flood of entertaining detail. We miss the deadly relevance and the cold impartiality of the seminar. But so long as a taste for good letters survives among those who use our English tongue, the reader in search of enjoyment will never resort in vain to the two Whig historians who have transmitted to posterity in a vestment of fresh and glowing colours one of the governing traditions of English public life.[24]

Writing history was still ahead of George, though. Having grieved for Macaulay, it was time for the demanding test of the Cambridge Tripos. The sociable George was easily distracted from the task of swotting, as he told Hannah.

> My dear Mother,
>
> Yesterday, as I was washing preparatory to rackets, there came a knock at the door, and I issued from my bedroom, covered with soap and shirtsleeves, full in the face of the Prince [of Wales]. He stayed for about quarter of an hour, talked about the pictures on the wall, etc...and then began to abuse the men up here for not hunting. He reiterated the wish he had expressed on Sunday about my hunting, so, as the royal desires jumped with mine, I am going out for the first time on Friday...A day's hunting will be the very thing, and just relieve one's mind for a day from the vexation of the coming examination.[25]

Hunting with Bertie, the Prince of Wales, was thoroughly enjoyable for George – 'My classics present a much more pleasing aspect,' he told Hannah, although 'I am glad I never hunted before. It is much too entrancing for a man before his degree. O what will that degree be?'[26]

The dreaded Tripos over, the Trinity authorities sent the irreligious George down as a punishment because he had missed chapel too often. He did not have to kick his heels long before the results came. George came second in the 1861 Tripos, behind Abbott. Successful, undoubtedly, although Macaulay would have confessed to his private journal some disappointment that his dear nephew had not come top. Thankfully, Macaulay was not there to witness George's two failed applications for a fellowship at Trinity. Piqued, George decided not to sit the exam for a third time. Other opportunities were arising

– Charles Trevelyan was returning to India as finance minister, and offered to take his son along as his private secretary, partly as compensation for missing out on the fellowship. Such were the advantages of connections and social standing. But the golden boy was hurt by the Trinity rejection, as he made plain in a letter written to Charles in 1862.

My dearest father,

I really feel more than I can well express the pain that you are sure to feel when you hear the result of this examination. Neither Jebb nor myself are on the list. None of the examiners pretend to say that we were beaten. If I had been wise I should have taken warning by last time and spared you and myself a periodical humiliation. It is a most cruel thing to call an examination a competition, and then to give the prizes by seniority. Never again will I put my reputation in any hands but my own. The examiners all express themselves thoroughly satisfied with me, which is really adding insult to injury. With great love,
I remain,
Yr. aff. Son,
G.O. Trevelyan[27]

The failure wounded George precisely because he had spent his life preparing for the sunlit uplands of Trinity, inspired by Macaulay. But the narrow confines of academia were not for him. He threw what he was pleased to call a non-fellowship dinner, and left Trinity behind. He had made lasting friendships there – with Henry and Arthur Sidgwick, Edward Bowen, Henry Jackson, Montagu Butler, Harry Yates Thompson, and his dearest comrade Sir George Young. Already he was beginning to take an interest in the wider world. His New Year resolutions for 1862 included 'to learn to speak, to make an honest effort at political knowledge'.[28] Immediately after failing the fellowship for the second time, George sailed for India, leaving his rancour behind.

It was to be an instructive year for the 24-year-old. Confident, high-spirited, charming and funny, George had inherited Macaulay's sense of humour, and fortunately more of his looks than the austere Trevelyan features. He was all set to experience the world. And George's duties as private secretary to his father were none too arduous. There was a lot of travel and tiger shooting. Even the journey to India enabled George to indulge in his hobby of composing light verse. 'Fair dames, whose easy-chairs in goodly row / Fringe either bulwark of the P. & O.'[29] On arrival, the welcome for Charles in Madras delighted his watching son. Charles had been sent home as Governor of Madras in disgrace, only to return as finance minister for all India. George recorded the occasion in a letter to Sir Walter Trevelyan and his wife Pauline, the couple who were to leave Wallington to him. 'At Madras the whole business resembled a triumph. The attachment of the natives was really affecting. The sentence most in their mouths "This Governor[30] is the Governor of the Sahib people, but Sir Charles was the Governor of our people."'[31]

For Macaulay's nephew, steeped as he was in the tradition of narrative history, this was an opportunity to observe and chronicle the unfolding events in India after the 1857 Mutiny against British rule. George wrote descriptive, amusing and perceptive semi-fictional letters home, published first in *Macmillan's Magazine* and then as a book, entitled *The Competition Wallah*. This was a term used to describe the civil servants in India appointed after competitive examination, introduced in 1853 after the efforts of George's uncle and father. The obvious irony here is that George owed his post to nepotism, not the reforms advocated by his nearest and dearest. He was no competition wallah. But he created one, the imaginary Henry Broughton, who wrote letters to an old school friend back home. George's intention was, via Henry, to 'induce Englishmen at home to take a lively and effective interest in the native population of their Eastern dominions'.

The eleven letters, written by the composite figure of Henry to his friend Charles Simkins, are the fulfilment of a supposed pact the two have made. Should only one of them pass the Indian civil service examination, he will write a full account of his experiences to the friend left in England. George used this device to great effect, describing the worst excesses of the Raj in full detail. Satirical, comic and occasionally savage, the letters are the portrait of an age at a pivotal moment. Here is 'Henry' describing the arrival of an English sahib at a railway station.

> Suddenly, in the rear of the crowd, without the gates, there arises a great hubbub, amidst which, from time to time, may be distinguished an imperious, sharp-cut voice, the owner of which appears to show the most lordly indifference to the remarks and answers around him. A few moments more, after some quarrelling and shoving, the throng divides, and down the lane thus formed stalks the Sahib of the period, in all the glory of an old flannel short and trousers, a dirty alpaca coat, no collar, no waistcoat, white canvas shoes, and a vast pith helmet. Behind him comes his chief bearer, with a cash-box, a loading rod, two copies of the *Saturday*

Review of six months back, and three bottles of soda-water ... The Sahib walks with the freedom and easy insolence of a member of the Imperial race, walks straight into the sacred enclosure of the clerk's office, and takes a ticket, at five times the price paid by his native brethren.[32]

The determination of the Empire builders to live just as one did in England, despite the punishing heat of Calcutta, also provided much material for George, or rather his alias Henry Broughton.

You probably never waltzed in full evening dress round the inner chamber of a Turkish bath, and therefore can have no conception of the peculiar charms of the dance in this climate ... the waste of tissue during a gallope, with a partner in high training just landed from England, is truly frightful. The natives understand these things better. They let their ladies do the dancing for them, and content themselves with looking on.[33]

George was no great fan of the Indian character, as he saw it. In a letter called 'the Hindoo character', he claimed Hindus were lazy, work-shy and found it difficult to tell the difference between truth and lies. However, well versed as he was in the English class structure, George found much to appreciate in the Hindu caste system. 'He belongs to a social order, which dates back far into the depths of time, with innumerable well-defined grades and classes; with titles which were borne by his forefathers, when the ancestors of English dukes paddled about in wicker canoes.'[34]

Patrician as George's views were towards Indians, he was to become a staunch defender of their rights. The Lieutenant-Governor of Bengal, Cecil Beadon, invited George on a tour of the province in February 1863. Here the inquisitive historian saw the aftermath of the 1857 Mutiny for himself, visiting places such as the Little House of Arrah, scene of much bloodshed. He did not like what he saw, as he explained to Pauline Trevelyan.

The chief traces of the mutiny are not material but moral. It is no longer the fashion to show the slightest interest in the natives: the 'confounded nigger' style is the thing nowadays. The Englishmen who do not belong to the Government Service behave too much like Orangemen in Ireland. Every day there is a ferocious article against the natives in one or other of the Calcutta papers, and I fear there is more chance that this feeling will extend to the Civil Service than that the Civil Service will influence for good the Planters and Merchants.[35]

George's letters were initially well received in England, providing an amusing and insightful account of Empire life for those who had little idea of what the day-to-day existence entailed. But that all stopped with his letter entitled 'British Temper towards India, Before, During and Since the Mutiny'. In this, George was merciless in his portrayal of the non-official British community, the plantation bosses. 'These men had come to the shores of India for the sole purpose of making money. They were under no professional obligation of providing for the prosperity and happiness of the population, and indeed were too apt to regard their dark fellow-subjects as tools for promoting their own ends.'[36]

The philanthropic, liberal vision of what England could do for India was, George found, being challenged by the grasping and vengeful views of the next generation of English settlers, whose attitudes had been hardened by the Mutiny. George was shocked by the indigo plantation owners he met in Bengal, whose sole aim, he found, was to make their fortunes, not govern wisely and well. And he made Henry Broughton tell it like it was.

> The European settlers in India speedily acquired that contempt for the Bengalese which it is a law of nature that the members of a conquering race should entertain for the subject population among whom they live. As the Norman baron regarded the Saxon churl...so it was inevitable that the English planter should regard the ryot and the coolly. No one can estimate very highly the moral and intellectual qualities of people among whom he resides for the single purpose of turning them to pecuniary account...[37]

His account of how well-dressed Indians were horsewhipped out of the enclosure at the annual Sunapur race meeting by an Englishman did nothing for the image of the Raj either. 'One or two civilians said to each other it was "a shame," but no-one seemed astounded or horrified, no-one interposed, no-one prosecuted, no-one objected to meet the blackguard at dinner.'[38]

In London, this bold denunciation of his fellow Englishmen led to George's vilification by the *Spectator*. He was seen as spiteful, issuing 'a burst of civilian hate against the independent settler'.[39] George was unabashed. He wanted to make English people aware of the harshness and contempt with which so many Europeans in India treated the Indian population. Inspired by Macaulay, he accepted the right of the British to rule over India, but only if that rule contributed to the well-being of India. John Clive, the great authority on Macaulay, much admired *The Competition Wallah*, which he argued was 'as much a revelation of the general outlook of a young Whiggish Radical as it is an account of a sojourn in India'.[40] He considered the work to be a serious appeal by an English patriot for a revival of that spirit and for an end to race hatred on the part of English settlers. The sociologist Edward Shils went so far as to compare George's account of India with de Tocqueville's of America, both written by young men seeking to discern the lineaments of a foreign society in less than a year. Shils observed that while *The Competition Wallah* was not quite in the same class as de Tocqueville, it was not far off.[41]

Back in the mid-nineteenth century, Charles and Hannah were also proud of their one-time dilettante son, regarding the later letters as particularly worthy of praise. Charles, as a reformer, would have agreed with and probably subtly influenced much of what his son wrote. He was pleased to see George coming of age and obtaining 'a habit of work such as he has never had before', as he noted approvingly. The father now wished the son to go into politics, as he confided to a friend in August 1863.

> I have been particularly pleased at the way George has taken to Indian affairs...He...has imposed upon himself an improving exercise by writing about what he has seen. He will return with his mother and sister in October. An opening will I hope soon appear for his getting into Parliament. You know how much I have it at heart. It will be much the best for him, and I do not think it will be bad for the public – to give up his whole life to public affairs.[42]

George's Indian experience was completed with a grand tour of Agra and the Taj Mahal. By now he was struggling with the climate, and more than ready to return home. As Hannah wrote to her daughter Margaret, 'He has no colour, his cheeks are thin, his eyes look quite large, and his cheek bones are developed. There are some people who just cannot live here in India, and he is one.'[43] The heat might have disagreed with him, but India had sharpened George's sense of purpose. The author of *The Competition Wallah* had made a name for himself in literary London, and his clashes with the plantation owners had awakened his reforming instincts. He was to write a further successful book about the Mutiny, called *Cawnpore*, which described the massacre there in which, among others, various Trevelyan relatives died. The *Times Literary Supplement* considered this the best of all his Indian pieces:

> It displays for the first time in Trevelyan, barely twenty seven years old, the family gift for marshalling intricate and in themselves details so as to give a limpidly clear and arresting account of the main facts; and on occasion it shows a power of rapid, telling description...that his famous uncle would not have disowned.[44]

Pauline and Walter Calverley Trevelyan, who had engineered George's eventual inheritance of Wallington, were most taken with *Cawnpore*. They heard their prodigy read it aloud in two sittings. George warned them the book would offend many of his readers, because he had tried to 'imbue it with a spirit of tolerance towards the natives'.[45] Certain passages might seem 'deliberately provocative', such as this one: 'The truth was that it mattered very little to them (the Sahibs) whom they killed, as long as they killed somebody. After the first outbreak of joy and welcome the inhabitants of Cawnpore began to be aware that the English were no longer the same men, if indeed they were men at all.'[46]

George's social criticism and his no-holds-barred style were thoroughly approved of by Walter and Pauline. Friends of Pauline wept at the book's description of the massacre of the British by the Indians. George left nothing to the imagination when detailing the state of the inner apartment of the ladies' house at Cawnpore: 'ankle deep in blood. The pilaster was scored with sword-cuts: not high up, as where men would have fought; but low down, and about the corners, as if a creature had crouched to avoid the blow...'[47] Bertie, the Prince of Wales, told George over whist at Marlborough House that he was seriously grieved by the principles displayed by certain Englishmen in the book.

George had made his point about India, but it was not a subject that featured much in his long career. He made just one speech on India, years later in 1868 in the House of Commons. He argued that Indians should be given places in the Indian civil service, rather than have to sit competitive examinations. This was because, he suggested, although Indian youths were quick-witted and capable of getting high marks in the exam, they had moral and physical defects that could not be adequately tested. His rather dubious view of what he called the Hindoo character had not changed much over the years. George was aware that he could be seen as speaking in derogatory terms about Indians, so he reminded his audience that he was a sincere well-wisher towards India.

After his Indian adventure, George returned to London to make his debut into London society and politics. Comforted by the knowledge that he was to inherit Wallington, the house and 13,000-acre estate in Northumberland, his sights were now focused on getting into parliament, just as his father wished. Most notable Trevelyans, according to David Cannadine, the biographer of G.M. Trevelyan, were not the sort to make a party swing.[48] They were far too earnest and high-minded for frivolity, drinking and idle chatter.

Not George. The 1860s, he told his children afterwards, were the last decade in which society in the old sense of the word, the Trollopian, Jane Austen definition, really existed. As G.M. Trevelyan understood it, there was

one supreme set recognised by all others as being 'Society' par excellence. Entrance could neither be demanded nor purchased. The keys were held by the dames of certain great political and territorial houses, who in due consultation with their lords opened their portals to some not born within their magic circle, most often for political, sometimes for literary or personal reasons.[49]

George moved effortlessly into this revolving world of country houses, Mayfair townhouses and gentlemen's clubs in St James's. He describes the scene in his book of verse *Ladies in Parliament*, which brings alive the salons of the political hostesses, and the atmosphere in clubland at dawn.

For the town is just awaking,
And you will not meet a soul,
Save, perhaps, Lord Chelmsford taking,
His accustomed morning stroll;
Or some swells who've chanced to linger
Over their cigars and chats,
Trailing latch-keys round their finger,
As they loiter home from Pratt's.[50]

The shining star of this constellation to which George was now drawn was John Bright, the radical political philosopher. John Stuart Mill, author of *On Liberty*, was also to be found on the society circuit, and George hero-worshipped him from afar but thought him a bore in person. John Bright, the Quaker from Rochdale, he found worthy of true personal devotion. The American Civil War followed the course Bright had predicted, not the one mapped out by *The Times*, *Punch*, and the Whig and Tory leaders, which gave him prophet status. The young Whigs, such as the Cavendishes, the Amberleys and the Trevelyans, invited Bright into their drawing rooms, and he in turn made them more radical. Bright had many enemies, dismissed by George in verse.

Since every party strife began the world is still the same,
And radicals from age to age are held the fairest game.
As in the troubled days of Rome each curled and scented jackass
Who lounged along the Sacred Way heehawed at Caius Gracchus,

So now all paltry jesters run their maiden wit to flesh on
A block of rugged Saxon oak, that shews no light impression;
At which whoe'er aspires to chop had better guard his eye,
And toward the nearest cover bolt, if once the splinters fly.[51]

Full of youthful ardour as he was, George now tried for parliament. The general election of 1865 gave him the opening he had been looking for. He stood for Tynemouth in the North-east of England, a small borough that while not quite rotten, those having been mostly abolished in the Reform Act of 1832, was certainly open to manipulation. Previously staunchly Tory, under the patronage of the Duke of Northumberland and the Tyneside shipowners, the Liberals now thought they stood a chance. And one shipowner even joined George's election committee, driving him round on the box of a carriage drawn by four horses. Not being from Northumberland meant the young candidate had to endure a certain amount of ribbing from the locals. One jingle went like this.

Who's come to Tynemouth, full of grace,
With big black whiskers on his face?
Who fancies he can go the pace?
The Wallah![52]

The election result hinged on the way the Chirton estate voted. The farmers and tenants always voted with their landlord, whoever he might be. And so Sir Walter Calverley Trevelyan of Wallington, just up the road, helped George buy the Chirton estate for £61,000 – it was sold shortly afterwards, having served its purpose. As G.M. Trevelyan put it, 'The fact that my father, of all people, first entered parliament by such a road as the Chirton estate, indicates how little of a Radical he then was, and what were the limits of the electoral reform that had been affected in 1832.'[53] However, Raleigh Trevelyan says G.M. misunderstood the details of this transaction, and in fact Chirton was not purchased until after the election, precisely because George knew how it would look.[54] The first version certainly makes for the better story.

Palmerston's Tory party won the election of 1865, and bucking the national trend, George was returned as the Liberal member for Tynemouth, helped, or perhaps not, by that old trick of vote-buying. Gladstone told him this was 'the most surprising victory of the election. He was very excited and gushing, and Mrs Gladstone was wild with interest and eagerness.'[55] George had played the system to get elected, but now he immersed himself in the Reform Act of 1867, which further extended the franchise. He was able to sit in the

Commons next to his beloved John Bright, and watch the sparks fly as the Reform Bill was debated. Gladstone, the Liberal Party leader, was admired by George but not revered. As he wrote to his sister Alice in 1867, 'Travelled part of the way with Gladstone. He was reading nothing but a silly little Church goody book.'[56]

No chance of finding George with the Bible on his travels – Aristophanes was a more likely choice. Not that there was much time for reading. Parliament occupied much of his time, what with the Reform Act, and his support for Cardwell's army reforms. On the abolition of the purchase of commissions in the army, also one of his father's favourite causes, the young George felt Cardwell had not gone far enough. His maiden speech, a halting affair by his own account, was made in favour of university reform. And then there was the continuing social whirl, during which George met one of the other towering figures of the time. Here he is remembering how the new MPs of 1865 got to know one another.

> During the ensuing autumn, and early winter – what with foreign travel, field-sports, and country house parties – we fleeted the time merrily and carelessly, as people then did in that golden world...towards the end of the year 1865 the Dowager Lady Cowper invited a large number of guests to her seat at Wrest, in Bedfordshire. On the first evening Mr Disraeli took down the hostess; and, to my dismay, there was no chair for me to occupy except that which stood empty on his other side. It was a more trying ordeal than I anticipated; for Mr Disraeli did not speak to me once through all the dinner, or after the ladies left...then I broke the silence, and timidly and respectfully asked Mr Disraeli whether he had a strong opinion on the Patent Laws. 'I have,' he replied, 'no strong opinion upon any subject in the world.'[57]

Crushed by this typically languid reply from the great man, George was soon cheered, for Disraeli, 'clad in velvet of a showy and cheerful colour', did recognise him the next day, greeting him as the son of his old and valued friend Sir Charles Trevelyan. When Disraeli was Chancellor, Sir Charles was his senior civil servant. Once again connections had come to the aid of George, and Disraeli henceforth 'treated me with a flattering and rather mocking freedom, quite irresistible to younger men whom he was desirous to conciliate'.[58] Not that their political views collided – Disraeli, arch-monarchist, would have disapproved heartily of an anonymous pamphlet probably penned by George some years later, called 'What Does She Do With It?'. It accused

Queen Victoria of hiving off money from the civil list and creating a private fortune from public funds. And George supported women's right to have the vote – anathema to Dizzy.

Still, political disagreements notwithstanding, what a heady experience being courted by Disraeli must have been. George was starry-eyed for much of his early period in parliament, and not just because he was in the company of John Bright and Disraeli. He was in love. While campaigning for Gladstone's re-election in Lancashire in 1865, sent down as the triumphant victor of Tynemouth, he had met the Philips family of Manchester. Robert Needham Philips, wealthy merchant, free-trader and follower of William Cobden, was charmed by the brilliant youngster who charged into his campaign committee rooms. So was Caroline, Robert's daughter. Clever, pretty and interested in politics, Caroline was enchanted by the witty young George. A speedy engagement ensued, and then it was just as speedily blocked by Caroline's uncle Mark Philips, one of the Manchester MPs. Mark, despite being a Liberal, had ambitions for Caroline to marry a Lord. As the more powerful of the Philips brothers, Mark had his way. But Caroline, in her quietly determined way, was not going to marry anyone except George, and ultimately thwarted her uncle. It took Caroline two years to change her uncle's mind. Distraught, George went travelling on the Continent, nursing his bruised emotions.

For a lovelorn liberal in search of distraction, Garibaldi's valiant campaign to reunify Italy was full of romantic appeal. George and his travelling companion Lord Lorne went in search of the heroic figure. While in Paris for the Universal Exhibition, the pair decided on impulse to try to reach Rome in time to witness Garibaldi's invasion of the Papal States. They managed to get an audience with their hero. In a letter to *The Times* many years later, in 1924, George recalled the event.

> We…learned that on the previous day Garibaldi had been entirely defeated in a decisive battle at Mentana, and that he was returning in a train with his Staff and personal followers, and might be expected within a couple of hours. At about 10 or 11 in the morning the train came in…
> We presented ourselves respectfully to the General, and he received us simply and cordially – Lorne as the son of those who had been his principal entertainers in his visit to England in 1864, and me as the Member for Tynemouth and North Shields, to which port he had sailed as a merchant-captain in the intervals of his soldiering…it was the worst moment in his long life of uphill struggle; but he met, and surpassed, my expectation of him as a noble and modest hero;

something more homely than I expected, but none the less loveable and admirable on that account.[59]

This encounter had many ramifications. The romantic appeal of Garibaldi was absorbed by G.M. Trevelyan, who was to write about the Italian general and his achievements. More immediately, meeting Garibaldi was some compensation for George, quietly grieving over the loss of Caroline. He was soon brooding more publicly in Florence, into the sympathetic ear of Lady Frederick Cavendish. 'She said she knew there was something the matter with me, and challenged me to tell her what it was. I told her, and she kept the secret, which I cannot remember telling anyone else. And she gave me an eager and beautiful sympathy.'[60]

Uncle Mark Philips finally capitulated, ground down by the silent but serious resistance of Caroline, who rejected all other suitors. In July 1869, quite unexpectedly, Mark gave his consent to the marriage he had opposed so vehemently. George wrote joyfully to Caroline: 'And so it is all over; and we are to be happy and sorry, and overworked and idle, and successful and unlucky together all the rest of our lives. Your father was very, very kind about it; and it is pleasant to see how relieved and happy he seems.'[61]

Uncle Mark was gracious in defeat. He wrote to George, 'The days of Clarissa Harlowe[62] are fortunately known no more, and Carry declares that she can expect happiness only as your wife. I fear you will not felicitate yourself upon becoming connected with a gouty old uncle, but I will try to behave well and not be cross.'[63]

That very same day, the happy groom-to-be-received this from his Florentine soulmate.

Dear Mr Trevelyan,

Didn't I always so say! And ain't I the very wisest and best of prophets and advisers? God grant you may both be as happy as we are, for many long years.

Very sincerely yours,
Lucy C.F. Cavendish[64]

In September 1869 George and Caroline were married, and were seldom parted until Caroline died 59 years later, to be followed after only eight months by a grieving George. This was an enduring love affair – as their son G.M. Trevelyan put it, 'They grew into one another by mind and habit so that I used often to wonder how one could survive alone.'[65] During one brief separation in 1908, George wrote to Caroline, 'I am never unhappy for a few days with work and solitude; for that amount of solitude, brief, and at long intervals, introduces an element of contemplation and recognition into one's feeling about the person whose presence makes one's life.'[66]

Caroline filled in the long hours while George was writing or politicking by painting. She had no wish to share the limelight with her husband – she later turned down the public-speaking opportunities offered to her as the spouse of a prominent politician and historian. While other liberal wives became political hostesses and agitated for women's suffrage, Caroline stayed in the background. Described by one servant as 'just if not generous',[67] Caroline's tight accounting methods were learnt from her father, industrialist, who taught her that counting the pennies carefully was the way to get rich. She exuded sweetness and light, but could be extremely steely. As the head gardener at Wallington wrote, 'Seldom did I see her ruffled. Whether this outward calm was due to a rigorous self-discipline or inherited I cannot say. Only I know from what she told me, her father could ring the changes with some clang when things didn't just run smooth.'[68]

Life was good for George in the late 1860s – he had found love, and well-connected love at that. Caroline would eventually inherit Welcombe, a vast Victorian mansion near Stratford-upon-Avon that is now a luxury hotel. And he had a new parliamentary seat that wasn't as rotten as Tynemouth. In the general election of 1868, he was elected as the MP for the Scottish border burghs. The land of Hawick, Selkirk and Galashiels echoed with history, from the Jacobite rebellion to the novels of Sir Walter Scott, much to George's delight. And the constituency was only 40 miles from Wallington, the stately home to which he was heir. To add to all this, the golden boy was given a junior job in government by Gladstone, as Civil Lord of the Admiralty. The caption to a 'Spy' cartoon in *Vanity Fair* summed him up thus:

> A busy, pushing man is Mr Trevelyan…He can scarcely find life long enough for all the forms of activity in which he would indulge. He is in every 'movement' that shows itself on the surface of the eddies and whirlpools of our modern politics…For ever writing, speaking, questioning, moving, dividing, agitating, he had, so far, seen his labours bear no inconsiderable fruit…He is a popular Doctrinaire, ready with remedies for all things, and very eager to apply them. He is not always exactly accurate in his facts. His 'views' are those of an audacious leader writer for the daily press. He is a Liberal.[69]

On the verge of making it big he may have been, but at this point the gold begins to flake off George. He was not a successful politician, and nor was his son Charles Philips – neither were good at compromising, both gave up much too easily. The iron resolve of Charles Edward had not been transmitted to his son – Macaulay's nephew had books he wanted to write, a wife he adored, and, while he loved the all-consuming atmosphere of parliament, the rigours of high office were not for him.

The Education Act of 1870 gave George cause to fall on his sword. While establishing publicly managed 'board schools', the act also increased the state grant to Church schools, making them a permanent part of the new education system. This disappointed many liberals, who believed in curbing the power of the Church, not entrenching it. George wrote to the Education Secretary, 'I regard this matter as one not of expediency, but right and wrong.'[70] He objected most strenuously to the fact that the government had dealt a blow to the endowment of denominational schools in Ireland, yet only partially applied the principle. He explained to Gladstone, 'I cannot compromise my future action in this matter as I am quite unable to support or to abstain from opposing any important concession to the denominational system.'[71] In his resignation statement he called the proposal a parasitical growth that ought never to have been attached to the bill. The *Spectator* thought his resignation most odd.

> Mr G.O. Trevelyan, Civil Lord of the Admiralty, appears to be possessed of that extremely rare and inconvenient article, an over-sensitive conscience. He cannot endure to vote for a Bill increasing the grant to denominational schools, and has consequently resigned. When an ambitious man gives up his chance of a career from a conscientious scruple we have nothing to do but to respect his principles, even if we cannot, as in this case, appreciate his actions.[72]

Gladstone was not at all impressed by this show of principle, and left George out in the cold for a decade. As G.M. Trevelyan wrote, 'My father had put himself back ten years and more in the race up the ladder of political promotion, on the lower rungs of which he had made so early and so promising a start.'[73] George never regretted his quixotic decision, insisting that for him there was something stronger than self-interest or fear of ridicule. Principled independence was his chosen path.

Out of office, he was able to pursue a more radical agenda. Together with Sir Charles Dilke, he campaigned against excessive military and royal

'A busy, pushing man is Mr Trevelyan...' George Otto Trevelyan drawn by Spy Cartoon for *Vanity Fair*, 2 August 1873. Courtesy of the Trustees of the Trevelyan family papers.

expenditure. In April 1872 he introduced into the Commons a resolution calling for the extension to the counties of the household suffrage that Disraeli had granted to the boroughs in 1867. Following the Reform Acts of 1832 and 1867, further extension to the franchise was greeted with the parliamentary equivalent of a raspberry. The resolution got only 70 votes. But George did not give up, and in each of the following seven sessions he reintroduced his proposal, either as a resolution or a private member's bill. His case was relentlessly logical. By now three million householders were excluded from the franchise simply because they lived in areas that were not parliamentary boroughs. Therefore the anomaly existed 'that a man who spins wool at Barnsley could make a worse voter than a man who spins it at Bradford'.[74] He argued persuasively that rural householders were being neglected because they were disenfranchised, while urban problems received far more attention. His persistence meant that when Gladstone's second administration took office in 1880, it was committed to further extension of the franchise, which was finally carried in 1884 with the third Reform Act.

The life of a backbencher gave George more time to write too, without the inconvenience of red boxes to attend to. And he could do some more reading and travelling at last. Or rather, Caroline could listen to him reading aloud. As this letter to his sister Alice from Milan shows, this was a time for revisiting the classics to which Macaulay had introduced him. 'We are reading Gibbon. The excellence of it is astonishing. That a man should have read through such an amorphous immeasurable mass of antique rubbish and yet retain such wit, vigour and imagination... '[75]

Then he tells Alice, 'We are reading Hogg's life of Shelley... It is a wonderfully amusing compound of vanity, silliness and cleverness, and gives a better picture of Shelley than any book gives of any other individual.'[76]

George read and reread Thomas Carlyle's *Sterling*, inhaling the style his uncle Macaulay had dismissed as a noxious ism. All this reading was preparing him for his task of writing a *Life and Letters of Lord Macaulay*. Not until 1874, when Disraeli won the general election, was he free to begin this work – the opposition years gave him the space he needed. Hannah had been on at George to begin the project earlier – she was to die in 1873 without reading the biography of her beloved brother, written by her darling son, that she so desired. The *Life* was published in 1876 to immediate and widespread acclaim. The author was thrilled by the reception. As he wrote to his sister, 'Nothing has given me so much satisfaction as to find that the eminent literary men, who were not overfond of my uncle qua literary man, have been won over by his private personality. Witness Carlyle, Morley, Leslie Stephen, and Froude.'[77]

John Morley, like George a politician and an author, even went so far as to say that the *Life* was a better book than Macaulay's *History of England*. Carlyle, a rival of Macaulay's, was lavish in his praise to George:

> I have nowhere found in any biography, not even in 'Boswell's Johnson', a human life and character more clearly, credibly and completely brought home to the conception of every intelligent reader...Your own part of the affair I think you have performed to admiration: nothing hidden and yet no offence given.[78]

Carlyle, now a firm friend, called the younger man a 'pullis Jovis',[79] a fortunate youth. And George did seem to live a charmed life. Even an attempt to blackball his membership of the Athenaeum Club, then a favoured haunt of literary types, failed. Some of the elderly military members had not forgotten his support for the abolition of the purchase of commissions, and sought revenge – but a well-publicised campaign, with a nomination paper signed by Carlyle among other luminaries, resulted in his election by 389 votes to 20. Carlyle, then 82, came to the Athenaeum for the vote to canvass support for George. Happily elected, all the new member of the Athenaeum really wanted to do was write. As he told his brother-in-law Henry Holland,

> The secret of my life is that I have a craving for literature, like that of some people for drink, and, till it was worked off, I could settle to nothing. Perhaps the most perfect simile would be that of a young man who is desperately in love, gets over it, and then goes about his business in peace afterwards.[80]

The next book George longed to write was *The Early History of Charles James Fox*, a portrait of eighteenth-century society and its leading Whig political light. Fox was something of a boy racer, brilliant and irresponsible, and the book provides today's reader with an insight into a bygone radical aristocratic milieu. The *Times Literary Supplement* described the book as

> Saturated with spirit, he could play with the characters of the time, as if they were familiar living acquaintances, and always had at his finger tips the bit of gossip to illustrate a man or the manners of his great little world. He brings out, as no other historian has done, the almost unique condition of English politics and society of the eighteenth century, when a few powerful families with their hangers on monopolized the plums of office

and of sinecures as a matter of course, so that it became almost a matter of chance if a man capable of government rose to the responsibilities of office.[81]

George never wrote anything equal to this – it was his hour of triumph. Many have been inspired by the portrait of Fox and his circle. Aneurin Bevan, founding father of the NHS, knew the book so well that some suspected he modelled himself on Fox. Michael Foot, Labour Party leader in the 1980s, and devotee of Bevan, said, 'It's a perfect book, because it's just one of the greatest biographies in the English language. It's the most wonderful story; it makes you in love with Fox, and understand why he was the greatest Liberal figure of that period.'[82]

Having finished his Fox book in time for the general election of 1880, George was beginning to miss the world of politics. Apart from his annual franchise proposals, he had played little part in Westminster life during the opposition years. After Gladstone retired, George, like the other radicals, supported W.E. Forster's candidacy for leadership of the Commons. But Hartington was victorious, and his cautious approach was not to George's liking. After the Bulgarian massacres of 1876, George supported Gladstone's campaign against Turkish misgovernment. Otherwise he devoted himself to his writing. So it was rather arrogant of George to be put out when, after the Liberal victory in 1880, Gladstone initially failed to give him a job. But then, at the eleventh hour, he was offered the position of Vice-President of the Board of Trade under Joseph Chamberlain. George declined, regarding it as the equivalent of political extinction, since Chamberlain would handle all the important departmental business in the Commons. Shortly afterwards, *Fox* was published by Longman and was a tremendous critical success, which impressed the Prime Minister. In November 1880 Gladstone came back with the tempting job of Civil Lord of the Admiralty. The Prime Minister wrote, 'You have used the time alike with energy and with judgement for the public services, for the literary world, and for your own reputation.'[83]

This offer suited George's vanity – his superior, Lord Northbrook, was in the upper chamber, so he got to speak for the navy in the Commons. In his acceptance letter to the Prime Minister, he was gracious: 'To have on record in your hand that I have employed my time not unworthily, is as high a reward as I can imagine.'[84]

Writing to his father Charles, George was elated, saying, 'It is a post of great independence and influence…Gladstone's letter is everything that could be wished for.'[85] A letter to Henry Sidgwick, his Trinity contemporary, positively drips with satisfaction:

> To be appointed by Gladstone to a post of serious business straight from books is a protection against the sort of comments which the critical would make. My intense enjoyment of the work leads me to think that he sees the fact rightly, that I am not a literary politician, but a somewhat one-sided dogged personage who never cares for anything but his ends.[86]

George did not have long to enjoy the Admiralty job. His determination was about to be tried and tested in Ireland, just as his father's had been. The subject this time was not famine but Home Rule. The parliament of 1880 returned the Irish nationalist Charles Stewart Parnell and his bloc of supporters, who wanted Home Rule for their country. To get it, they pursued a policy of obstruction in the Commons, which gave Gladstone many headaches. Meanwhile in Ireland itself, the Land League was pressing for agrarian reform – the subsequent unrest there brought a draconian clampdown from the Chief Secretary W.E Forster. Parnell was imprisoned, and let out when Gladstone ordered a change of tactics. Forster resigned, and Lord Frederick Cavendish, whose wife Lucy had encouraged George's love affair with Caroline, was appointed in his place. No sooner had Lord Cavendish landed in Ireland and begun to walk, in the company of his under-secretary Mr Burke, across Phoenix Park to his new home when disaster struck. The two men were stabbed to death by Irish assassins called the 'invincibles', who opposed not only the English but Parnell too. The uproar this double killing caused in England and Ireland moved John Morley, like George a politician and author, to describe 'a society on the eve of dissolution'.

Into this violent atmosphere came George, appointed to replace the murdered Lord Cavendish. Dilke had refused to take the job without promotion to the Cabinet, forcing Gladstone to look elsewhere. Five days after the Phoenix Park killings, George was thrown into the job. It came at a time of great personal distress to him. His sister Alice's husband, Stratford Dugdale, lay dying after he had tried to rescue colliers trapped by the collapse of a mine he owned in Warwickshire. Dugdale's death, portrayed as heroic by the press, moved Gladstone to tell George it was such deeds that gave him hope for the country. George wrote to his sister,

> It is heart-rending to think of your grief, and my enforced absence. I never felt anything so much. The state of the country here is very sad; but you

must not think of me in actual danger. The question is one of precaution and no device is neglected. It was a very different risk that made your husband's death so truly glorious.[87]

All-night sittings in parliament were frequent, and there George faced the wit and the venom of the Parnellite opposition. During two years as Chief Secretary he answered over two thousand[88] parliamentary questions, many of them fiercely hostile, on every conceivable aspect of the administration of Ireland. At one point, our radical aristocrat told his tormentors that 'though he might be an Irish Secretary he was still an English gentleman'.[89] Not a comment likely to endear him to his opponents, one might think, but in 1883 George wrote this to Alice:

> Somehow or other, the Irish members have a strange and almost ineradicable liking for me. Healy the other day talked of me as singularly courteous and genial, 'and this,' he said, 'though I do not forget the Richmond incident,' which meant that I had put him in prison for four months out of the last five.[90]

Parliamentary guerrilla warfare aside, most of George's time was spent in the Chief Secretary's Lodge, attempting to run Ireland from day to day. Or, rather, contain the country. The lawlessness subsided a little, and George and his superior Lord Spencer, Viceroy of Ireland, were relieved but realistic. Both were dismayed by the coercive tactics of previous British administrations in Ireland, and wished to avoid becoming partisans of the Orangemen. Neither fooled himself into thinking he had 'solved the problem' of Ireland. George told Alice in August 1882,

> Things are mending here, fast and surely, as far as crime and disorder in general are concerned, though I fancy that there is more probability than ever of some sensationalist crime. It is an odd atmosphere to find oneself in: and very unlike what I should have chosen for myself. The little boys are very happy, and Carry tolerates it. It is her way to take things as she finds them. The garden and the grounds are beautiful.[91]

The little boys were Charles Philips, Robert Calverley, and George Macaulay, the historian-to-be, who later described how 'unconsciously a sense of the drama of English and Irish history was purveyed to me through daily sights and experiences, with my father as commentator and bard'.[92] The everyday drama of Ireland was taking its toll on George, who at only 46 began to turn white of hair and beard. He wrote to his sister Margaret,

The effect of getting used to what is bad in Ireland is that you get more and more disgusted with the whole thing. The perversity of everybody who either writes or speaks is something inconceivable. If these people were left to themselves, we should have a mutual massacre; unless they are not quite as brave as they pretend.[93]

George was well guarded while in Ireland – the assassination of Lord Frederick Cavendish had appalled England. Even when visiting his father at Wallington, the Irish Secretary travelled with his security detail. Wallington's ever-observant head gardener, Edward Keith, recalled an unusual shooting party late in 1880.

> A shoot had been arranged in the home woods. We were beating up that narrow part of the west woods nearing the Fountains. We were crowded together, Sir Charles and his son only walking with the beaters…A well got-up person had been walking not far from the Irish Secretary's side all the morning, whom I had taken for a probable private secretary. 'Rabbit back!' rang out from Jimmy Thornton. Mr Trevelyan wheeled, fired and missed. Crack! rang out a shot to my side. A colt revolver smoked in the right hand of my neighbour. A rabbit was struggling on the ground some twenty yards away, a bullet hole through its body. The supposed private secretary was the famous detective, Moore of Scotland Yard, one of the most deadly shots in the country, ready at any moment to hole any fanatical Irishman that dare raise hands against the late Secretary's successor. Mr Trevelyan nodded his admiration of his protector's skills. Sir Charles looked on with a sickly smile, visualising black deeds. Jimmy Davison, sucking a short black cutty pipe in his clutched hand, nearly swallowed the filthy clay bowl, baccy and all, as he jumped clear, believing the hole was through him, not the rabbit.[94]

Highly strung and sensitive, George found the experience of administering Ireland a draining one. He was worn down by the pressures, and disillusioned about his prospects. In December 1882, he told his political mentor Sir William Harcourt he feared Dilke's promotion to the Cabinet had damaged him, since the radical wing of the party now had a representative at the top table. Harcourt persuaded him not to moan to Gladstone, but the following year George told the Prime Minister he should be in the Cabinet to give him more authority in the Commons over the Parnellites. By July 1884 George couldn't take any more, and wrote to Gladstone asking to be removed from a position that was 'not human life at all'. He felt his 'nerves, health, happiness and self respect'[95] were being sacrificed as he faced the Parnellites night after long night in the Commons.

Gladstone rewarded him for the Phoenix Park years in 1884 with a job in the Cabinet, as Chancellor of the Duchy of Lancaster. There George saw his project, the County Franchise Bill, pushed through parliament, a further extension of voting rights that the Lords bitterly opposed. Queen Victoria was persuaded to mediate with their lordships, after George made representations to her. She wrote in her journal of 29 October 1884, 'Mr Trevelyan I find very agreeable and sensible, and not a violent Radical, as he used to be.'[96] The author of 'What Does She Do With It?' had mellowed to the point where he saw the uses to which a constitutional monarch could be put. The County Franchise Act was passed, Gladstone was delighted, and George presented the Grand Old Man with a medallion of Charles James Fox. Relations were not to remain so cordial.

The general election of December 1885 saw Gladstone in power, but Parnell's 85 Home Rule MPs held the balance of power between the Liberals and the Tories. Chamberlain declared that, after the Reform Acts, this election result demonstrated how 'government of the people by the people has at last been secured', and he and other liberal radicals looked forward to at last reforming the House of Lords if not the monarchy. But the Irish question was to dominate politics of the 1880s. Gladstone announced his conversion to Home Rule, which divided his Cabinet and his party and resulted in his government surviving for only eight short months. George became Secretary of State for Scotland, hoping to be able to influence the Cabinet discussions on Home Rule. His experiences in Ireland had left him profoundly sceptical about the wisdom of this policy – partial Irish devolution he might have supported. But Gladstone opted for total Home Rule, unacceptable to Chamberlain and to George, and both quit office in 1886. In his resignation statement, George explained that he could not accept the Land Bill under which Irish landlords were to be expensively paid off. And he was very concerned about the risks involved in transferring responsibility for law and order to an Irish nationalist government. On Home Rule, George parted company with his mentor Harcourt and many other influential colleagues such as Spencer, who had come to the conclusion that the policy was the only way of pacifying Ireland. Harcourt described George as sitting in Cabinet throughout the long debates like a melancholy owl.[97] Gladstone lost the vote on Home Rule in the Commons, and in July 1886 called an election, deepening the split in the party. George stood as a Liberal Unionist, uncomfortably allying himself with the Conservative cause, and lost his borders seat to a Gladstonian Liberal by only 30 votes.

A spectacular U-turn followed. George, unlike other whigs, was not happy as a Liberal Unionist. After a round-table conference early in 1887, he allowed himself to be persuaded to rejoin the Liberal Party, sharing Harcourt's optimism that it was possible to negotiate an end to the split. Gladstone for once took George's concerns seriously, abandoning his idea of a major land-purchase scheme, and accepting the principle of continued Irish representation at Westminster. This enabled George to save face, and declare that the new Home Rule proposals were significantly different to those over which he had resigned. George moved back into the Gladstone camp in July 1887, standing as a Home Ruler in a Glasgow by-election. Chamberlain was furious, regarding this behaviour as tantamount to personal betrayal. How could the man who had resigned from the Cabinet over a point of principle suddenly overcome his supposedly heartfelt convictions? G.M. Trevelyan's explanation for his father's inconsistency is 'not that he loved Caesar more, but that he loved his enemies less'.[98] George was uncomfortable being on the same side of the Irish argument as the Tories, whose motives for opposing Home Rule he abhorred. As he wrote to Alice, 'The fact is that hatred of the Irish is the one good card the Tories have, and they must work it. But where can it lead them? They must go forward, for the nature of hatred is that it grows hotter unless the causes are removed.'[99]

George felt out of place. In swallowing his objections to Home Rule, he was inevitably attacked as a 'political weather-cock', suffering the scorn of the newspapers and his one-time Liberal Unionist allies. As he wrote to Alice, 'The violence of the Liberal Unionist papers is scandalous. Far worse than the Conservative. I am very glad that we are going to fight it out. Ever since I said that the Liberal party ought to be reconciled, they have been abusing me; and they may just as well have something to abuse me for.'[100] In parliament but in opposition, George busied himself with the estate of Wallington, which he inherited upon his father's death in 1886. Then George's wife Caroline was left the red-brick splendour of Welcombe in 1890. Life was pleasantly divided between Wallington and Welcombe, with the summer spent in Northumberland and the winter in Stratford. George loved to shoot game at Wallington, and to play toy soldiers with his sons. The great battles of the nineteenth century were re-enacted over the uncarpeted floor of a large, draughty room, with several thousand lead soldiers. George's running commentary helped instil a love of military history in the little boys.

Political office intruded once more into the life of the country gentleman – in 1892 Gladstone made George Scottish Secretary for the second time. Harcourt tried to persuade the Prime Minister to promote his protégé to Colonial Secretary but failed. Queen Victoria, who lived on her Balmoral estate in Scotland, having virtually retired from London life after Prince Albert's death, took a keen interest in George's brief. She had definite views on Crown appointments, and let the Scottish Secretary know exactly what she was thinking. George used to say to his children that the Queen was 'a very great lady',[101] although he could have done without her tremendous interest in decisions such as who was to be appointed professor of philosophy at a particular Scottish university. After Gladstone's retirement, George retained his post, even though Rosebery admitted to the Queen that he would not have appointed him as Scottish Secretary. In 1894, George voted for a private member's motion in favour of Scottish Home Rule – more than a hundred years later, that dream was finally realised with the establishment of a Scottish parliament. In his previous brief tenure as Scottish Secretary, George had persuaded parliament to pass a bill designed to remedy some of the grievances of the crofter tenants in the Highlands. This too is an issue that the Scottish parliament revisited more than a century later.

George retired from the Commons in 1897, his political career at an end. Patrick Jackson, who assessed him for the Oxford *Dictionary of National Biography*, found his political beliefs difficult to categorise.

> His reverence for Macaulay, his intellectual background, and his proud sense of family tradition might have led him to become an orthodox whig. In his writings he certainly looked back nostalgically to the days of Foxite whiggism. But he inherited from his father a more forward-looking interest in administrative reform.[102]

Gentle, sensitive, but also vain, George consistently overestimated his political potential, hoping at one point to be made Chancellor. A radical in the context of the 1870s, he supported reform of the army, extension of the franchise not only to the counties but to women, and land reform in Scotland. His resignations were ridiculed, but, as Patrick Jackson says, such disinterested actions are vital to the health of democratic politics.

Politics over, George, aged 59, plunged once more into writing. His next venture was more controversial – he attempted a history of the American Revolution, despite never having set foot in the country. His friends wanted him to complete his life of Charles James Fox – they used to say there ought to be an act of parliament to compel him to do so. But George would not be dissuaded from his course – he wanted to tell the story of how many in England opposed the policy of George III towards America. Never popular in Britain, his six-volume history of the revolution was well regarded in the United States, where it challenged the received wisdom. The books, which have much charm, paint a picture of a king at odds with many of his people in his treatment of the American colony. None other than Theodore Roosevelt, President of the United States, enjoyed George's depiction of the revolution. He wrote to the author in 1904, just after he had been re-elected to the White House.

> In my hours of leisure (during the campaign) I did a good deal of reading. I re-read your history of our Revolution and liked it more than ever, but came to the conclusion that you had painted us a little too favourably. I also re-read both your Macaulay and your Fox, and then re-read Macaulay's History. When I had finished it I felt a higher regard for him as a great writer, and as in the truest sense of the word a great philosophical historian, than I have ever felt before. It is a pretty good test of such a history to have a President who is also a candidate for the Presidency read it in the midst of a campaign.[103]

'A kindly old man.' Sir George Otto Trevelyan at Wallington with his grandchildren Theo and Pauline Trevelyan, 1910. Courtesy of the Trustees of the Trevelyan family papers.

Other influential Americans also enjoyed the history of the Revolution – Henry Cabot Lodge, John Hay and Elihu Root placed their admiration for the work on record. The author Henry James, by then a family friend, wrote this appreciation when the second volume was published in 1903.

Dear Sir George,

I should be a poor creature if I had read your last two volumes without feeling the liveliest desire to write to you…The American, the Englishman, the artist, and the critic in me – to say nothing of the friend! – all drink you down in a deep draught…the book's being so richly and authoritatively English, so validly true, and yet so projected as it were into the American consciousness, that will help to build the bridge across the Atlantic…and you bring home to me…what a difficult and precarious, and even might-not-have-been, Revolution it was…[104]

Fondly received in America, here the history of the American Revolution made little impact. Even G.M. Trevelyan, fond son that he was, found the work unsatisfactory.

…the last volumes in particular show an exaggeration of his tricks of style and a curious inability to bring the work to a logical ending. Yet the vigour and artistry of the narrative is that of a master, though in a style less in fashion in the twentieth century than in the nineteenth. It was not so much that his powers had declined, as that his mind had ceased to move with the age…the 'American Revolution', to English readers at least was a voice from the past. The style of thinking and writing had great merit, but it was subtly out of fashion.[105]

Patrick Jackson writes that although enjoyable and well written, the revolution books are

overlong and repetitive, with an excessive reliance on the theme that the loss of the American colonies was due to the stubbornness and stupidity of George III and his ministers. The colonies, by contrast, are depicted in a heroic light, and it is hardly surprising that the work was much more popular in the United States than in Britain.[106]

Still, the six volumes created for George a firm friendship with Teddy Roosevelt. Both were all-consuming readers of the same kind of history and literature, and had a similar world-view. As Joseph Bishop says, 'Roosevelt's characteristics as a letter writer are conspicuously displayed, because in

Trevelyan he had a correspondent who was peculiarly responsive to his own intellectual tastes and knowledge...Each put his mind to the other's, and the result was a correspondence of rare interest and value.'[107] Roosevelt had been variously a rancher, a historian, a reformer, a hunter, a military hero and, of course, president. George was not outdoorsy like Teddy, but politically they seemed to be in sympathy, despite their seemingly incompatible labels of radical Liberal and Republican. Roosevelt went on to be the most successful third-party presidential candidate in US history when he stood for the Progressive Party, on a platform which George thoroughly approved of. The pair corresponded avidly, with letters flying to and fro over the Atlantic for twenty years. Their correspondence began when Teddy was Governor of New York. He had kindly received Charles, George's son, when he was touring the US. Charles, as we shall see, instantly hero-worshipped the rambunctious Roosevelt, and returned to Wallington full of tales of his greatness. George, as a thank you, sent Teddy a copy of his history of the revolution. Teddy subsequently spent many an evening at the White House reading history written by one Trevelyan or another.

> ...I have read your son's[108] Age of Wycliffe with great pleasure. Pray congratulate him from me on all that he is doing. I find reading a great comfort. People often say to me that they do not see how I find time for it, to which I answer them (much more truthfully than they believe) that to me it is a dissipation, which I have sometimes to try to avoid, instead of an irksome duty.[109]

Roosevelt's views on the proper writing of history, and his dislike of pedantic scholars, chimed absolutely with George's opinions. Here is the President criticising 'these small men who do most of the historic teaching in the colleges'.

> A thousand of them would not in the aggregate begin to add to the wisdom of mankind what another Macaulay, should one arise, would add. The great historian must of course have the scientific spirit which gives the power of research, which enables one to marshal and weigh the facts; but unless his finished work is literature of a very high type small will be his claim to greatness.[110]

Roosevelt said he would only serve two terms in office, and towards the end of the second he was planning another of his great hunting trips, which would include a detour to England to stay with George at Welcombe.

If I can visit England without having my own ambassador or anyone else call on me, without being expected to see anybody I didn't already know, I should love to meet you and Selous and Buxton and Arthur Lee, and to see the English lanes in the spring, and stop at English country inns, and see a cathedral here and there…But if all this is impossible, and I have to go thru the dreary farce of unspeakably foolish formal entertainment at the cost of people in whom I take not the slightest real interest, why I shall come straight back from Africa to the United States.[111]

In November 1908, Roosevelt wrote to George from the White House, the election over, his chosen successor Taft victorious. Teddy was regretting his decision only to serve two terms.

Of course if I had conscientiously felt at liberty to run again and try once more to hold this great office, I should have greatly liked to do so and to continue to keep my hands on the levers of this mighty machine. I do not believe that my President has ever had as thoroly good a time as I have had, or has ever enjoyed himself as much…

Your new edition of the Life of Macaulay came and I have reread the whole volume with the delight it always gives me…I have made up my mind that I will have to take some books on my African trip, and the special piece of resistance is to be Macaulay's complete works – to which I may have to add your American Revolution. My son Kermit, by the way, I was rather pleased to find, among his books for the voyage has included Homer in the original.

Kermit and my elder boy Ted have both chuckled over your inability to tell me the best translations of the Greek tragic poets on the grounds that you were old fashioned enough to read them in the original…I never got so that reading any Greek or Latin author in the original represented to me anything other except dreary labor.[112]

In 1910 Teddy came to England, after his shooting tour of Africa, where he paid a 'cheerful and joyous'[113] visit to his long-time correspondent at Welcombe. The photograph of the pair shows the ebullient Teddy next to the shy but delighted George. Their letters became more numerous as the First World War took its bloody course. Both men had sons in uniform. George wrote to Roosevelt in 1915,

This morning I read the sentence in which you set forth the MORAL side of the Munitions of War question – whether they were to be employed for the rescue of Belgium, or for her continued enslavement…You know that you are my hero and always will be ... I would pray 'God bless you' in your great objects, but that word is of ill-omen to me.[114]

The events of the First World War confirmed George's view that it was the most unmitigated calamity, marking the end of the civilisation to which he belonged. He didn't believe England could have kept out of it with any honour, yet the bloodshed dismayed him. He felt old and out of touch, and depressed by the wider world. G.M. Trevelyan was serving with the Ambulance Corps on the Italian front, a source of great anxiety to his father. When G.M. returned in September 1918, he went on foot from Hexham station to Wallington. George walked to the top of Shily Hill to meet his favourite son, 'and there,' he said afterwards, 'like Laertes, I wept upon his breast.'

Offered a peerage before the war, by Asquith, George declined, saying he had not the time to play a full part in political life. Only a few months earlier, displaying the talent for nepotism which all Trevelyans appear to have held dear, he had written to Asquith, the Liberal Prime Minister, complaining that Charles Philips Trevelyan, his eldest son, had been left out of government. Asquith made a peace offering of a peerage, but relations were strained.

Charles Philips claims he made George refuse the honour.[115] The old man was awarded the Order of Merit in 1911, which provided the imprimatur of establishment approval for his achievements as a writer and politician.

From then on he began a retreat into the past, a place he felt at home. He and Caroline lived in almost complete seclusion at Wallington and Welcombe, reading aloud Cicero, Theocritus, Shelley, and of course Macaulay. Caroline painted landscapes in the style of Corot, while George translated ancient Greek for his own amusement. When she wasn't painting, Caroline bustled around in her grey silk gowns, 'like a toy mouse on rollers'.[116] The couple

The Historian and the President. After corresponding for years, Sir George Otto Trevelyan and Theodore Roosevelt finally meet at Welcombe, 1910. Courtesy of the Trustees of the Trevelyan family papers.

had a house full of servants – a cook, maids, a butler and a doorman. Lady Marjorie Weaver, George's granddaughter, recalled a kindly old man who, when not in his study, could be seen bent over his extensive collection of jigsaw puzzles. Kitty, another granddaughter, described going to visit him at Wallington.

Grandpapa's study had opaque glass in the door, and I could see his blurred figure stooping over his desk. He was then in his seventies and was hunchbacked with much thinking and stooping over books. I knocked, went in, found him benign; but didn't like him, for the age span was too great. He gave me chocolate drops out of a drawer and started holding a brilliant conversation, about when he was in Gladstone's government. The brilliance was all on his side; I didn't say anything and after a time forgot to listen, till he called me back with a bump by saying: 'And you remember, my dear, what Lord Desborough said in 1887?'[117]

In old age, George would often reflect self-importantly upon his past. A radical liberal he might have been in his youth, but in his seventies he reminisced in much the same manner as the Tory squires Trevelyans were supposed to be so different from. This made him an easy target – H.G. Wells enjoyed parodying the whole Trevelyan family in *The New Machiavelli*. This paragraph about a new MP receiving advice from a senior parliamentarian is a not at all well-disguised dig at George.

We dined with the elder Cramptons one evening, and old Sir Edward was lengthily sage about what the House liked, what it didn't like, what made a good impression, and what a bad one. 'A man shouldn't speak more than twice in his first session, and not at first on too contentious a topic,' said Sir Edward.

'No.'

'Very much depends on manner. The House hates a lecturer. There's a sort of airy earnestness –'

He waved his cigar to eke out his words.

Little peculiarities of costume count for a great deal. I could name one man who spent three years living down a pair of splatterdashers. On the other hand – a thing like that – if it catches the eye of the *Punch* man, for example, may be your making.[118]

In his final years, George did a lot of pontificating and reading, and very little else.

Unlike his industrious father Charles Edward, he was not much of a landlord. Repairs were neglected, wages were stingy. An old farmer on the Wallington estate told George's head gardener Edward Keith, 'I think nowt of your new master. Sir Charles never passed my door wi'out looking in. Sir George seldom bothers to enquire whether you are dead or alive.'[119] George was aware that he had run Wallington down. Shortly before his death, he summoned Mr Keith to the house. This was not an easy encounter for the loyal servant, who recorded George's opening gambit.

> 'During the last few days I have been looking over many of my father's papers, relating to his activities not only on the estate but connected with county affairs, and I am struck by the amount of work he must have got through in such a short space of time. Tell me,' he said, fixing me with that steady eye of his, 'what you thought of him, and let me know candidly from your point of view how far I have failed to live up to that high standard he set me as a model landlord.' And here he gave vent to one of those chuckling laughs so delightful to hear in his old age.[120]

Poor Edward Keith was now on the spot. He tried to be tactful.

> 'Sir Charles was always planning and working for the improvement of the Estate, the happiness of the people connected with it, and the pleasure of those who were to follow after...I am afraid, Sir George, however much useful work may have been done since his death, in all fairness to his memory we must own up to it that on his own initiative he accomplished as much in seven years as your agents have got through in forty odd years.'

George took this assessment manfully, telling Mr Keith he'd spoken the truth. Estate management had never been his strong point – it never held the same fascination for him as books did. He wasn't a countryman either. As Mr Keith put it, 'he lacked that definable something which remains ever the possession of those whose adolescent days have been spent exploring the brooks and dales or tramping the windswept moors of bleak Northumberland'.[121]

Charles Philips, George's son and heir, was just as damning about his father's abilities as a landlord. In a letter to Jennie Lee, Charles attributed his conversion to socialism in part to George's appalling management of Wallington.

> He was only a rent receiver. He did nothing for the community. He left the estate to a second rate agent. He wearied out an absolutely first class bailiff by turning down every suggestion for improvement. He was bitterly jealous

of every move of mine to get him to plant or even look after the wood... Like any rank Tory squire he used to say that he never made a penny out of being a landlord. In fact for forty years he made between one thousand and two thousand clear profit, if the expenditure on his carriages, his dogs, his garden and his house are reckoned as they should be his private expenditure... his farewell talk to his family, whether he was conscious of it or not, was a rather incoherent explanation of the way he had saved money into this great fortune. Miser I don't call him; but a man with a hopelessly distorted idea of the uses of money.[122]

George made a great deal of money from Wallington and from his books – he left over half a million pounds to his children. While deliberately not spending on the estate, he was happiest pottering around in his library, with Caroline. G.M. Trevelyan writes that in his eighties, George had 'an undue shrinking from social intercourse, a fear of having visitors in the house, though in fact when they were there he talked to them with his old eagerness...'.[123] In fact George was shy, and old age only confirmed his shyness. At least he knew where he was with his books, and his Carry. Edward Keith noted that she was the ideal wife.

Lady Trevelyan was never a lover of London life, the rush and glitter of the London season did not fit with her quiet and orderly ways. I know from what she confided to me that the sweetest hours of her life were those spent at Welcombe and Wallington, in the midst of her family... Lady Trevelyan shirked publicity. She was of the old school, contented like Mrs Gladstone and others of that ilk to minister to and watch over the best interests of her husband.[124]

In January 1928 George's beloved Caroline passed away at Welcombe. He lived long enough to approve this inscription on her tomb: 'By nature courteous and gentle towards all, and full of tender concern for the welfare of others. A skilful painter of the landscapes she loved so well. Above all singularly blest in almost sixty years of married life.'

George had no wish to live without Caroline. He wanted to bow out at Wallington, and with great effort made the final journey from Warwickshire to the Northumbrian countryside he loved so very much. He sat alone in the great library at Wallington, reading the classics, telling his grandchildren, 'She's calling for me, she's calling for me.'[125] Shortly after his ninetieth birthday he died, and was buried next to his father in Cambo churchyard. 'Death of a great literary Victorian,' was the verdict of the *Daily Express,* 'the

last notable link between the present day and Macaulay, Ruskin and Carlyle.'
His heir Charles Philips described him as 'nearly a very big man'.[126] Patrick
Jackson saw in his political career a strain of genuine radicalism but little in
the way of solid achievements.

> Trevelyan cannot be rated as a major figure in either politics or letters
> when compared to the greatest of his contemporaries…Perhaps
> Trevelyan's main claim to be remembered is that his career reflected a
> consistent integrity that sprang from family pride and from deep-seated
> radical convictions which were more important to him than ambition and
> self interest.[127]

On his deathbed, George was muttering about Macaulay, his lifelong role
model in letters and politics. 'He was a common man,'[128] he said repeatedly.
In his closing moments the radical aristocrat seemed pleased to have risen
above the solidly middle-class roots of Uncle Tom.

4

THE ROMANTIC CRUSADER

Dashing, handsome, wealthy, sporty, and ideologically left-wing, Charles Philips Trevelyan was quite unlike any of the family members we have encountered hitherto. The elder son of George and Caroline had a promising early career but ultimately did not reach the dizzy heights his parents hoped for. Bertrand Russell thought him the least gifted of the trio of Trevelyan brothers.[1] Beatrice Webb, his friend, described him as 'a man who has every endowment – social position, wealth, intelligence, an independent outlook, good looks, good manners'.[2] His eventual achievements were uneven – temperamental and fond of resigning, he was not a natural politician. Elected a Liberal MP in the dying days of the nineteenth century, he later joined the Labour Party, after passionately opposing the First World War and becoming a leading member of the Union for Democratic Control. Charles was a Labour Cabinet minister in that party's first ever government of 1924, and again from 1929–31. As a member of the landed gentry in the party of the people he was a walking anachronism, yet he championed causes such as raising the school leaving age. As a socialist, he left the family estate of Wallington to the National Trust. His own privileges and gentlemanly pursuits always remained intact, though, and he took care to live in Wallington until the end of his days, a crack shot to the last. Glamorous and very attractive to women, Charles Philips enjoyed a close friendship with Jennie Lee, and in his seventies fathered a child out of wedlock with his secretary at Wallington, Edith Bulmer. Leonard Woolf described him as having 'a mind and a body of immense toughness; physically his energy and mentally his curiosity were indefatigable'.[3]

Charles Philips Trevelyan was born on 28 October 1870. His parents, having waited to marry until 1869 because of the opposition of Caroline's influential uncle, lost no time in starting a family. Charles entered into a world of high-minded liberalism underpinned by a wealthy lifestyle. The family lived in three different houses year round – while parliament was sitting, life revolved around Ennismore Gardens in London, convenient for George, a Liberal Cabinet minister under Gladstone. Then there was Welcombe, the red-brick mansion in Shakespeare's county of Warwickshire, the country house of Robert Philips, and a Christmas and Easter retreat for his daughter and her family. Summers were spent at Wallington, which Charles was to inherit, and ultimately leave to the nation. There he learnt the arts of rabbit and pheasant shooting. Charles's devoted companion during these peripatetic years was his nurse, Mrs Prestwich, or Booa, the nickname bestowed by her three charges. Throughout the long and varied lives of the trio of Trevelyan brothers, Charles Philips, George Macaulay and Robert Calverley, the poet, Booa was always on hand with a kind word or an encouraging letter. She was Charles's 'teacher, arbiter, comforter, much loved and loving friend'.[4]

When Charles was ten years old, and his father George was back in government after his wilderness years, it was decided that the time had come for the heir apparent's formal education to begin. In 1880 Charles went to a prep school called The Grange, where the headmaster, Reverend C.G. Chittenden, held progressive views on education. George and Caroline packed their eldest son off with lengthy notes about his ability and health concerns. The headmaster replied:

> I am much obliged for your notes. Such information is always valuable.
> I am not at all concerned to learn that you do not think him clever, and
> that he learns slowly; but I am very glad to hear that he is reasonable. A
> reasonable boy is, in all aspects, a more satisfactory pupil than a merely
> clever boy. You may depend on our not expecting too much from him.[5]

But George Otto would always expect much of his son and heir. A brilliant classical scholar himself, influenced by Macaulay, George was impatient for his eldest son to progress in Latin and Greek. The Reverend Chittenden wrote back to the ambitious father,

> I am afraid my boys often seem backward, but it is really a gain that a boy
> should be able to construct a simple Latin sentence before he begins to

translate much – as it is in Greek, that he should read the characters fluently before he attempts much else. Charles seems to be a very intelligent boy. Like most intelligent boys he gets weary of the amount of Latin and Greek grammar made necessary by our Public School system: but that is the fault of the system rather than the boy.[6]

Under the watchful eye of his understanding headteacher, Charles became Head Boy at the Grange. Not bad for one rated only as 'reasonable' by his parents. From there he progressed to Harrow, the setting of George Otto's academic success that had so delighted Macaulay fifty years earlier. Charles was not academic, but he was athletic, and made the school football team, something the resolutely unsporting George Otto could never have achieved. Politics was the common ground between father and son, since Charles could not correspond with his father in the language of the classics. Growing up in the household of a radical liberal had a great influence on the anxious-to-please Charles, as he later related in a letter to his friend the Labour MP and minister Jennie Lee: 'It is from him I got my radicalism, and my faith in the final good sense of my fellow citizens, my hatred of privilege, my detestation of the House of Lords. I had it in greater measure even than he…'[7]

Yet for all George Otto's radicalism, he chose for his sons a school that was a symbol of the conservative establishment. The boys were the token Liberals at Harrow, as Charles's account of the atmosphere at school during the 1885 general election makes clear.

We have had one of the most exciting and interesting weeks that I have known. The Conservatives in the school are absolutely furious. There is a Liberal Committee room nearly opposite Dr Welldon's, and on the windows are posted various Liberal placards. The Conservative candidate, Ambrose…an awful ass who can't speak decently from stammering…has not put up any placards yet. So the Conservatives in our House, with the help of a rich banker, Baring, whose son is in the School, got a placard…and…they had about five hundred printed. While all this was going on, the Conservatives in the School got more and more enraged with the Liberal Committee rooms. Till yesterday they contented themselves with hooting and knocking at the door. Then, they began to pelt the Bobbies…about six police joined in and they got Robinson and Johnson down to the police office and they are to be tried tomorrow…[8]

Firmly in the Harrow Conservative camp at this point in history was the young Winston Churchill. He was a few years below Charles, who was never

'Teacher, arbiter, comforter, much loved and loving friend.' Charles, Robert and George Trevelyan with their nanny, Miss Mary Prestwich, at Wallington. Courtesy of the Trustees of the Trevelyan family papers.

very impressed by Britain's future wartime leader. This is Charles to his father on the subject of the Churchill family.

> Had the pleasure…on Thursday, of shaking hands with Randolph Churchill; an honour I should think the Tories thought I was not exactly entitled to…He was bringing his son down here for what is known among us by the expressive name of the 'skews' exam. I should have thought his son ought to have at least aspired to the highest exam if not the schol.[9]

Later, Charles was gleeful in recording Winston's early lack of scholastic promise: 'Lord Randolph's son has taken Third Fourth. He is last but one in the school!! An ex-Chancellor of the Exchequor's Son!!!'

By 1901, when both men were in the House of Commons, Charles was rather more admiring of the bumptious Churchill: 'He is undoubtedly a big man…inordinately ambitious. But whatever line he takes, he will always bring out the best and most reasonable side of it. I like him personally. He amuses me and is first rate company with all his egotism.'

Charles finished at Harrow in 1889, before Churchill did, and, like his father and great uncle before him, he then went to Trinity College, Cambridge. George would have contemplated no other path for his eldest son. However, Charles was not as academically brilliant as his father – his talents lay elsewhere, and he was drawn at once to the Cambridge Union. George advised his son to drop the student politicking, as it would interfere with his studies. Anxious that his first-born would fail to achieve the obligatory family first, George even suggested that his son should take up Chapel, breaking with his own atheist views. Charles reluctantly conceded on both points. Despite being good-looking and well connected, the gauche young Charles was finding social and academic life at Trinity a trial. By giving up the Cambridge Union he lost the one arena of college life he felt confident in. During his second year, Charles suffered from nervous depression. In his final year, his depression deepened. He knew he was not going to achieve the first his father longed for. 'I think I realise now that it has been the prospect and the feeling that I was not up to the standard in the work that has ruined my time here.'[10]

When, in the summer of 1892, Charles discovered that his degree was a second, he was desolate. Much as he had predicted this public failure to live up to the family tradition, it was still painful.

> Things are past the point of redemption. Oh it is so horrible. All my courage is gone, all my strong self confidence, all my hope. The very

brightness of my prospects as the world would say, is a curse on me! What can it lead to but the repetition of the same miserable story of inadequacy and inefficiency in the end?'[11]

Charles's biographer, A.J.A. Morris, suggests that he found Cambridge life tough because he did not really know how to make conversation. As Charles wrote to his mother, 'I cannot get on with people. I do not care to take part in their drivelling conversations and flabby amusements. And I have not the wit to make them talk and do anything worth the while of a rational being.'[12] Morris puts this surprising inability to communicate down to Charles's rather rarefied upbringing.

> Trevelyan had been brought up in a home where, amongst the male members at least, declamation was the more usual form of communication. He was more used to a company regaled by lengthy discourse on the niceties of parliamentary procedure, the tyrannies of the House of Lords, the fatuity of royalty, or the pleasures of classical literature, than to be entertained and be entertaining with unselfconscious, inconsequential chatter.[13]

Charles endured Trinity, rather than embracing it as George Otto and Macaulay had done. This he saw as a failure of his own making, rather than an unsuitable choice forced upon him by his overbearing father. The three years left him thoroughly sick of 'intellectual excitement… Of Macaulayism, Trevelyanism; intellectual cleverness in general seems so unsatisfying.'[14]

Free from the agonies of undergraduate life, Charles threw himself into campaigning for the Liberals in the summer of 1892. He helped ensure the re-election of his father's old friend John Morley. But the oppressive nature of institutional life soon returned. His parents, in their wisdom, decided he should become private secretary to Lord Houghton, appointed Lord Lieutenant of Ireland by the Liberal Government. George and Caroline thought a spell in Dublin Castle would help Charles's social skills. The young George had greatly benefited from his time in India – but the son was not cut from the same cloth as the father. Charles told his mother he found going to Ireland 'with a whole crowd of ADC's [aide-de-camps']…was rather too much like going back to school. There's the same sense of having got among a whole lot of incompatible companions and the dread feeling that one will never get on with them.'[15] And in working in Ireland, he was following once again in his father's footsteps – George had been Chief Secretary to Ireland.

Charles found he had very little to do over the Irish Sea, apart from attend ceremonial occasions, which he found ridiculous, not wanting to 'prance about in gold lace and white inexpressibles through an Irish season in Dublin Castle'. Gladstone's Home Rule Bill was inching its way through the Commons, yet virtually all the other gilded young men serving as ADCs were opposed to the measure. Charles, who supported Home Rule, found this isolating, as he told his mother.

Tonight Lord Houghton was at play with some of the party. I stayed with others. Afterwards one of the men spoke of politics and Home Rule bitterly, in that high-handed, distainful, superior way that only Tories can speak, spurning their hearer's opinions, getting the ruder and more blatant if they see he objects. He spoke of the Irish as ruffians, and used the worst sort of language towards them. He knew no better. There was no retort without the eloquence which I do not possess. Such are the pleasures of belonging to a Home Rule Government.[16]

Charles was shocked by the lack of concern for the Irish people among those he called 'these supercilious gentry'. He made Irish acquaintances outside the Castle, taking himself off on long walks to escape the tedium of life inside. The Trinity depression returned, as he felt without a role or purpose. His parents finally relented, the fit of the blue devils lifted, and Charles left Ireland. He desperately wanted to become a Liberal MP, and a radical one at that, his politics having been forged by his experiences in Dublin Castle. George, well connected as he was in the Liberal world, was already putting out feelers. Charles was grateful. 'I cannot tell you how much I appreciate the manner in which you have taken the greatest trouble to make the political world realize my existence and have kept on the alert for any favourable chance of getting me a good seat at the next election.'[17]

Rich and well connected, it did not take long for Charles to receive his first approach. Some Mid-Lanark Liberals asked him to enter their selection process, for a safe seat. However, the constituency in the end preferred the more experienced candidate, Edward Caldwell. Charles's self-doubt surfaced once more as he told his mother that, as usual, he had failed.

It is the same with me everywhere and with everything – in college work, love and politics; everything made easy for me up to the crucial point …False encouragement of kindly but bad judges and inadequacy at the finish. I feel again here that I have been pushed with the best intentions and no doubt full belief in me, without the foundation of work and knowledge which is necessary.[18]

The Mid-Lanark selection process taught Charles the importance of doing one's homework on a constituency, and made him realise he must improve his public-speaking skills. His fits of depression were conquered for the moment. In December 1893, the Liberal seat of North Lambeth came up. George did his bit promoting his son, and Charles won through from a shortlist of four, much to the displeasure of some local Liberal members. However, Charles hung on to fight the seat in the 1895 general election, promising in his manifesto 'to labour in the cause of progress'. This was the election in which the Liberal Party was split over Home Rule – Charles, a supporter, stood as a Liberal Radical just as his father was on the other side of the debate as a Liberal Unionist. Charles, who dashed around the constituency with a coach in four, lost by 400 votes to the anti-Home Rule candidate, the famous explorer of Africa Henry Morton Stanley, who twenty years earlier had found Livingstone. Defeat, but Charles was not discouraged, knowing this valuable training had helped him over what he called the 'Asses Bridge of rhetoric'.

At this point, Charles became acquainted with Beatrice and Sidney Webb, the founders of the Fabian Society. Uncomfortable with his social privileges, and concerned by inequality, Charles was still searching for a philosophy to articulate the views he held so deeply. The writings of John Ruskin appealed to him, with their emphasis on fighting injustice. The Webbs provided concrete ideas on what government could do to help the lot of the common man. Living in London with his parents, Charles was one of many earnest young liberals who frequented 41 Grosvenor Road, the home of the Webbs. H.G. Wells, who satirised Charles as the would-be politician Willie Crampton in *The New Machiavelli*, summarised the hold the articulate Webbs had over those like Charles: 'It was natural I should gravitate to them for they seemed to stand for the maturer, more disciplined, better informed expression of all I was then urgent to attempt to do.'[19]

Life with the Webbs wasn't all worthy policy discussions, though. Charles enjoyed the Fabian gatherings, which had their share of larks. Here he is describing an outing to Beachy Head:

We have monopolised the Hotel, except the bar, which is filled with tourists and fly men during the middle of the day. Till eleven and after five we have the whole place and the whole Head to ourselves. It is glorious weather...and Mrs Webb has had to borrow glycerine for her sunburns. I am teaching the whole party to bicycle...Mrs Webb will soon be proficient. Mr Webb is hopeless, and with an impatience unreasonable in a man who has devoted years to converting London to Collectivism, abuses the bicycle for not 'balancing' during his first lesson. Bernard Shaw is at this moment industriously tumbling about outside...We have an enormous library contributed by different members of the party which nobody reads because we are either out all day or talking.[20]

Charles found George Bernard Shaw captivating company, and was greatly influenced by his ideas and approach. George Otto and Caroline, Lady Trevelyan received enthusiastic letters full of praise for the Shavian analysis.

Shaw gives the best exposition of the state of things one could hope to hear...His great point is that the ordinary man cannot, and that the leaders at present do not do any elaborate thinking either about the theory or the detail of politics. This indictment is generally absolutely true...the dilettante character of our leadership at present is an evil which we younger men feel more and more everyday.[21]

Charles's confidence grew, and his feelings of inferiority lessened as he found both a philosophy and a set of friends to go with it. Through the Fabian Society Charles made another important friendship, with the Liberal Herbert Samuel, a bond that was to reinforce his new-found philosophical leanings and eventually lead him to change political allegiance. Herbert Samuel and Charles were both interested in the emergence of the new Independent Labour Party, and had sympathies with socialism while remaining radical liberals. Herbert Samuel, later a Liberal Home Secretary, introduced Charles to the Rainbow Circle in 1895, a discussion group of 'Liberals of the Left and Socialists of the Right'. Ramsay MacDonald, who would later appoint Charles to his first Cabinet, was the secretary of this earnest group. Charles told his mother: 'Samuel and I have been trying to thrash out difficulties at the Rainbow Circle with the thinking Socialists. I think we make them come down a little from their ideal eminence – certainly we get our own minds clearer as to what we want.'[22]

Even in the late 1890s, years before he joined the Labour Party, Charles was intrigued by socialism. In Boston in 1896, he made a speech that shows how his thinking was progressing.

I have the greatest sympathy with the growth of the socialist party. I think they understand the evils that surround us and hammer them into people's minds better than we Liberals. I want to see the Liberal party throw its heart and soul fearlessly into reform so as to prevent a reaction from the present state of thugs and the violent revolution that would inevitably follow it.[23]

As Charles engaged in serious debate and analysis, his parliamentary ambitions were progressing. The Liberals of Elland in Yorkshire were interested in offering him their relatively safe seat once the sitting member retired. Charles was delighted. George helpfully paid for an experienced and able parliamentary agent to nurse the seat for his son, while the next member for Elland went off on a world tour with the Webbs, as one did in those days. His travelling companions, who had just completed their mammoth work on the trade unions, were now turning their attentions to an exciting-sounding comparative study of local government. In March 1898 the trio sailed on the RMS *Teutonic* for America, followed by Honolulu, New Zealand and Australia.

Charles wrote letters home during this nine-month odyssey, which were published as a diary after his death. Leonard Woolf wrote the foreword to the book, observing how the letters depicted a class and an era that no longer existed. Woolf detects in Charles's letters the 'psychology of the ruling class', as the elder son of Sir George Otto Trevelyan and the great nephew of Macaulay accepts the fact that 'he is a member of an international elite with the privilege of entrée into Society'.[24] And Charles was invited to lunch with governors of States, judges of the Supreme Court, millionaires, heads of universities, and ambassadors, who showed him everything from a debate in congress to a football match. As Woolf records, 'only once did one of the "top people" hesitate to see Charles, but it was only because he did not realise who Charles was; as soon as he realised that Charles was a son of Sir George Otto Trevelyan, he opened his arms in welcome.'[25]

Charles's letters describe how the Webbs, those egalitarian social reformers, travel in a 'state cabin'[26] across the Atlantic. Sidney and Beatrice are always very concerned about being in the best available hotels, which the robust Charles finds rather restrictive, not to mention ideologically suspect. The Webbs keep getting their pocketbooks stolen, so Charles has to finance them. While the travelling party is in America, the country is on the brink of declaring war with Spain. Lunch is arranged with Teddy Roosevelt, in years to come pen pal of George Otto and future President, who is then the Naval Secretary in Washington. Charles, always impressionable, falls under Roosevelt's spell – his 'tearing spirits'[27] are quite irresistible.

The life and soul of the party – as of all parties when he is present – was Roosevelt. Of course all the talk is about the war. I had a most interesting half hour, hearing about all the commanders of the American battle ships, the probably naval policy, the methods of warfare…But to have a talk at such a time, when he has got the navy in hand which will probably be fighting in a week, is delightfully exciting…I can tell you it is an exciting thing living in the midst of a nation preparing for war.[28]

Charles finds the larger-than-life Teddy Roosevelt, who is able to be both swashbuckling and erudite, utterly charismatic. He is

a noble and practical character, and will go further than any man I have yet seen. He is a brilliant and epigrammatic talker which makes him the life of any company. If he fails in making a big name for himself, it will be because of some act of jovial daring. He is dying to fight himself at this moment, and if an army did go to Cuba, he would go with it and throw up his secretaryship.[29]

The British Ambassador to Washington, Sir Julian Pauncefote, arranges for Charles and the Webbs to be shown around the Senate. Charles finds him a 'fatherly old boy, quite solid, respectable, stupid, imperturbable as a British Ambassador should be. His daughters are the natural result, nice and stupid, such a contrast to the average American girl.'[30] The comparison with his new hero Roosevelt is unfavourable: 'Never was democratic effectiveness and aristocratic diliatoriness more marked than passing from Roosevelt to Pauncefote.'[31]

While travelling in Pittsburgh, Charles discovers that Roosevelt has indeed given up his post so he can fight the Spanish. 'Friend Roosevelt has resigned to my immense disgust in order to take up a command in the army. No man has the right to resign a position of such supreme importance as the command of the Admiralty at such a juncture. I shall tell him so.'[32]

As his idol Roosevelt joins the battle, Charles leaves the Webbs, no match for the charismatic future President when it comes to personal appeal, and tours America by himself. He goes for long and dusty walks, reads poetry, flirts with pretty girls, and admires the American spirit. Everywhere doors are thrown open to him because he is related to the well-known historians Macaulay and Sir George Otto Trevelyan. From Chicago, Charles writes, 'Here I may say there is the most universal knowledge among all the educated people of GOT's writing. He is quite a household word.'[33] While pointing out how Charles's path across America was smoothed for him by connections,

Leonard Woolf acknowledges his diligence. 'Wherever he went, every minute of his day is spent in interviewing every kind of person, from statesmen to trade unionists to farmers. He inspected minutely every kind of institution and organisation from a legislature or Supreme Court to a primary school.' Woolf finds him 'a professional in the art of government, the technique of administration … he is passionately interested in history and politics, in the way people live, how they are educated, how they rule or are ruled'.[34]

Reunited with the Webbs in San Francisco, the travelling party departed for Honolulu by ship, for more comparative studies of local government. Charles's mother Caroline was most concerned that while crossing the Pacific in an American boat he would be taken prisoner by the Spanish. Her eldest son didn't take the threat very seriously.

> You will have received a letter from Webb by this time to say that we may have to risk capture by the Dons between Honolulu and New Zealand. It seems unavoidable, but the risk is so trifling that I do not mind it. It will be a spice of excitement and will warrant packing my revolver on the top instead of the bottom of my trunk … I expect Webb and I together would impress a privateer captain with the importance of the British flag. I do not fear a Spanish prison. I only fear a Spanish hotel, and the long voyage to it.[35]

The ship was British, not American as Lady Caroline had feared, and the voyage was uneventful. On board, the Webbs were purposeful as ever. 'Mrs Webb has been writing her diary, which will be the Pepys of the nineteenth century. Webb has read all the books available on board upon any solid subject.'[36] Also on the ship were American officials preparing to announce the annexation of Hawaii, which Congress had just decreed. One consequence of this was the disinheriting of a Trevelyan family acquaintance on the island, Princess Kaiulani. She could not become Queen now the Americans had claimed Hawaii as a state. Charles went to look up the Princess without a throne, whom he'd met in London, and they went surfing in Waikiki, complete with canoes and garlands of flowers. Charles found the Princess greatly depressed. 'It is a horrid position to be placed in. She is too European, civilized, attractive, to marry a native. But in Europe of course she would always be regarded as half-savage … I feel very sorry for her; but not enough so to become a royalist and raise a counter-revolution.'[37] The Princess sent Charles off with a present of three dozen coconuts, but he wrote home, 'I am not going to marry her any more than an American heiress.'[38]

While Charles was learning the benefits of playing rather than working, the Webbs were still busily engaged in their comparative study of local administration. They found politics in Hawaii to be less corrupt and more effective than in America. The next country to investigate was New Zealand. There the weedy Webbs and the courageous Charles parted company once more. The party was due to visit Napier, to investigate meat-freezing factories of all things, but the bridge over the river Mohaka was down, and the river was a raging torrent. Undaunted, Charles decided to swing across the river using a rope cage.

> The crossing was of course impossible for the unathletic Webb or even the masculine vigour of Mrs Webb... our host fixed up a board with ropes attached to a pulley... my valise with a few clothes, third volume of Wilhelm Meister, the precious Letter III and my precious razors was tied by a rope to the side of the board. I bade an affectionate farewell to the Webbs wishing them a speedy crossing, and mounted my car.[39]

The 100-yard crossing was an adventure, in which Charles lost his faithful valise, and had reason to be grateful to the Harrow gymnasium for teaching him how to use ropes. The Webbs, watching from the far side, cheered Charles and then returned to the inn they were staying in, imprisoned by the high waters. 'They will have to wait however long it takes. It is a pity they are not on their honeymoon. But, they are still sufficiently devoted to enjoy some hours tete a tete a day. But I am afraid the meagre literature of the inn and my bag will hardly fill in the interstices of more than 24 hours.'[40]

From the mini-adventures of New Zealand, it was on to Australia, for yet more interviews and visits and evaluation of public life. Charles by now was thinking of liberal politics in England, and how he could make a difference upon his return. He wrote to his close ally Herbert Samuel: 'I think the chief effect of my tour politically speaking, is to make me more of a land reformer than before. The availability of land is the supreme difference between old and new Britain.'[41]

Later in life, Charles concluded that his American experience had radicalised him in a more profound sense.

> Before the first war I lived chiefly with my own class. The only time I had ever felt I was in the society I wanted was when I was in the United States in 1899, where at last I plunged into an egalitarian world where everybody talked to everybody and not up or down to them. It was only when I joined the Labour Party that I found I could get the same atmosphere in England.[42]

Shortly after Charles's return, the opportunity to play a real part in political life presented itself. The Liberal member for the Elland was prevailed upon to retire, forcing a by-election in February 1899. The agent George had retained for Charles while he was overseas, Jack Marshall, had canvassed the seat in true Liberal fashion. But this would be a tough fight. Charles, armed with a magic lantern, decided to hold a series of lectures in Elland, telling the constituents about what he'd learnt during his travels. He was an easy target for his Tory opponents, who mocked him in verse, in the manner of Kipling.

As got a lantern too,
Clever Chawles;
With a magic slide,
Limelight Chawles.
An' 'e'll lecture, an' 'e'll spout
Till the bally gas goes out,
An' the more people rise and shout,
'No more Chawles'.

As a bloke 'e's right enuff,
Dear ole Chawles,
But 'is politics is stuff
Rubbish Chawles.
You 'ave lost your bloomin' way
As you'll see one Wednesday
When to Foster[43] you will pay
'Omage Chawles.[44]

Chawles won the day, however, and was elected with a majority of nearly a thousand votes over the Tories. At last, after what he considered to be his many setbacks in life, he had achieved something – Member of Parliament at the age of just 29. George Otto, that hard taskmaster of a father, was delighted. 'My Dear Boy, it is a very great success, and of a sort which proves how very important it was that the fight should come when it did. The seat has not only been won but saved…Congratulate Mr Marshall for me. It is what he promised us…It is a great relief – and triumph.'[45]

Charles had won the approval of his father, but almost immediately the two had a serious falling out over the Boer War. George, as a Gladstonian Liberal of the old school, could not support the war. Charles, who had come under Teddy Roosevelt's spell and believed in liberal internationalism, justified the British Government's intervention as necessary 'to remedy a situation in the Transvaal intolerable to self respecting Britons'.[46] His brother George Macaulay sided with their father, disliking what was happening in the concentration camps. George, then studying at Cambridge, took his elder brother to task.

> For God's sake don't go to your constituency and make a 'statesmanlike' speech. Go and attack the government, who can't make peace or wage war, but seek to end it by threatening or bullying, and making clemency impossible. Have you also considered the statistics of mortality in the concentration camps for August? In five years time, even if the rate of death does not increase, they will all be dead.[47]

The end of the Boer War gave the family an opportunity to patch up their frayed relations. Charles was never again so gung ho in support of adventures abroad, and from the Boer War onward he moved steadily to the left in foreign affairs. The dawn of the new century saw Charles immerse himself still further in parliamentary life and serious causes. To Caroline, Lady Trevelyan's mind, her eldest son was doing well but lacking that crucial ingredient for a grown man – a wife. Charles knew what his mother was thinking. 'I have promised to tell you if I fall in love or make up my mind to marry anyone...You need not be afraid as far as I am concerned that I shall commit myself in a hurry. It is vastly more likely I shall never marry at all.'[48]

An inaccurate prediction, as it turned out. Gertrude Bell, the Arabist who famously drew a line in the sand before lunch marking out the border of Iraq, had a half-sister called Molly who caught Charles's eye when he visited the Bell family home in London. Molly (Mary) Bell was the granddaughter of a millionaire ironmaster from Durham, Sir Isaac Lowthian Bell, fellow of the Royal Society and Liberal MP. Molly's father, Hugh, inherited the title along with three quarters of a million pounds at the turn of the twentieth century. Hugh Bell's first wife, mother of Gertrude, died of pneumonia after childbirth, and he married Florence Olliffe, whose father was a well-known Irish surgeon. Their three children, Molly, Elsa and Hugo, were bought up in Redcar. Molly was musical and charming, and, as Caroline, Lady Trevelyan used to say, the pretty one of her three daughters-in-law.

Molly was smitten when she first met Charles at 95 Sloane Street in London. She wrote in her diary, 'Charles Trevelyan, Sir George's son was here. He is a dog.'[49] Despite this mutual attraction, all did not proceed smoothly at first. Charles, just like his grandfather, preferred to talk of tariff reform, Home

Rule and raising death duties while courting. Molly, who thought herself a 'bit of thistledown'[50] intellectually, found Charles ungallant when confronted by her ignorance. The nascent romance withered for a year. The eleven-year age gap suddenly seemed too much to Molly. Then, during the social season of 1903, the pair met at a party and Charles, feeling lonely and unloved, was not so domineering. Charles was still intent on improving Molly – suggesting she read Morley's *Cobden* and a course of philosophy. But he was more encouraging and less hectoring then before. Molly still knew that 'mine will generally be the under side in a discussion, and you will ride triumphantly over my flattened corpse'.[51] In September 1903 Charles asked Molly to marry him, and she happily accepted. Molly's ironmaster father Hugh Bell affectionately called Charles a 'damned serious gowk', quite unlike his daughter, who had been brought up to play the piano, sing a bit and then become a wife and mother. Despite their differences, Charles's heartfelt philosophical views charmed Molly. And he never hid from her his own assessment of his abilities.

> When I read Gladstone's Life I feel my own nothingness, and I am constantly anxious that in your newness to affairs you should not make pretty dreams for yourself of great successes for me … I have not the quickness, variety or imagination of outlook which can possibly enable me ever to deal with the complicated revolutions of our national politics. I can only do my duty. And so little do I think there is any good chance of rising to any high position with my mediocre store of knowledge and ability, that I shall try less and less to try for position and more and more to take a line I think right … my desire is to imitate Gladstone's openness and rectitude.[52]

As befitted Molly's background, the wedding was a society affair, held at Holy Trinity Church in Sloane Street, London, on 6 January 1904. The bride wore white satin, the groom a frock coat, and they were attended by five bridesmaids. Molly's mother, Lady Bell, would have none of Charles's atheism, and he acquiesced, his famous intransigence tempered by love. The honeymoon was in true Trevelyan style – walking a hundred miles in Cornwall. They were a well-off pair – Charles had inherited money from his grandfather, and Molly had a private income from her grandfather's success in the iron trade. They built a house in Great College St, Westminster, complete with a division bell. This enabled parliamentary guests to come to dinner and attend critical votes in between courses. Charles and Molly frequently entertained, providing Molly with taxing etiquette issues. 'Did a Bishop take precedence over a Baronet?'[53] she wondered. Molly was well versed in how one should behave. Jennie Lee stayed with the Trevelyans the night before she was to be introduced into parliament, and Molly schooled her expertly for the ceremony.

A short time before I was to leave for the house, Lady Trevelyan had an inspiration. Standing at the far end of her long L-shaped drawing room, she told me to go to the other end and come slowly towards her, three steps at a time, bowing as I advanced. I needed that rehearsal for otherwise I might have made a most ungainly parliamentary debut, bowing from the waist as I walked towards the Speaker's chair, but forgetting to lower my head.[54]

The diplomat Sir Humphrey Trevelyan described Molly as indomitable, with the air of 'having just stepped out of an illustration to a Victorian novel'.[55] Courageous and energetic, she bore Charles seven children, one of whom died young, and then in later life had to endure her husband fathering a child, Martin, with his private secretary Edith Bulmer. The half-sister of Gertrude Bell

'To my childlike eyes they were a godlike couple.' The engagement photograph of Charles Philips Trevelyan and Molly Bell, September 1903. Courtesy of the Trustees of the Trevelyan family papers.

was formidable, but, forty years into married life, this episode reduced her to silent fury. Such marital tension was not even on the horizon when Charles and Molly first married. Their daughter Kitty recalled how loving her parents were.

> Father was dark, took life seriously, and seemed a mixture of Celt and Roman, while Mother was fair and radiant, like a Greek; to my child like eyes they were a godlike couple. They loved us children, and were very much in love with each other; they were both gifted and beautiful; they had enough money and enough time, so that is how I thought life was for all people. One day they were kissing each other lovingly when Mother said to us, 'Your father and I wonder whether it is all right to make love to each other when you children are there.'[56]

Molly devoted herself to becoming the perfect political wife, but before too long wanted to move beyond the role of supportive spouse. As Pat Jalland, historian of Victorian women, has noted, 'Molly…passionately desired an active partnership but had to acquiesce in her husband's traditional view of marriage; she had the greatest expectations and consequently made the greatest sacrifice as a political wife.'[57] Molly read widely, as Charles wished, and with her unforced charm and natural ability as a public speaker soon became very popular in the constituency. The doyenne of Liberal political wives, Lady Aberdeen, congratulated her on a speech she made in 1905: 'It was charmingly done and very much to the point…Both on public and personal grounds I rejoice in you as a recruit.'[58] While nursing her baby daughter Pauline, Molly campaigned actively during the 1906 election, feeding the infant in committee rooms between events. She frequently spoke herself, as her diary records. Here is the entry for 4 January, when she had two engagements: 'Spoke quite well at both… back to nurse Pauline at 4.30. Out at 6.15 to three meetings of Charles'.'[59]

According to Pat Jalland's analysis of Charles and Molly's relationship, her political education and aspirations for partnership were proceeding too fast for him. Molly assumed his radical political ideas would naturally translate into an equal role for her in his political life, when actually Charles was more of a traditionalist than she had realised. As his career stalled, he withdrew from her. Molly sought comfort in her thirty-year task, the needlework tapestry that hangs at Wallington showing the Trevelyan family legend. She could not hide her unhappiness from Charles.

Don't you realise how the important side of your life is getting every day further from being a part of me? ...I never doubt for one instant that you love me enormously, far better than anything else. But I am getting to see now that it is my beauty and my cheerfulness that are the reasons of that love. I think I can never be now what I so long to be – your chief friend in every way. Sonny, I do love you so, and it is not kind to leave me so much out of your life...I know that often, constantly, every day, I fail to come up to your standard of intelligence, and so political interest. I fail largely because there is so little point in caring for your interests, when you do not care to share them with me, nor to encourage my efforts, nor to show that you understand my desire to share in your life, by opening it up to me and telling me every day the ups and downs...Dear, our life together can never be perfect until we share everything...I fear that I am getting dull and narrow, caring for your daily welfare more than the larger side of your existence.[60]

While Molly was frustrated with Charles, his father was too, although for different reasons. Sir George Otto, impatiently watching from the wings, willing his eldest to succeed, was not content for the young MP to progress at the same rate as all the other callow backbenchers. He was forever firing off letters to leading Liberal figures, asking when Charles would be given a job in government. In 1908, humiliated by seeing yet another Cabinet reshuffle go by without a place for a Trevelyan, Sir George decided the time had come to pull some strings. He wrote to the Liberal Prime Minister Henry Asquith:

Since our party came in, full recognition has been given to past services of those who, in the old days, served the country and the cause, by the employment of their sons and relatives who were worthy of a chance in the career of administration. Now that several younger men have been placed in office, while my son is left out, I must protest, once for all, that I feel the exception made in our case very deeply.[61]

This from the man who in his youth had questioned the hereditary role of the monarch. Asquith wrote to Charles, assuring him he had not been passed over, and promising a place in Cabinet once a fitting vacancy arose. In October 1908 the post of Under Secretary at the Board of Education was on offer. It wasn't quite a seat at the Cabinet table, but Sir George and Charles were thrilled. The rightful order of things had been restored. Charles remained in the Board of Education until the outbreak of the First World War in 1914, but he moved increasingly leftward, wondering aloud why the Liberals did not cooperate more with Labour on common ground. The foreign policy conducted by George Otto's old friend and Northumberland neighbour Sir Edward Grey, the Foreign Secretary, left him further disillusioned. Charles came to the view that policy was being conducted in secret and imposed upon parliament. Then, after he heard Grey address the Commons, Charles knew he had to leave the government. 'Let every man look into his own heart, his own feelings, and construe the extent of the obligation for himself,'[62] Grey told the hushed Commons. He spoke of Britain's obligations to France, which made war against Germany inevitable. Charles told Molly, 'I never was clearer in all my life...We have gone to war from a sentimental attachment to the French and hatred of Germany.'[63] In a letter to his constituents, on 5 August 1914, he explained his reasons further.

> However overwhelming the victory of our navy, our commerce will suffer terribly. In war too, the first productive energies of the whole people have to be devoted to armaments. Cannon are a poor industrial exchange for cotton. We shall suffer a steady impoverishment as the character of our work exchanges. All this I felt so strongly that I cannot count the cause adequate which is to lead to this misery. So I have resigned.[64]

George Lansbury's view of Charles's move was that 'he must have known when he resigned that he was giving the death blow to his career, and the courage which compels such a step is not to be distinguished from the courage of a soldier who falls in battle'. Charles's prospects within the Liberal party were indeed now fading fast, but with typical energy he threw himself into the fledgling pacifist movement in Britain. This anti-war grouping included Ramsay MacDonald, E.D. Morel, Arthur Ponsonby, Arnold Rowntree, Bertrand Russell and the Liberal MP Philip Morrell. This loose federation became the Union of Democratic Control. Its objectives were the prevention of secret diplomacy by parliamentary control of foreign policy; negotiations after the war for an international understanding based not on governments but popular parties; and peace terms that would neither humiliate the defeated nations nor rearrange national boundaries so as to cause future friction between nations. In jingoistic wartime Britain, the Union of Democratic Control was accused of being a German-funded, unpatriotic and deeply suspect organisation. Charles, until now a scion of the liberal establishment, was cast out to the very fringes of public life. The mainstream of the Liberal Party loathed the UDC. Sir George Otto, a typical example, believed England's involvement in the war was a burden she could not have rejected, of which all true Englishmen ought to be proud. Charles's brother George also believed that in the end England had to enter the conflict. The two brothers, with their deep bond, became estranged. This rift hurt Charles far more than his father's predictable disapproval. As he wrote to Molly,

> I know that wisdom may begin to come to poor human beings through misery. But even I doubt when I see people like George carried away by shallow fears and ill-informed hatreds...It shows how absurdly far we are from brotherly feeling to foreigners when even in him it is a shallow veneer. He like all the rest wants to hate the Germans.[65]

This fundamental rift with one to whom he had been so close made Charles feel wretched, he confided in Molly. 'I am more discouraged by it than anything else because it shows the helplessness of intellect before national passion.'[66]

Molly's family were also pro-war – Charles was the odd one out, as the gung ho local press in his constituency were forever reminding him. This is his local newspaper, the *Brighouse Echo*, on the subject of family divisions:

> All of Mr Trevelyan's near relatives, and also those of his wife, are at present engaged in doing what they can to support the Government and further the cause of the Allies. There is unanimity of word and action on their part...Sir George Trevelyan...loses no opportunity of using his pen to indicate his approval of the policy adopted by His Majesty's advisers. Mr G.M. Trevelyan is supporting his friends the Italians who are united in the Grand Alliance. Sir Hugh Bell is indefatigable in his efforts to promote recruiting: Major Bell is with his regiment facing the enemy; Miss Bell is nursing the sick and wounded. They could hardly do more. Mr Trevelyan on the other hand, talks about peace – that is all.[67]

The *Daily Sketch* was even more scathing:

> With a man of Mr Trevelyan's views Elland[68] should be in Russia. Trevelyan would then have a very congenial atmosphere – in the Reichstag...England nor Elland has no place now for men of the Trevelyan stamp. We have no time to listen to his foolish and pernicious talk. It is a scandal that he should be in Parliament when he continues to preach these pro-German and utterly impracticable pacifist doctrines. Trevelyan must go.[69]

The Elland Liberals asked Charles to stand down, but he stood firm, quoting Burke's statement to the electors of Bristol. 'Your representative owes you, not his industry only, but his judgement: and he betrays you instead of serving you, if he sacrifices it to your opinion.' But it was hard for him to make waves as an anti-war MP. The leading lights of the UDC were either vilified or ignored by the majority of the press. Their speeches in parliament often went unreported. The UDC never caught the mood of the public, and remained the debating house of the intellectual left. Charles wanted to publish a pamphlet raising doubts about the atrocities being committed by the Germans in Belgium in the autumn of 1914. C.P. Scott, the editor of the *Manchester Guardian*, counselled against such a move.

> It would be expedient to hold back the pamphlet. The war is at present going badly against us and any day may bring more serious news. I suppose that as soon as the Germans have time to turn their attention to us we may expect to see their big guns mounted on the other side of the Channel and their Zepplins flying over Dover and perhaps London. People will be wholly impatient of any sort of criticism of policy at such a time and I am afraid that premature action now might destroy any hope of usefulness for your organisation [the UDC] later.[70]

C.P. Scott's fear of the German Zeppelins hovering in the sky above England summed up the fears of many in the country, and shows just how far to the left Charles was in relation to his nation. However obscure and irrelevant the UDC was to most British people, it did influence the post-war policy debate. The historian A.J.P. Taylor described the UDC as succeeding where the Foreign Policy Committee and all its other predecessors had failed.

> It launched a version of international relations which gradually won general acceptance far beyond the circle of those who knew that they were being influenced by the UDC…a Trade Union branch in 1915 passed unanimously a resolution on war aims; and then, on someone pointing out that this reflected the policy of the UDC, as unanimously rescinded it. Later on, the resolutions were to be passed, and there was no rescinding.[71]

Taylor credits the UDC with bringing the notion of a League of Nations into the public arena.

Despite the UDC's lack of immediate, high-profile impact, Charles's doggedness impressed those who knew him, including the author George Bernard Shaw. Innocent as he was in the ways of parliament, Shaw suggested Charles should be bold enough to make a definite 'bid for the Leadership of the House'. Charles did not have enough support to even contemplate such a move. But Shaw flattered him.

You have great advantages: you have an unassailable social and financial position, intellectual integrity and historical consciousness, character, personality, good looks, style, conviction, everything they lack except cinema sentiment and vulgarity. If you feel equal to a deliberate assumption of responsibility it is clear to me that you...can very soon become the visible alternative nucleus to the George gang and the Asquith ruin...I have been lately saying on occasion, 'What about Trevelyan?' and the only objection is that you seem to have specialised too much as a Pacifist.[72]

Shaw was understating it when he wrote that Charles's pacifism was a barrier to his advancement – during the First World War, being a pacifist made advancement through the conventional political routes impossible. Another political opportunity was opening up for Charles, though, The Independent Labour Party had similar views on foreign policy to the UDC. Charles, as a radical liberal, had always been interested in Labour's agenda. Now, in the intolerant wartime atmosphere, both groups were drawn together. In 1915, he wondered aloud about joining the ILP in a letter to E.D. Morel, before deciding against.

I am inclined that I can be more useful to the UDC by being identified with no political party. I am clear that it would be fatal to any progress with the Liberals for anyone to take a definite step towards political change of allegiance who is in a prominent position against us. We cannot yet tell at all how the political situation will develop. There is no hurry.

His attraction to the Labour Party did not dwindle, though. Charles wrote an article in a journal called *The Nation* in 1917 entitled 'Can Socialism and Radicalism Unite?'. His short answer was yes. The longer polemic went like this:

Our lives have been spoilt by compromise, because we tolerated armament firms and secret diplomacy and the rule of wealth. The world war has revealed the real meaning of our social system. As imperialism, militarism and irresponsible wealth are everywhere trying to crush democracy today, so democracy must treat these forces without mercy. The root of all evil is economic privilege...Where shall we find the political combination which will offer us resource in its strategy, coherence in its policy, and fearlessness in its proposals?[73]

J. Pollack McCale, an old Harrovian acquaintance, was appalled by Charles's intellectual journey. 'Do you,' wrote the apoplectic correspondent, 'in the utter tosh you write at a time critical for our country, wish to turn

Europe into a commune with Lenin as Prime Minister and Ramsay MacDonald as deputy? Do you wish to introduce us to the luxuries of Bolshevism, murder, rape and pillage, or do you merely wish to see your own country ruined?'[74] Such was the atmosphere of wartime Britain. Charles felt increasingly drawn to the Labour Party, and alienated from his class. As the war drew to its bloody close, he announced he was joining the party of socialism. His mother was predictably frosty.

> Your decision to join the Labour party is, of course, a trouble to us. I hope you will get on with your new friends and not let them lead you into deep waters. It will make a considerable difference to you and your family but you have doubtless considered everything. I had hoped that after the war we might find ourselves all more in sympathy on public affairs.[75]

Charles replied:

> I think from your letter you are looking from the wrong angle at my action in joining the Labour party. I of course knew that you would regret my leaving the Liberal party, but there is nothing unnatural, sudden or surprising about it. You talk of 'my new friends'. In the first place I have worked in close comradeship with several of the leaders of the Labour party for four years. There is nothing to choose in personality, ability, or character between them and the pick of the Liberal Cabinet, with whom I previously associated in politics. But beyond that at least half my Liberal friends are either joining the Labour party now or are on the verge of joining it…Any amount of my private friends of the same education, and, if that matters, social position, are joining now. I don't want to make you realise this in order to make you uncomfortable about the Liberal party, but in order that you may be comfortable about me.[76]

Charles's parents never were reconciled to his departure from the Liberal fold. But for their oldest son, changing parties meant he was finally able to break free from the dominance of his father's ideas. As he told Jennie Lee in a letter written towards the end of his life, George Otto had always regarded socialism as cranky, which had influenced Charles greatly. 'Consequently as I grew politically conscious, I found myself hostile to him and thwarted by him. Not being an original mind I was dependent on my surroundings. I was furiously hostile to the land system, but not clever enough to become a socialist in practical politics…'[77]

In a 1920 book, *From Liberalism to Labour*, Charles explained his conversion at length, to his parents and the outside world. Before 1914, he argued, a radical could do more for social reform as a Liberal than in the Labour Party. But the failure of the Liberals to prevent secret diplomacy before the war, and their failure to prevent the Treaty of Versailles afterwards, meant that they were a spent force. Instead, the basis of Labour foreign policy would be friendship with Russia. Together they would overthrow Versailles, liberate Germany and defeat the French. A.J.P. Taylor noted, 'Though Trevelyan later became an extreme Socialist, there was not a word in his confession of faith about nationalization or the capital levy. Foreign affairs alone had carried him into the Labour party.'[78]

The voters took some time to accept Charles as a Labour man. Standing in the 1918 post-war election as an independent Labour candidate, Charles was crushed. Not until 1922 did he regain a seat in parliament, as the Labour member for Newcastle Central. In the December 1923 general election, the Tories were the largest single party but without an overall majority. Labour had 191 seats, making them the second biggest party, and King George V invited Ramsay MacDonald to form a government in January 1924. Soon afterwards, Charles was summoned to a meeting with the new Prime Minister. He told Molly, 'I no longer have six children – I have six million.'[79] Charles was to be President of the Board of Education with a seat in the Cabinet. His parents' pride in his achievement went some way towards masking their misgivings over his desertion of Liberalism. Sir George, pleased that the family tradition of high office had finally been upheld by his heir, wrote:

> It is a very great advantage indeed in any genuine and important office, to go to a department the working of which you familiarly know. It is a saving to time, and a source of confidence and comfort, which no one can imagine who has not experienced it, and likewise experienced its opposite. To be the one man in a great office who knows nothing about the processes and the one who has to make the decisions, is a most bewildering business. My father, even, felt it, and said that in his first fortnight at the Treasury he saw the snakes coming out of the papers in his dreams at night. Well, you have as long a family tradition of official work to keep up as George has of book-writing, and I have no doubt you will do it worthily.[80]

When Tony Blair in 1997 promised that a Labour Government would focus on 'education, education, education', he was consciously echoing the priorities of that first Labour Government seventy years earlier. The party in the twenties regarded improving educational standards as a moral obligation. Charles, conscious of the advantages of his Harrow background, wanted the children of the workers to have the same opportunities as those of the wealthy. He proposed to do this by expanding secondary education and raising the school-leaving age. Charles built on the ideas of R.H. Tawney, whose goal was secondary education for all. The break between primary and secondary education at the age of 11 was Charles's initiative, and he obliged schools to provide senior classes for children aged 11 to 14, an important step towards the universal provision of secondary education. H.G. Wells, who had so cruelly mocked the would-be politician Charles ten years earlier, was now impressed. He wrote this letter in October 1924: 'I think your work for education has been of outstanding value…I have watched your proceedings with close interest and I am convinced that there has never been a better, more far sighted, harder working, and more unselfishly devoted Minister of Education than yourself.'

Raising the school-leaving age to 15 was more of a battle. In 1930, the year after Labour formed a second government, Charles introduced a bill in the Commons that ran into difficulties with Roman Catholic MPs on the Labour backbenches. More children at school for longer meant improving the facilities of most schools. The Catholic bishops pressurised their MPs to come up with as generous a financial settlement as possible. Charles, an atheist wary of the power of Church schools, was prepared to go some way towards meeting these concerns, but did not want to entrench the power of the Catholic lobby. He wrote this letter to his old friend Bertrand Russell in 1929, outlining the dilemma:

> I represent a constituency [Newcastle Central] swarming with Irish Catholics. I would rather lose my seat than give the priesthood a bigger power in the schools. I am absolutely determined that the Labour party shall not get into the hands of any religion, least of all Catholic.
>
> My anchor is the appointment of teachers. If I could get that into the hands of the public I would concede a great deal in other directions. Scotland has dealt with the question as well and as tolerably as it probably can be. The schools are wholly in the hands of the people and teachers are appointed by the local authority. The task is tougher in England with the old Church of England on our back and the 6000 school areas.[81]

If Charles was going to give extra money to the schools, he wanted concessions in return for the extra money. As the letter outlines, his proposal was for Catholic schools to resign control over their teachers to the local authorities in return for the cash to extend their premises. This was not popular. The government was defeated on an amendment sponsored by Labour's Catholic lobby, and then the Lords rejected the bill. In a letter to Molly, Charles's frustration with Prime Minister Ramsay MacDonald was apparent: 'MacDonald detests me because I am always quite definite and won't shirk things in the approved style. He will let me down if he possibly can, the real wrecker [is not the House of Lords] it is MacDonald with his timidity.'

Distressed and despondent at the failure of his precious bill, Charles resigned from government once again. In his letter of resignation to the Prime Minister, he made clear the extent of his overall disillusionment.

For some time I have realised that I am very much out of sympathy with the general method of Government policy. In the present disastrous condition of trade it seems to me that the crisis requires big Socialist measures. We ought to be demonstrating to the country the alternatives to economy and protection. Our value as a Government today should be to make people realise that Socialism is the alternative.[82]

The very day that Charles resigned, 19 February 1931, he amplified his criticisms of MacDonald, whom he could not stand, at a meeting of the Parliamentary Labour Party in the Commons.

I have for some time been painfully aware that I am utterly dissatisfied with the main strategy of the leaders of the party... The Labour party is going to be the power of the future however long it takes to evolve leaders who know how to act. But it is as in an army. The leaders for the time must settle the strategy. The officers who can command the battalion can retire, but they must not rebel. I have taken the one step of protest open to me. I resign my position as an officer and become a private soldier.[83]

In a letter to his brother Bob, Charles was pleased with the impact of this hand grenade.

On Tuesday I caused a terrific sensation by saying outright that we should never get anywhere until the leadership was changed. Somebody had got to say what masses of people have been feeling for the past year. Fortunately I don't in the least care what happens to myself and I infinitely prefer spending such time as I have away from the House of Commons administering this estate and other things in Northumberland effectively than administering education with my hands tied by the Tory party and the House of Lords.[84]

However, Charles's cousin and parliamentary private secretary Morgan Philips Price was not impressed by the whole episode. He believed it showed up Charles's weaknesses as a politician.

> He is a man with no great power for thinking out a problem but he relies on instinct which is generally right. 'When in doubt rely on instinct' is a phrase I have heard him use. Unfortunately he has the Trevelyan characteristics of impulsive action alternating with periods of gloomy depression. He rushed out of cabinet without consulting anyone (I, his PPS, learned of his action from the wireless) and he did not give any reason for his action in public. He only made an attack on Macdonald in the Parliamentary Labour Party meeting which, without the necessary explanations and reasoning was not understood and his action (instinctively sound) was generally condemned by the rank and file of our party. I had a difficult two or three days after his resignation. He had gone North to Wallington, and I did my best to defend him in the Lobbies from our members but I wrote Charles a very frank letter in which I reported what was said about his action and his manners. He has a genius for doing the right thing in the wrong way.[85]

Charles was not one for concession and compromise, and just like his father he was not really temperamentally suited to the realities of political life, where principle is so often sacrificed to pragmatism. As with George Otto, Charles promised much but never quite delivered. The pair frequently resigned from office, without leaving an enduring mark on the body politic.

Once out of office, the lure of Wallington, with its attractive lifestyle of shooting and socialising, was for Charles far greater than that of opposition life at Westminster. Two years earlier, in 1928, his parents had died within months of one another. Sir Charles Trevelyan, as he was now known, had at last become master of Wallington. As he took a back seat in public life, so he could live the squire's life to the full. The sight of the latest Trevelyan family in situ at Wallington greatly impressed the American Mrs Winchester Bennett, whose daughter had married into the dynasty.

> We were ushered into the large dining room, where a long mahogany table was set out with twenty three places. All around the walls were open shelves containing a priceless set of Chinese ceramics, the wedding gift of Miss Wilson who married Sir John Trevelyan. Molly had six children, and they were all there for tea with visiting friends, also one married daughter with her two babies. When Uncle Charlie finally made his appearance, I

thought he was one of the handsomest and fascinating men I had ever met.[86]

Wallington was in a state when Molly and Charles inherited it. Grand from the outside, it was in need of urgent repair. The roof over the main hall, Sir Walter Calverley Trevelyan's pride and joy, was about to fall in. The 13,000-acre grounds had been neglected, the tenant's houses were in a state of decline. Sir George Otto had not been a good landlord, caring more for the classics than the condition of the cottages on the estate. Charles and his wife set about making improvements. In April 1929 they invited their tenants to Wallington to celebrate their silver wedding anniversary. Good socialist that he was, albeit an aristocratic, mansion-owning one, Charles marked the occasion with a grand gesture to the people.

You are all aware that I am no friend of the system which by pure chance makes me rich and a thousand others poor for life…I want you to know that I regard myself not as the owner of Wallington and the people of Wallington, but as a trustee of property which under wiser and humaner laws could belong to the community…I want you to feel that to come and see Wallington is on your part not an intrusion but a right…We would like to think that the pictures, the china, the books, the woods, the garden, are possessions for all the people around here to cherish or to use…

We have often expressed the opinion in public that it would be a fine thing if the Nation were to give family allowances where there are children in the family and that would be one of the best methods towards a wider and juster distribution of wealth. We intend to give an allowance to every family on the estate of 2/6 a week for every child from birth till such time as it leaves school or college. The allowance will be paid every month by Lady Trevelyan to the mother of the family…[87]

Family allowance, or child benefit as it is known today, was not provided by the government until after the Second World War, following the Beveridge Report. Charles was 16 years ahead of public policy in setting up his own private scheme. Through such generous acts did he rationalise the contradictions of being a socialist baronet. The most extravagant of Charles's gestures was to leave Wallington not to his eldest son George, but to the National Trust, in 1941. This was in line with his socialist principles, leaving the great house to a grateful nation, but he retained ownership of the place until he died. It was an ideological move, but also a pragmatic one – he knew future generations would struggle with the cost of keeping up the great house, especially with death duties to be paid. This speech by Lord Lothian on the threat to the English stately homes had influenced his thinking:

> I venture to think that the country houses of Britain, with their gardens, their parks, their pictures, their furniture, and their peculiar architectural charm, represent a treasure of quiet beauty which is not only specially characteristic but quite unrivalled in any other land. In Europe there are many magnificent castles and imposing palaces. But nowhere, I think, are there so many or such beautiful country manor houses and gardens; and nowhere, I think, have such houses played so profound a part in moulding the national character and life. Yet most of these are now under sentence of death.[88]

Charles could not bear to think of Wallington declining, with future generations forced to sell off the fine collections of china, or cut down the woods to meet tax bills. He was already opening the doors to the public on a weekly basis, so leaving the house to the National Trust was a natural progression. As Charles acknowledged in a radio broadcast explaining his bequest, not all baronets felt quite as he did.

> There is one great reason which makes it easier for me than for most people in my position to make this initial move. To most owners it would be a terrible wrench to consider alienating their family houses and estates. To me, it is natural and reasonable that a place such as this should come into public ownership, so that the right to use and enjoy it may be forever secured to the community. As a socialist, I am not hampered by any sentiment of ownership. I am prompted to act as I am doing by satisfaction at knowing that the place I love will be held in perpetuity for the people of my country.[89]

This decision did not go unchallenged within the ranks of the family. John Dower, Charles's son-in-law, asked, 'You're leaving the house to the National Trust, but living like people you disapprove of. How can you justify that?' 'I'm an absolute eccentric Englishman,'[90] came the reply. The arrangement whereby Charles kept a life interest in Wallington meant the sacrifice was to be made by his family and not him. The real loser was Charles's heir George Lowthian Trevelyan, later a renowned New Age thinker, who had hoped to turn the house into a further-education college. The late Marjorie, Lady Weaver, Charles's middle daughter, said that George was devastated when the house was left to the Trust. 'George was very unsure of himself,' she recalled, 'but if my father believed something, he did it. I don't think he was a very aware person.' Marjorie summed up her father's attitude to Wallington as 'he'd give it away but he was going to enjoy it as long as he could'.[91] Whether George Lowthian knew of Wallington's fate in advance of the announcement is disputed. Sir Geoffrey Trevelyan, George's younger brother, says he can remember sitting in the parlour with his five siblings as his parents delivered the news. Molly wrote, 'Our own decision has been arrived at after discussion and agreement with our six children.'[92]

George Lowthian's biographer Frances Farrer says that, although the decision cannot have been a complete surprise to him, the final realisation was a terrible blow. George's friend Rhoda Cowen says, 'It happened that George was staying with us at our London house in Phillimore Gardens when he opened *The Times* at breakfast and saw that Wallington had been given away. It was quite dramatic! It was the first time anybody had given away such a place. George was dreadfully shocked, he stood quite still, went white, and was silent. Then he said the oddest thing, I shall always remember it: "My hairbrushes don't belong to me any more!"'[93]

George Macaulay, in a letter to his brother Bob, thought that on balance leaving Wallington to the Trust was a favourable move. His active interest in the Trust had played a part in Charles's decision. In a neat twist, as chairman of the Trust's Estates Committee, George received the house from Charles on behalf of the nation. But even G.M. felt the decision was hard on his nephew, who had lost more than just his hairbrushes.

> Of course it is possible to take the view that the house and estate ought not to be left to the National Trust at all. Prior to the war I did not take a decided view on this question, but I clearly perceived that my brother was determined to do it...I am bound to say that the circumstances of the war and the probable state of things after the war make me more favourably disposed towards the plan in its general aspect...it would be financially impossible for George or anyone else to continue to run the estate burdened with death duties without their selling the treasures of Wallington or large parts of the estate, or both...I confess I think George has been hardly treated in not being more consulted and given a more definite place in the arrangement. But in the old days he showed no interest in Wallington, and his father is absolutely determined (in theory) not to treat him as an 'eldest son'.[94]

Charles, as usual, didn't seem to care what anyone thought of his decision. After the formal transfer to the National Trust, he wrote to his brother

George, 'The Deed is now accomplished and the old place has a future if there is a future for anything.'[95] The 'old place' does indeed have a future – Wallington is thriving in the National Trust's hands. Many thousands have enjoyed visiting the house and the grounds over the years. In 2004 Wallington received 165,654 visitors,[96] the highest number ever in all the years of Trust ownership. Even in 2003, when the house was closed for major refurbishment works, nearly 120,000[97] visited the gardens. Charles would be delighted to see how Wallington's appeal has endured down the ages. The family connection has been retained. Patricia Jennings, Charles's youngest daughter, has lived for many years in a flat in the house.

Not that Charles made life easy for the National Trust. James Lees-Milne, country houses secretary for the organisation, thought Charles was having his cake and eating it by giving the house away yet living in it until he died. Charles continued to behave in the manner to which he had become accustomed. During the Second World War, he had a crown painted on one pillar of Wallington's entrance gate, and a hammer and sickle, the symbol of Soviet Russia, on the other pillar. This presumably demonstrated his dual loyalties to the sovereign and left-wing politics, while infuriating the other landowners. James Lees-Milne was horrified. 'I deplore the hammer and sickle business more than I can possibly say. I should equally deplore Conservative slogans slashed upon National Trust gate piers, or Nazi Swastikas.'[98] He mentioned the matter to G.M., who said the Trust could do nothing.

Others found Wallington and its chieftain equally frustrating. The diplomat Sir Humphrey Trevelyan, a cousin who visited Wallington, found the place and the master full of contradictions. Humphrey could not reconcile the soap-and-blood-splashed copy of Macaulay's Thucydides[99] in the library with the hammer and sickle either.

> I used to have an odd feeling… that there was something not quite natural about the picture presented by life at Wallington, the picture of the Trevelyans as spiritual if not actual descendants of Macaulay, soaked in history, and, as it were, living in it, and of Charles, dominating the scene, a man of broad acres and great substance who was at the same time a rebel storming the battlements of Tory imperialism as the champion of the 'people'. I do not mean that it was consciously stage managed: it was the consequence of the illogical position which Charles had created for himself, of his attempt to reconcile two basically irreconcilable positions.

To those who didn't know Charles, his persona seemed perfectly convincing. A reporter for *The Times* wrote this approving assessment of the man:

> Sir Charles is not a showman. The homely Norfolk jacket, cycling breeches and hose, and heavy hob nailed boots are his favoured dress. Even menial tasks he does not scorn. He will paint a gate on his estate alongside a labourer. He will dance a country dance on the lawn at Wallington with visiting school children.

Harriet Trevelyan, Charles's great niece, worked as a GP in the Wallington area during the 1960s. She found that the hammer and sickle episode, Charles's politics and the bequest to the National Trust had combined to cause such resentment with the local landowners that, even eight years after Charles's death, she was not welcome in some of the big houses.[100] Charles wouldn't have minded. He knew the local grandees couldn't stand him, as he explained once:

> My well to do neighbours in the county and Newcastle are from their point of view right in detesting my attitude. I am very dangerous to their way of life because I know only too well what I am aiming at. It is a much more serious thing to the existing order when not only are pious opinions expressed that it is an unsocial thing for private people to own country houses and castles and thousands of acres, but when they are actually surrendered as a matter of principle. I am not troubled in their thinking me a traitor. Indeed I hate their loyalties. I am much more concerned that the masses understand what I am doing, and feel that the world is changing in the direction they never really hoped to see twenty years ago.[101]

Still, Charles's generosity had its limits. Harriet recalls how Wallington's GP, George Cormack, suggested to Charles that council houses could be built on estate land, an idea that was poorly received. Harriet remembers her great uncle as more complicated and less honest than his brother George.[102] Charles's daughter Kitty adored her father, yet also found him maddening.

> I never knew anyone who was so successful at holding complete opposites within his being, yet making a round whole of these opposites. He was an aristocrat of mind and heart and blood, yet he was a socialist by conviction; he was a born dictator, having his own will into the last detail, yet he believed in democracy, that no one must have power over another, that every soul must be free. These opposites caused no conflict in him, only in those with whom he had to deal. [103]

Illogical and contradictory the Wallington set-up was, but it did enable Charles to hold court at house parties, and keep in touch with his political friends once he ceased to play an active role in government. After the Northumberland Miners' Picnic in Bedlington each year, the main speaker would come and stay with Charles at Wallington. Clement Attlee, Hugh Dalton, Frank Wise, Jennie Lee, Nye Bevan and Hugh Gaitskell were among the Labour luminaries who enjoyed strawberries and cream on the terrace and picnics in the grounds. After dinner, parlour games were played, which many guests found utterly intimidating. Molly, Lady Trevelyan was the ringleader in firing off questions at unsuspecting visitors. Who was the English general who won Blenheim? Which is the largest stone dome in the world? James-Lees Milne captured the atmosphere of Molly in game mode:

> After dinner, I am worn out, and long for bed. But no. We have general knowledge questions. Lady Trevelyan puts the questions one after the other with lightning rapidity. I am amazed and impressed by her mental agility, and indeed by that of the daughters, who with pursed lips shout forth unhesitatingly answers like a spray of machine-gun bullets. All most alarming to a tired stranger. At the end of the 'game', for that is what they call this prep school examination, they award marks. Every single member of the family gets 100 out of 100. The son-in-law gets 80, Matheson[104] (who is also a clever man) gets 30. I get 0. But then I am a half wit. Deeply humiliated I receive condolences from the Trevelyans and assurances I shall no doubt do better next time. I make an inward vow that there never will be a next time.[105]

In fact, Lees-Milne had to endure several more such evenings in the company of Molly and Charles.

> My host and hostess were extremely cordial but alarming. He was a handsome man with piercing eyes and a mouth which turned up at the right side into a kind of sneer which was disconcerting. She, tall, poised, and bustling...spoke in a brittle staccato with a North Country intonation rather like Lord Curzon's. Both husband and wife struck me as academic, the reverse of pleasure-loving, over-political, and trailing the threadworn coat of Socialism. My aesthetic eye saw them as out of harmony with the artistic background of Wallington. But they were gracious in the way that the right – or should I say the left? – minded are with sinners from the wrong end of the spectrum.[106]

The family certainly had a well-developed sense of its own superiority. For guests robust enough to survive the ritual humiliation of the parlour games, shooting was usually the next part of a weekend visit. Charles and his brother George, who lived a few miles away at Hallington, greatly enjoyed a day's shoot on the Northumberland moors. Charles was a crack shot, and went on shooting into his eighties, by which time he probably should have stopped, as his eyesight was not what it had been. Charles's great nephew Tom Trevelyan recalls Charles firing at some birds and not seeing the young Tom right behind his target. Tom looked down at his coat and saw the pellets bouncing off the heavy tweed. His companions were amused but said nothing to Charles. One did not criticise him, or his brother George.[107] Harriet Trevelyan describes another shoot, this time at Houstead's, site of a Roman fort. It was supposed to be a rabbit shoot, as the pheasant season had finished. A pheasant flew up and Charles shot it, claiming it was a 'flying rabbit', much to the discomfort of the gamekeeper, who was not fooled.[108]

Charles was the autocrat of Wallington, running the place exactly as he pleased. This extended to his personal life. In 1931 a young woman called Edith Bulmer came to work as his personal secretary, a role that gradually expanded until she helped him run the estate at Wallington and assisted with his political work. Edith lived in the house, and was about the same age as Charles's older children Pauline and George. She was a committed Labour supporter, an ardent walker and youth-hosteller, and like Charles very active in the People's Theatre in Newcastle, a group with socialist roots. Edith starred in a People's Theatre production of George Bernard Shaw's *St Joan*, which Charles saw. Kitty Trevelyan portrayed Edith thus:

> I was in Wallington, in one of the corridors by the Central Hall, when Father came up to me and said: 'Kitty, I want you to meet Saint Joan,' and I saw Edith for the first time. She was as tall as me, slim and longfaced, with a Roman nose – shy without awkwardness – a rare woman who went beyond the bounds of masculinity and feminity...We took long to get to know each other; Northumberland was as familiar to her as the contours of her long calm hands, and we walked the moors together, or padded quietly down the wood walks to watch the herons fishing on the ponds. She never showed emotion, though she had plenty...It was almost though she had no ego with which to be aware of herself.[109]

Some years after Edith came to work at Wallington, she and Charles became intimate. By 1939, the wider family was aware of the relationship.

Letters from Janet Trevelyan, Charles's sister-in-law, to her daughter reveal a crisis precipitated by the baronet's decision to take Edith on a political visit to Russia with him. At this moment, Charles's older children Pauline and Marjorie realised what was going on. Janet wrote,

> At least they have decided to let their mother know that they all feel very strongly about it and back her in anything she wishes to do but of course we emphasised in our talks to Pauline that to bring on a family crash might be the very opposite of what her mother wanted. She could have had that at any time! So I don't know how it will turn out, but I'm sure it can't do any harm for Molly to know she has her children's love and sympathy. And it may go further and get E.B. out of Wallington without a crash. Charlie is not always so utterly dead to good feeling, though he is such a colossal egotist.[110]

Molly, interestingly, did not want a public row about Edith. She still adored Charles and was willing to put up with the situation, despite the anger of her children. Molly and Edith, wife and mistress, had abided by a certain unspoken code of conduct until the Russian visit upset everything. Janet wrote,

> I've been hearing from Pauline and Molly herself this week, and they've all decided that no open demonstration must be made against Miss B. It would bring the whole structure down, and the curious thing is that Molly herself has a considerable regard for her. She has 'played fair' for the past five years, and so has C. apparently, and as for this Russian journey it was Molly herself who planned it, with a complete disregard, I'm afraid, for the talking propensities of ordinary mortals. But Molly and Charles still have a deep and fundamental love for each other and she is hoping, poor dear, to get him back more completely in the last few years of life. That certainly ought to be the reward of all her patience![111]

In 1943, Molly was rewarded for her patience by the arrival of Charles and Edith's baby. Edith, aged 39, gave birth to Martin Bulmer, who was never publicly acknowledged as Charles's son. For Molly, who had come to an accommodation of sorts and lived with Edith's presence for ten years, the unthinkable had happened. Charles had fathered an illegitimate child at the age of 72. Tongues were wagging in Cambo. This letter from Molly's daughter Kitty to Ann Gillie, a family friend, was written two weeks after Martin's birth.

> Mother is in a terrific state. I am not going to write of it because I think every thought in the wrong direction increases the difficulty for her. I am

at bottom very sorry for her. I fear she may go visit E in which case I'm sorry for them both but largely for E because when feeding a baby it's terrible to be attacked, as don't I know! But every day is a gain. She has spoken no word to Father or me. But luckily George[112] was here, so he got the brunt of it and was most helpful. I don't think she has taken offence at not being told sooner.[113]

Molly was determined to use this mortifying event to finally get Edith out of Wallington. Even though Charles had cheated on her so publicly, she was still the loyal wife, concerned about his standing. As she wrote to Ann Gillie,

> If he were an obscure person living in a small street, it would not matter. But he is a very prominent person, living in a great house and in the public eye. His good name will suffer. She ought to be made to see that.
>
> You say she has been happy at Wallington. Let her keep the recollection of those years, and not start a new period there (or thereabouts – if not

'If he were an obscure person living in a small street, it would not matter. But he is a very prominent person... His good name will suffer.' Sir Charles Philips Trevelyan, with his lover Edith Bulmer, greeting the writer George Bernard Shaw at Newcastle Central Station, 1936. Courtesy of *Newcastle Evening Chronicle*.

actually living in the house) which cannot be as happy as the former period, because she will have brought obloquy upon him.

The curious thing about the whole story is that he is devoted to me. Of that I am absolutely certain. He has the greatest concern for my happiness, and is deeply distressed if I am not happy.

I can envisage a new era at Wallington when he and I can draw together again as companions for the last years of our lives if the tension of her presence is removed, both from my life and from my children's. But if I have to be called upon to live down his mistake in letting her come back, the relations between him and me will be very difficult.

What has throughout been my great sorrow is losing him. I love him so deeply. I have never looked at another man for 40 years. I miss his companionship beyond words. I have so often longed for someone to turn to for help and advice, and comfort, and I have asked myself who I can turn to. My sister? Kitty? George? And then quite suddenly I realised who I yearned for. It was the old Charles, not the Charles of today, but the Charles he used to be, to whom I could say everything, from whom I had nothing to conceal, no thought I couldn't say. When we first married, we agreed never 'to let the sun go down upon our wrath.' If there was any misunderstanding, we always talked it out before we went to sleep.

We can never do that now. We just say, 'well, goodnight,' and kiss each other. If the burden of her person were no longer there, I think we might recover much of the lost ground.

Grow old along with me.
The best is yet to be.
That might still be possible.[114]

Molly wrote again to Ann Gillie, in September 1943. She remained adamant that Edith should not move back to the Wallington estate with her baby, a view Charles would not accept.

I had a heartbreaking talk with C on Wednesday night, in which I was told again and again that I was wrong, narrow, bitter, cruel. No amount of public criticism affects him in the slightest degree. All he cared for is to carry his own wishes, completely regardless of suffering to anyone else, because he regards all his opponents as so wrong that it is better they should be made to realise it. While he talked, I began to question whether the view I take is wrong: but in sober thought I still feel convinced it is not wrong, and I should be knuckling to brute force if I altered my views. So there will be no change in attitude…All I can do is to keep silence, out of loyalty to the wonderful past I have had in my married life.[115]

In October, Molly wrote once more to Ann:

Although I feel you are right as to the ultimate decision lying between the three of us, I see this difficulty: whatever I do or say, the other two will always think 'This is only another effort on M's part to oust the woman she is jealous of'. I fear that nothing will ever eradicate that opinion, in spite of the fact that all jealousy is over long ago. I have accepted the position of second string, and have built up for myself a life full of interest and vigour outside my home. So it would be a tremendous help to all of us (for our children agree with me in thinking it would be better if E were to leave altogether) if someone who stands outside the ring could make C and E see a new point of view – that he is clinging to her as a companion for his own benefit, although by so doing he is hampering her life and her development: that E's first duty now is to her boy, and that she should be free to live her own life with him and for him, which she cannot do if she stays in this neighbourhood. There is a great feeling of animosity against her, and although she may put a nonchalant mask on, she cannot help being conscious of it, and that consciousness will re-act upon the boy, to his detriment. What C has never been willing to do for me, he may be willing to do for her – i.e. let her leave.[116]

But Charles ignored Molly's wishes completely. After the birth, Edith lived two miles away with her friends the Towbs, a Jewish family from Newcastle, and then lodged in Cambo village, close to the house. Four years later Edith and Martin moved to a cottage across the courtyard from the big house. So much for Molly's determination to get the pair off the estate.

Charles's relationship with Edith was an enduring one – it lasted over twenty years, until she died, a month before he did. The pair identified very much with the dilemma of Edward VIII, who abdicated because he could not marry Wallace Simpson, an American divorcee, and remain King. Martin Bulmer has a copy of a Laurence Houseman novel called *John of Jingalo*, a story of a monarch in difficulties, which Charles gave to Edith as a Christmas present in 1936.

Despite the age difference – Charles was old enough to be Edith's father – the two shared an enthusiasm for politics and political literature. Molly, who as a young wife had longed to share the political side of Charles's life, had long since backed away from it following his disapproval. Edith probably shared more of Charles's political ideals than Molly ever did. During the Second World War, Edith taught for the famous Army Bureau of Current Affairs, credited with contributing to the Labour landslide of 1945 by educating the soldiers. Her letters to Charles contain many references to their joint desire to improve the lot of ordinary people. Here she is writing to him after he attends an event marking 100 years since the deaths of the Tolpuddle Martyrs:

> I'm glad Tolpuddle was a satisfactory do … it is fairly full circle, as you say, but one hundred years! I'm impatient and want things to move in the right direction faster than they do.
>
> I love you
>
> Edith[117]

Martin Bulmer reflects that it was almost as if Charles was a bigamist and had two wives. He likens their relationship to that between David Lloyd-George and Frances Stevenson for over thirty years from 1913 to 1945. Lloyd-George was married to his wife Margaret, who lived in North Wales, while Frances acted as his private secretary in Whitehall, and eventually lived together with him in Churt in Surrey.

Charles knew how much the family, particularly his puritanical brother George, disapproved of his relationship with Edith – but he simply didn't care. George was the only family member who ignored Molly's instruction not to confront Charles about his relationship with Edith. Janet Trevelyan described George's outburst: 'He sticks to it that it was a Good Thing to behave like a thunderstorm to him and E.B. just that once. He doesn't think that he could talk quietly to C. about it all, as he feels it so deeply… '[118] Tom Trevelyan, Charles's great-nephew, remembers going on a shoot at Wallington one day when Charles saw Edith in the distance and waved. George stiffened and laid a hand on his leg. 'Charles,' he rebuked his brother, 'no.'[119] Tom saw this as a gesture that said it all – Trevelyans were supposed to be above the temptations to which ordinary mortals succumbed.

As to whether there were other women in Charles's life before Edith, it is hard to say. He was certainly attractive and flirtatious. He was a very close friend of Jennie Lee's – although her biographer Patricia Hollis does not suggest they had an affair. The age gap between Jennie and Charles was much the same as between Charles and Edith. He, something of an elder statesman in the Labour Party, provided Jennie with financial and emotional support throughout her career. The Labour MP Frank Wise, Jennie's lover before she married Nye Bevan, died of a brain haemorrhage while crossing a stile at Wallington. Charles immediately rushed to London on the sleeper train to comfort Jennie – only when he arrived could she allow herself to weep, as Patricia Hollis records. It was Charles who asked Nye to look after her in the wake of Frank Wise's death, a move that led to their marriage a year later. Jennie's political counsel was always important to the aristocratic grandee of the Labour Party. When he wanted to give money to Labour candidates standing in the epochal 1945 election, which Labour won by a landslide, Jennie suggested he pay the deposit for one Michael Foot, then a young unknown. Foot hinted to me that the two had an affair – 'they were both good looking people',[120] as he put it. Jennie herself, in a letter to Frank Wise, described herself as 'an over-vital animal' with the temptation to love others. '…because I love you better and more completely than any other man, does not still my curiosity and even temporary infatuation for others. The borderline between friendship and passion in the relationship of any man and woman is always precarious.'[121] Whatever the truth of their relationship, Charles turned out for Jennie throughout her turbulent personal and political life. When she campaigned in Cannock in 1945, Charles was one of the star turns at her rallies. He, along with Nye Bevan and J.B. Preistley, drew huge crowds, and Jennie won with a thumping majority. To her, Charles was a steadfast friend who 'sustained me through all kinds of stormy weather'.[122]

Labour's victory in that pivotal election gave Charles great satisfaction. His gift of money to ten or so candidates in 1945 was important to him as well as to those who benefited. Michael Foot recalled how he was standing in Plymouth, his home town, which had never been Labour. 'To my amazement, about ten days before the election I was sent one hundred pounds from Charles Trevelyan…it was a lot of money in those days…it pretty well paid for most of the expenses. One hundred pounds was a tremendous gift.'[123] As a member of the first Labour Government of 1924, Charles watched with pleasure as the welfare state he had advocated for so long finally began to come into being. After losing his Commons seat in 1931, he remained involved in Labour politics for part of the next decade, though he refused offers to stand again for parliament. An approach from Churchill for a war role in London was also rejected. Charles was by that time 70. He wholeheartedly supported the war against Nazi Germany – how times had changed since August 1914. This time, George Macaulay wrote to his daughter Mary, 'I am the pacifist and CPT the jingo – within limits.'[124] Charles greatly enjoyed being Lord Lieutenant of Northumberland, an appointment made by Ramsay

MacDonald that annoyed the local gentry still further. The position was considered a perquisite of the Percys. He made Wallington a centre of radical activity in the North, visited by People's Theatre working parties and young people of the left. No longer a participant in public life, he became an avid correspondent from behind his desk at Wallington. Copies of Hansard were stored under the stairs, and he followed the world's course closely. Leaders all over the world, from Stalin to Nehru, received unsolicited letters from Charles. With typical self-belief, he assumed that it was his right to dispense such advice. As an admirer of the Soviet Union, having visited in the thirties, he retained his admiration for the Communist regime until the events in 1956 in Hungary changed his outlook. On the eve of the Second World War in 1939, Charles was worrying about how the British public perceived the Russians. Stalin received this advice from the old man:

Dear Mr Stalin,

I am concerned that the British public are today generally less well-informed about Soviet Russia than they were, and more estranged from your people. This is no doubt partly due to the pro-fascist policies of our present government and to the prejudices and distortions of the capitalist press. But not nearly enough is being done to counteract these deliberately hostile elements…It is customary in England to hear yourself classed as a dictator in the same breath with Hitler and Mussolini. Whereas all British workers, Liberals and anti-fascists in our country need to be made to understand that you owe your ascendancy to the confidence of a free and democratic people, constantly renewed.[125]

Charles suggests the British public could be won over if it was easier to visit Russia: 'It is worth more than anything else to enable increasing numbers of intelligent English visitors to see the country.' He concedes that 'the placing of Soviet news in Britain is of course difficult because of the deliberate hostility of most of our capitalist press. But some new technique of simple and direct pronouncements from the Kremlin would be useful at critical moments…' The letter ends with an offer to discuss these matters in person when Charles is next in Moscow.

In 1954, the Indian Prime Minister Jawaharlal Nehru was sent this despatch from the elder statesman:

I have just read that you are considering retirement from your position as ruler of India. I hope you will think many times before you decide on the step. Though I have no claim to your attention, I am certain that I represent the views of many Englishmen. I am the only surviving member of the first Labour cabinet of 1924...If you were to retire now the world would lose the most balanced judgement of any of its rulers... your retirement at this time would deprive mankind of one of its chief hopes of stabilized peace.[126]

Nehru, who was an admirer of G.M.'s history books, took the trouble to reply to his eccentric correspondent.

It is rather difficult to explain the condition in India and the rather special position which I hold here...I would undoubtedly exercise considerable influence on policy and the Government's activities, whether I am in Government or not...I realise the difficulties, and it is because of this that my proposal was only a tentative one for consideration.[127]

To the very end, the adrenalin of politics, domestic and foreign, ran in Charles's veins. His grandfather Charles Edward had been a public servant and a statesman, his father had been a nineteenth-century Liberal minister and mainstay of Gladstone's administrations, but Charles for most of his working life was something slightly different, a twentieth-century professional politician with a propensity to say what he believed, and face the consequences – hence his resignations from office during the First World War and in 1931. Of course, his private income enabled him to be so forthright – he wasn't dependent on the salary of an MP. But his engagement with first radical Liberal and then left-wing Labour politics was genuine and all-encompassing. His disillusionment with the Soviet Union following events in Hungary in October 1956 was succeeded in the final 15 months of his life by a developing interest in the potential of Communist China as a model for the future. These deep political preoccupations were shared with Edith.

Charles was physically and intellectually vigorous to the last, commanding, interested and questioning what was going on in the world. In a letter to Jennie Lee in his twilight years, Charles reflected on what he had achieved, and why he had not gone further.

I have nothing to grumble about in regard to my life as a whole. I have done better than I deserve a long way. But I always feel that I was unlucky in having as the most important people with whom I had to deal, Ramsay MacDonald and George Otto Trevelyan. We had to suspect and eventually dislike each other because our natures and our faiths were so different. But my father had none of the personal bitterness and meanness of J.R.M.[128]

Yet difficult personalities aside, Charles was pleased with his independence of thought, as he explained in another letter, also written in his final years:

> What made me any use in the world was having to stand nearly alone in the first war. Since then I have never found it hard to take my own line and have found out the way to do it. I discovered that if you believe a thing sufficiently strongly there is no need to fear isolation or unpopularity...If you see what you think is right clearly enough, there is really no difficulty. Most people's minds are rather mixed and foggy.[129]

In January 1958, aged 87, Charles Philips Trevelyan died at Wallington. His first cousin Morgan Philips Price wrote that 'his sincerity often led him to be intolerant of other people's opinions, and with a greater degree of tact he could have accomplished much more of what he wanted; but that was not his nature. On the other hand, nobody could question his idealism.'[130]

5

CLIO'S DISCIPLE

The dead were and are not. Their place knows them no more, and is ours today. Yet they were once as real as we, and we shall tomorrow be shadows like them ... the poetry of history lies in the quasi-miraculous fact that once, on this earth, once, on this familiar spot of ground, walked other men and women, as actual as we are today, thinking their own thoughts, swayed by their own passions, but now all gone, one generation vanishing into another, gone as utterly as we ourselves shall shortly be gone, like ghosts at cockcrow.[1]

I f ever a man were destined to write history, the story of generations past, it was surely George Macaulay Trevelyan, youngest son of George Otto. He was named after his father and his distinguished great-uncle, literary historians both, and became the best-known and best-loved historian of England in the first half of the twentieth century. J.H. Plumb, a fellow historian and devoted disciple, regarded him as the poet of English history, a unique phenomenon of our literature.[2] His *English Social History,* published during the Second World War, was a best-seller across the English-speaking world. His reputation has gone full circle in the forty-odd years since his death – from Grand Old Man of history, to member of the Great Unread, fit only for the second-hand bookshops of the world, to narrative historian whose shares may be rising once more. As his supportive biographer David Cannadine provocatively says,

> For those people who believe that the purpose of history is to write big books on large subjects that will reach a broad audience, he remains a

giant figure, a rather heroic figure, a splendid figure. For those who believe that the purpose of writing history is to spend time in archives, to be hugely erudite, to write very rarely, very badly, and only for your academic colleagues, then Trevelyan is the antithesis of everything they believe history ought to be all about.[3]

George Macaulay Trevelyan was born in 1876 at Welcombe, in Warwickshire, the youngest of George Otto and Caroline's three sons. Entering the world a fortnight before the publication of his father's *Life of Macaulay*, he was named in honour of his renowned relative, a prescient choice. Charles Philips, the eldest son, became as we have seen a Labour Cabinet minister, and Robert, the middle son, was a minor poet. It was apparent to the trio's many observers that George Macaulay was the brilliant one. In the assessment of Beatrice Webb, the Fabian, the youngest Trevelyan was gifted with 'far greater talent and power of concentrated work'.[4] Aware that he had been born into a high-achieving dynasty, G.M. wanted to take his place alongside Macaulay and George Otto.

At only six years of age, the future historian found himself living at the Chief Secretary's Lodge in Ireland. While his father George Otto was dealing with demands for Home Rule, in the grounds of the Lodge in Phoenix Park the young George was happily occupied. He remembered

> playing at marbles and hide-and-seek with a mild and gigantic Irish plain-clothes detective, named Mr Dunne, whom I regarded as my playmate, and who was incidentally responsible for the preservation of my small person. It was startling to discover one day that he took the opposite side about the battle of the Boyne.[5]

Through the Lodge gates, the 6-year-old boy and his guardian could see real soldiers – cavalry, infantry and artillery – drilling in Phoenix Park. 'Our grounds were like a private box for viewing these delights,'[6] he wrote. A caricature of the Duke of Wellington was carved on a beech tree on the lawn – he too had once been Chief Secretary of Ireland, as George Otto loved to remind his young son. G.M. could never understand how a general could be Chief Secretary – he wrote it off as one of the insoluble mysteries of childhood. Isolated as this existence was, he enjoyed it. There were 'gala days', when George Otto came up to his son's room and taught him how to play battles with lead soldiers. The father wrote in 1882,

> I have just contrived to set George playing at a 'city' instead of those eternal battles. It reminded me so of old days; except that his battles are

one continual revolution, in which the roughs, the police, the students of the University, the tradesmen and the 'gents' form different combinations, and always end by killing the whole of each other. He has no idea of the quiet flow of civil life. I am glad to say there are slight indications that Ireland is beginning to return to a state of things less resembling that of George's town.[7]

The three brothers played this game endlessly at Wallington, with their lead soldiers deployed across the vast expanse of the floor. As Bob Trevelyan, G.M.'s brother, recalled,

> Much of our pocket money must have gone towards purchasing those exquisitely packed cardboard boxes, each containing twenty or thirty infantrymen…all moulded, packed and painted at Nuremberg. Even now I sometimes dream of discovering and pillaging marvellous magic toy shops, rich with countless boxes of the oldest and best soldiers, and most precious of all, artillery – canon, gunners…[8]

One brother would be Wellington, the other Napoleon, while the third acted the part of impartial destiny. Many hours would be spent arranging the English and French armies – each with nearly two thousand lead soldiers – into the appropriate formations. Battles would often take weeks of hard work, and sometimes had to be left unfinished at the end of the holidays. The brothers became immensely knowledgeable about military strategy. Jennie Lee, the Labour minister, discovered how the Trevelyan brothers had wiled away the long hours of their childhood when she was on a trip to Belgium.

> What I best recall is Charles Trevelyan packing as many of his friends into a taxi as it would hold, then taking us to the field where the Battle of Waterloo had been fought. To my amazement Charles knew the position of every regiment during the battle and guided us around with all the zeal of a small boy playing at soldiers. Where was the near-pacifist, the stern upholder of 'peace by negotiation', the serious senior statesman? At that time I had not yet visited Wallington, the family home of the Trevelyan family. Later I discovered the secret. The whole of an immense attic floor was laid out with literally thousands of toy soldiers. Every one of the regiments that had fought at Waterloo was represented. Charles, his historian brother George, and his poet brother Robert may have disagreed on many things. But they were united in the joy they took in this relic of their childhood.[9]

This elaborate game, which George learnt aged six, continued well into his undergraduate days. In a letter to Bob written from Wallington during a Cambridge vacation, George updated him on the progress of the fighting:

> The battle is going on lazily. An attack of the Hills corps…has failed… At ten minutes before eight, the English guard corps begins to appear over Kip Hill, and Buonaparte being only just preparing to cross the lakes, it will be best for the Gonave Corps to gradually roll itself up down the road, to form a junction with him if possible, as they cannot hold their present position until Napoleon comes…If it is possible to hold the Wall Houses till Napoleon comes I will make them do so. If not, they must fall back on East Wallhouse.
>
> This seems to be the best plan, and I will conduct the operation unless you write to the contrary. If you would prefer to have the battle put off till you return, write to say so at once.

Once back in hall at Cambridge, George was still reflecting on his battle moves to Bob: 'P.S. The battle ended very quietly. A good many of the young guard were cut off in retreat. I think you would have probably won the hill in time…My plan was good and succeeded in the main but was so badly executed that the result was very paltry.'

Living history in Ireland, playing history in the nursery, the young George absorbed yet more history at the knee of his father. Travelling with George Otto was an act of historical education in itself, as G.M. described:

> He had the quality of making his companion feel the excitement that he himself felt at being privileged to see the battlefield at Waterloo, or the staircase in the tragic house at Delft at the foot of which William the Silent was murdered, or the places where the Tuileries, the guillotine and Salle de Manege once stood; and as to the Forum, the Palatine, the Campagna, they were holy ground, where history's most royal pageant had been played.[10]

The scenes of old murders, battles and revolutions gripped G.M. too. During a visit to Rome, George Otto took his youngest child to see the Janiculum, where he told him the tale of Garibaldi's defence of the Roman Republic. Years later, G.M. was to write his acclaimed biography of the unifier of Italy, a work surely inspired by his father. Just as George Otto the young liberal had been caught up in the romanticism of Garibaldi's adventures, so G.M. was captivated by the subject too. History had cast its spell. By eight years old, he had produced his first book, 'Brave Men of Britain'.[11] Written in an exercise book, with very few spelling mistakes, there are accounts of various battles in the Napoleonic Wars – all of which George had re-fought himself, minus the bloodshed, with his lead soldiers.

Even before he went away to school at the age of nine, George had begun his acquaintance with the works of his great uncle and namesake Macaulay. At Wallington, his mother Caroline read aloud to him the famous third chapter of the *History of England*, describing the state of the country in 1685, just before the Glorious Revolution. 'I remember so well Mama reading it to me for the first time when I was a little boy; it was in the library, and I used to lie with my head on the woolly rug against the fire and look up at the marble head carved on the mantelpiece, while she read.'[12]

All three boys went to Harrow, at the time a school favoured by wealthy Victorian businessmen, with a strong army tradition. Sporty, conservative, it was everything George was not. He felt himself to be a misfit, just as his brother Charles had before him.

> Wrapped in literary and historical imaginings which were a bore to my schoolfellows, I refused to make any effort to care for anything that interested them. I was utterly lacking in tact and adaptability to human surroundings. I remember a boy asking me, with a sneer, whether I knew the name of a Derby favourite; I did know, for it was the subject of general conversation that week, but said I didn't because I resented the tone of the question; my interrogator went away marvelling, to spread the news.[13]

In a letter home to his parents, George explained how he was holding out against the general Tory drift of Harrow: 'I keep the flame of my liberalism bright in this dark corner by taking in the *Daily News* and *Speaker*, and conversing with them for want of more articulate liberal friends.'[14]

George's chief comforter during the school holidays was his dedicated nurse, Mary Prestwich, 'Booa'. When Caroline, Lady Trevelyan married, she brought Mary to Wallington with her, to serve as her personal maid. Very soon Mary became the boy's nanny, and once they were grown she stayed with the family as their housekeeper until her death in 1923. Tall, dignified and devout, she was an evangelical Christian. Over her speciality treat of parkin, a Lancashire gingerbread of oatmeal and black treacle, this no-nonsense Northerner would tell her charges about the gospel of salvation. George took it all very seriously at first. 'I loved Booa, and her religion was mine until, at the age of 13, I learnt that Darwin had disproved the early chapters of the Bible; at that dire discovery, all the rest, I fear, fell away from me at once.'[15] He was an unbeliever for the rest of his life, but he gained from Booa a knowledge of the Bible, and a love of its most beautiful passages, which helped him in his writing of early English history.

George's childhood taught him that 'poetry, history and solitary walking across country were the three best things in life'.[16] At Harrow he fell in love with Shakespeare, Milton, Shelley, Keats and Tennyson – they came to mean quite as much to him as his father's gods of Gibbon, Macaulay, Carlyle and Ruskin. At Cambridge, he discovered Swinburne, Browning, Wordsworth and George Meredith. Holidaying at Welcombe, home of his grandfather Robert Philips, meant that George lived and walked in Shakespeare's Warwickshire. At Stratford, he saw his first play, Frank Benson in *Richard III*. As he played in the grounds of Welcombe, his imagination wandered. 'The large stretches of woodland to north and west, where I used to roam among the primroses, I imagined to be wrecks of the Forest of Arden, as perhaps some of them were.'[17]

In 1893 George went at last to his spiritual home, Trinity College, Cambridge, alma mater to Macaulay and George Otto. He had been longing for a change of scene, as he wrote to his mother: 'I live in literature, politics and history, and am burning for the world (be it only Cambridge).'[18] Now, finally, he was following directly in the footsteps of his forefathers. Macaulay had felt towards Trinity 'as an ancient Greek or a medieval Italian felt toward his native city',[19] and had developed the habit of walking through the college grounds, book in hand, morning after morning through the long vacation. George Otto wrote, 'Some there are who can never revisit it without the fancy that there, if anywhere, his dear shade must linger.'[20] This tradition George Macaulay consciously imitated. He wrote to Charles, 'Tell Papa I have been working several mornings walking up and down under the Library reading my note-books. I shall always do so when I can in future.'[21] Even the compulsory act of attending Chapel had its compensations, because it meant walking past Macaulay's statue every day. Conscious of his heritage and anxious to live up to the family name, George was using all the self-possession and self-control he could muster to emulate the eminence of his relatives. As Beatrice Webb noted,

> He is bringing himself up to be a great man, is precise and methodical in all his ways, ascetic and regular in his habits, eating according to rule, 'exercising' according to rule…he is always analysing his powers, and carefully considering how he can make the best of himself. In intellectual parts, he is brilliant, with a wonderful memory, keen analytical power, and

a vivid style. In his philosophy of life, he is, at present, commonplace, but then he is young – only nineteen![22]

Trinity created a powerful network of friends for the aspiring great man – Maurice Amos, later a judge in Egypt, Ralph Wedgwood of the pottery family, George Moore, the philosopher, and Ralph Vaughan Williams, the composer. Elected a member of the Cambridge Apostles, an elite within an elite, George was a contemporary of Bertrand Russell, who became a friend, as well as Desmond MacCarthy, the literary critic, G.H. Hardy, the mathematician, and Lytton Strachey, of Bloomsbury fame. Strachey and George rubbed along rather uncomfortably in the Apostles. They had a running disagreement over homosexuality. The Apostles had celebrated homosexuality, if not actually practised it, since the 1830s, but George disapproved heartily, puritan that he was. Strachey, who was gay, mocked George frequently in his letters – particularly his habit of roaring 'So and so's a sodomite!' Strachey was not especially fond of the strait-laced George, and made fun of his habit of dining in college on macaroni, rice and stewed prunes washed down only with soda.[23] 'The simple life', as Strachey referred to the hearty way in which George and his brother lived. Strachey's animosity continued once both men had graduated.

> On Wednesday morning I trudged off to Trevy, to tell him I could not do my Voltaire article in time for the January number. He didn't seem to mind, and at once launched into lecture after lecture. It was truly awful. Everything he said was stupid and rude to such a painful degree! In addition to all the old ordinary horrors, he has now become curiously numb and dumb...I believe he's disappointed, almost embittered, and perhaps he doesn't like Janet anymore. His book has come out.[24] Does he think he's immortal? Does he consider that in 200 years' time this passage will be his only memorial? Mort aux vaches![25]

Rather more in tune with George was his most beloved friend from Trinity, the poet, athlete and climber Geoffrey Winthrop Young. This was a second-generation Trinity friendship – George Otto and Sir George Young, one of the first alpinists, were devoted friends too. Together the younger generation created a game that lives on to this day. In 1898 George and Geoffrey dreamt up 'The Hunt', a version of 'Hare and Hounds', played out over the Central Fells of the Lake District each late May Bank Holiday weekend. Human hares chase after human hounds, up and down the peaks, over several days. It is not for the faint-hearted or the unfit, but it is a living legacy of G.M. Trevelyan and Geoffrey Winthrop Young's friendship. If I narrow my eyes, the craggy features of my father racing across the fells blur and become those of his grandfather, a hundred years earlier.

Close as he was to Geoffrey Winthrop Young, the most important relationship in George's life at this point was with his older brother Charles Philips. The two were very different – Charles, as we have seen, was dashing, glamorous, and rather like his father George Otto, too fond of resigning to ever make it as a successful politician. George was serious, determined, and meticulously grooming himself for greatness. Yet the pair shared a love of literature and the great outdoors, and both were at the turn of the twentieth century liberal in their politics. Charles and George were prone to depression, or 'blue devils', and through their correspondence they comforted one another. As George wrote soon after arriving at Cambridge, 'I discovered with surprise, that probably very few people have friends, intimate in the way that we are intimate, on whose arm to lean when the unnameable darkness falls. Possibly other people are not troubled by the unnameable darkness as we are. But be sure I need you as much as you need me.'[26]

Because George destroyed almost all his correspondence before his death, not wanting anyone to write a fashionable 'psychological' biography of him, more of his letters survive than Charles's replies. When Charles was troubled by an unsuccessful love affair, George wrote,

> Half your life you are in good spirits and can make yourself delightful to anyone, especially to the family, while the other half you are in the Blue Devils…and so unless I, David, am there with my harp, Saul sulks away in a corner, and spins ridiculous theories about Democracy absorbing his domestic affection etc. Out on it! Know yourself, don't theorize about yourself.[27]

Literature was George's answer to depression. Just as Macaulay had comforted himself by reading after his sister Margaret died, so could Charles. But he had to read the right sort of book – not *The Egoist*, but Browning's *Paradise*, where one could 'find glimpses there of your higher self'. Even in 1902, George was still exhorting his older brother to read properly.

> It is not necessary to become a metaphysician, but it is necessary to feel the inner truth of our great heritage of English poets, and of Carlyle's Sartor, to roll them under the tongue of our mind, to have by heart the tags that appeal to you, to live in them, to be converted to them since they alone are religion – ![28]

Self-improvement is a theme running through George's letters – and that sense of destiny, which he felt not just for himself but for Charles too. 'You and I are made to do work in this world and thereby to get some share of fame, not enormous fame or work, but enough to satisfy us and the world we serve. I have Napoleonic determination that this shall be so for myself and for you too, and you are not going to drop behind.'[29]

'He is bringing himself up to be a great man.' The young George Macaulay Trevelyan by the sundial at Wallington. Courtesy of Tom Trevelyan.

This high-minded rectitude, vaulting ambition and distinct lack of a sense of humour irritated quite a few of their circle. As already mentioned, H.G. Wells parodied Charles and George Trevelyan cruelly and at great length as the Crampton brothers in *The New Machiavelli*, published in 1910. Wells made Charles into Willie Crampton, the politician, 'rich and very important in Rockshire',[30] who eventually becomes Postmaster General. George is the younger brother Edward Crampton, with a 'strained' and 'unmusical' voice, who is at work 'upon the seventh volume of his monumental life of Kosciusco', making him 'one of those unimaginative men of letters who are the glory of latter-day England'.[31] Wells, just like Strachey, found the Trevelyans' self-importance and tendency to dominate conversation rather trying. He took his revenge in fiction.

> Good Lord! What bores the Cramptons were! I wondered I endured them as I did. They had all the tricks of lying in wait conversationally; they had no sense of the self-exposures, the gallant experiments in statement that are essential for good conversation. They would watch one talking with an expression exactly like peeping through bushes. Then they would, as it were, dash out, dissent succinctly, contradict some secondary fact, and back to cover. They gave one twilight nerves. Their wives were easier but still difficult at a stretch; they talked a good deal about children and servants, but with an air … of making observation upon sociological types.[32]

Such observations left George unmoved. He would probably have dismissed that kind of talk as jealousy, the product of an inferior mind. His Napoleonic qualities led him to define very early on the way in which he was going to leave his stamp on the world. In the autumn of 1895, he told Charles, 'I have definitely, and I believe finally, chosen the amelioration and enlightenment of others as the first object, instead of the pursuit of truth as truth.'[33] History for the many, not the few. Like his great-uncle, and his father, and his father's fellow nineteenth-century liberals John Morley and James Bryce, George believed that history's primary purpose was its didactic public function.[34] Now it had to be written. At Cambridge in 1895, Lord Acton was appointed Regius Professor of Modern History, and George threw himself at the feet of the great man. He worked obsessively hard, so much so that he had a nervous breakdown, but in 1896 he achieved the expected first in the Tripos. 'If I get a second I shall be the most unmitigated humbug since Tolstoi's Napoleon,'[35] he wrote beforehand. He went on to read for his fellowship dissertation, choosing the Peasant's Revolt of 1381 as his subject.

Appointed the first ever history fellow at Trinity, his seamless rise continued, and his first book, based on the dissertation, was published by Longman in 1899 – *England in the Age of Wycliffe*. Another dynastic ambition was achieved here – Longman had published George Otto, and the son took great pleasure in the connection. Soon afterwards George gave up academic life temporarily. With the cushion of a sizeable private income, he did not have to depend upon the Trinity stipend. He did not want to become a professional historian – perhaps he found the confines of college life too restrictive, the scrutiny and judgements of others too intrusive. He certainly had no time for the bitchy world of the professional scholar. Instead, he was able to write his books independently. He taught at the Working Men's College in London, and worked on his next book, *England Under the Stuarts*.

Teaching was George's welcome distraction from the horrible events in South Africa at the end of the nineteenth century. The Boer War made him miserable, not least because it caused a family row. George Otto, his father, was against the war, Charles was in favour of it, and George started off by being on the same Liberal-imperialist side as his brother but then became deeply troubled. Horrified by the concentration camps, in which Boer children were dying of measles, George asked, 'Can we lightly destroy the rising generation of a whole people? ... I think we are very guilty to this nation.'[36] Let down by the Liberal leadership, detesting the jingoism of the Conservatives, George was downcast. In what was to become a lifelong habit, he wrote to *The Times*, that bulletin board for the great and the good, calling for the concentration camps to be moved to healthier climes near the coast. As a man who felt he was part of the history of the nation, George was always prone to depression when the wider world acted in a way he could not comprehend. Modern society concerned him, with its rush towards industrialisation, and resulting emphasis on leisure time, all of which he feared would destroy the spirit of active social involvement responsible for so much beneficial change. The Conservative Party he saw as indifferent to injustice – and so he concluded, in a letter to his father, society itself had to change:

> I believe that in order to get a new spirit in the upper and middle class, or rather in a small proportion of those classes – the classes that possess wealth and power and hold the country in the hollow of their hand – in order to get them to do things, the entire belief in 'progress' and 'the benefits of civilisation' must be destroyed, or at least combated tooth and nail. Only when there is a general discontent, not merely this or that, will the spirit of saving society begin. It is to individuals first, rather than the

masses, that I hope to appeal...with the world going, as I conceive, to ruin, for causes much more fundamental than the mere South African error, or even the mere strength of Toryism...it is impossible to act and work as one would act and work in a classical period of literature and politics. Once one has faced facts they are tolerable and even interesting.[37]

George was profoundly ambivalent about academic history – which is partly why at this point in his life he had left Cambridge to teach in London. He wanted to be a literary historian, to draw outsiders in to his view of the past, rather than to exclude the uninitiated. Lord Acton's successor as Regius Professor of History at Cambridge, John Bury, declared in his inaugural lecture that history was not a 'branch of literature', but was in the process of becoming 'a science, no less and no more'.[38] George, sitting in the audience, bristled, reminded of how yet another distinguished Cambridge historian, Sir John Seeley, had told him how Macaulay was a 'charlatan'.[39] George spoke out, writing first an article and later an essay maintaining that for history to be read and respected it must be presented in a literary and artistic form. While history should be scientific in that it should be accurate and faithful to the facts, he argued that it could not discover the laws of cause and effect of any event, for the facts in the end were interpreted by the imagination, intellect and sympathy of the historian. To make his case, George described what might be felt and thought during a walk in the gardens of St John's College, Oxford – the headquarters of Charles I's court during the opening year of the Civil War.

Given over to the use of a Court where days of royalty were numbered, its walks and quadrangles were filled, as the end came near, with men and women learning to accept sorrow as their lot through life; the ambitious abandoning hope of power, the wealthy hardening themselves to embrace poverty, those who loved England preparing to sail for foreign shores, and lovers to be parted for ever. There they strolled through the garden, as the hopeless evenings fell, listening, at the end of it all, while the siege guns broke with ominous iteration...The sound of the Roundhead cannon has long died away, but still the silence of the garden is heavy with unalterable fate, brooding over besiegers and besieged...[40]

Beautifully written, elegiac and haunting, conjuring up a picture of the King's court in its final hours through the use of imagination and facts combined – the passage sums up both George's approach to history, and everything his detractors despised about his work. To J.H. Plumb, student, friend of George's and fellow Cambridge historian, those few hundred words have an incomparable beauty of tone.

Having read such words as these, who could doubt that here was a great artist at work; at work in a medium, the writing of history, in which scholars have been plentiful and artists rare. But why did Trevelyan choose to use his gift of imagination in history rather than poetry?... One overwhelming reason cried aloud in the... quotations above, that is his preoccupation with Time.[41]

This, it must be said, is currently a minority view among academic historians. Sir Geoffrey Elton, the historian who eventually succeeded George as Regius Chair at Cambridge, denounced his predecessor as a 'not very scholarly writer', who produced 'soothing pap', 'lavishly doled out' to 'a large public'.[42] Professor J.P. Kenyon in *The History Men* maintains that George was an 'insufferable snob', overwhelmed by 'mandarin complacency' with 'socially retrograde views',[43] who, what's more, did no archival work before he was 50, never wrote a learned article and had only one officially accredited research student. Dr J.C.D. Clark was even more damning, claiming George was guilty of 'shallowness', 'superficiality' and 'glibness'.[44] A more modern critic, Stefan Collini, finds that

> Trevelyan was able to write with an easy familiarity about the families who had for so long ruled England, and yet in some ways his inherited sense of his destiny was a handicap: there were certain kinds of questions it didn't dispose him to ask... he was not prompted to be critically reflective about the assumptions and concepts he brought to the writing of history. In an important sense, Trevelyan was not an intellectual.[45]

However, Richard Evans, author of *In Defence of History*, concedes that while George's views have for a long while seemed old-fashioned, '[o]ne consequence of the post modernist incursion into history is to make their emphasis on poetry and imagination seem contemporary once more; but poetry and imagination that are disciplined by fact'.[46] George's greatest defender is his biographer, the historian David Cannadine. Cannadine painstakingly demolishes the argument that his subject was not an 'academic' historian, demonstrating the breadth of his original research. He takes issue with the view that his subject was a nostalgic patrician longing for the ordered world of the eighteenth century, in which the landed gentry held sway. Cannadine argues that 'in his power to recreate the past, and to inspire in others the passion to explore it further, he had no equal in his day and has had no equal since'.[47]

And there I shall leave the professional historians, with their competing views about George's place in the pantheon. My purpose is not to settle an argument about historiography, but to try to illustrate the personality of the man. George himself made no further forays into the debate about the nature of history – he found the spectacle of historians scrapping amongst themselves rather unedifying. And anyway, by 1903 he was in love.

George's first beloved, Hester Lyttleton, rejected him, or rather her family did, on the grounds of his atheism, bringing on a fit of the blue devils. But with Thomas Carlyle to comfort him, and the great man's book *Sartor Resartus* as a companion, George reflected on how privileged his life was despite his heartbreak. In June 1900 he spent a weekend at Carlyle's birthplace of Ecclefechan, and felt inspired. 'The postman of Lockerbie for instance, with whom I talked yesterday, whose grandfather knew "auld Tam" here as a lad, to this poor postman and many others of all ranks and fortunes *Sartor* is and will always be the word of life...'[48]

Carlyle helped heal the wounds of George's first love – and the cure was completed by Janet Penrose Ward. She was the very model of a Trevelyan wife – intelligent, public-spirited and, like her husband, to be part of what Cannadine calls the overlapping aristocracies of birth and talent. Janet was the great niece of Matthew Arnold, poet and critic, and the great granddaughter of Dr Thomas Arnold, the reforming headmaster of Rugby School. As her father-in-law-to-be wrote, 'She pleases herself by the recollection that her grandfather, Doctor Arnold, saw the *Lays of Rome* in Manuscript, and persuaded their author to publish them. Macaulay had doubts whether they would take a place in English literature.'[49] Caroline, Lady Trevelyan saw Janet as the clever one of her three daughters-in-law. Janet's father, Thomas Humphry Ward, was the art critic of *The Times* and her mother, Mrs Humphry Ward, was a popular novelist, anti-suffragette campaigner, and pioneer in the welfare of London children. Janet too worked tirelessly for that cause, raising the money to save the Bloomsbury playground now known as Coram's Field from developers. She was made a Companion of Honour in recognition of her fund-raising efforts in 1936. Fluent in Italian, Janet was a member of the British–Italian League, instrumental in the creation of the British Institute of Florence, and the author of *A Short History of the Italian People* as well as a biography of her mother and a memoir of her son Theo. She was, in short, no slouch.

Janet's upbringing meant she was more than equal to the task of marrying into the Trevelyans. Lord Rennell used to say that she knew more Greek than any woman he had ever known.[50]

Janet's aunt Julia married Leonard Huxley, and their children Julian Huxley, the scientist, and Aldous Huxley, the novelist, became G.M.'s cousins by marriage. A clever child, Janet was reading Carlyle at 16, impressing Julian Huxley, and preparing her for marriage to George, that Carlyle devotee. Bertrand Russell described Janet somewhat patronisingly as

> one of the most loveable people I have ever met. She has not much to say and I often find the talk flagging when I am with her, but she is filled full of generous loves and friendships, and honest and sincere in a very rare degree. She is ignorant of the world, as everyone is who has met with nothing but kindness and good fortune. This gives her the pathos of very young people, and makes one long to keep sorrows away from her, well as one may know that that is impossible.[51]

Janet was well suited to George. Both were high-minded, eschewed flashy, fashionable company, and had family traditions of intellectual rigour and achievement to live up to. A pretty child, with enchanting ringlets, Janet grew into a handsome woman who spent little time on her appearance, regarding such preoccupations as self-indulgent. Although fiendishly bright, Janet did not go either to boarding school or university. She was educated at home. Mrs Humphry Ward was instrumental in the setting up of Somerville, the women's college at Oxford, but, rather mysteriously, she did not want her own daughter to benefit from the education there. As a leading opponent of the movement for women's suffrage later on, the battleaxe novelist had some contradictory ideas about the status of women. John Sutherland, Mrs Humphry Ward's biographer, observes that Janet had 'a brain and a mind of her own. Mary Ward did her best to cultivate the one and to curb the other.'[52] Rather than let her go to college, Mary set her 17-year-old daughter the task of translating Adolf Julicher's commentary on the New Testament from German into English. That gigantic, unutterably tedious task took Janet four years. The 635-page translation was published in 1904. Sutherland suggests that Mary Ward was trying to break Janet, to 'give her a taste of the same self-flagellating discipline by which Mary had controlled her own "wildcat" nature as a schoolgirl'.[53]

There was little frivolity in Janet's teenage years. Mary Ward was extremely possessive of her daughters, choosing their clothes and controlling their social lives as best she could. Janet, like her elder sister Dorothy, was actively involved in her mother's good works. Janet's introduction to philanthropy was telling stories on Monday evenings to the underprivileged children of central London. More than a hundred youngsters aged between three and ten crammed into the Passmore Edwards settlement building in Tavistock Square, Bloomsbury, to listen. The subject matter was eclectic – once Janet put on a magic-lantern show of seventeenth-century history to 136 children sitting on 76 chairs. It's almost as though she was auditioning for the role of George's wife.

Dorothy never married, and devoted her life to serving her mother and the settlement. She was the unpaid assistant upon whom Mary Ward depended heavily. Janet had no intention of staying so close to her mother. Much as she adored her, she didn't care for the Stocks set of dim aristocrats and high Tories. Janet's disdain for her mother's innate conservatism must have made the liberalism of the Trevelyans most attractive. Once the epic German translation was complete, Janet was ready for marriage. The fact that her mother initially disapproved of George only increased Janet's determination.

Over the Christmas of 1902 Janet spent a few days at Wallington, going for lots of long walks,

> nearly always with George and liked him better than ever – he's so splendidly keen about everything, and has such a tremendous feeling for the trees and the earth. Also he's writing a solid History of the seventeenth century in England, and his learning [at 26] is something quite appalling. I found that Biblical criticism was absolutely the only subject on which I could stand up to him at all. (Oh no, I'm forgetting Birds – he doesn't know about birds).[54]

George wrote later that in marrying Janet 'I also acquired another family proof reader to which my subsequent writings owe so much...This was the most important and fortunate event of my life.'[55]

Mary Ward was impressed by George's pedigree, his education, his money and his prospects. His atheism was a serious stumbling block for the novelist best known for *Robert Elsmere* – she used the Church of England as the setting for much of her work. George wrote to the Wards in April 1903 to propose marriage, provoking much harrumphing from the indomitable Mary. The family was holidaying in Italy, without Janet. Dorothy's diary records the reaction of the formidable authoress. 'This has been a memorable day, for talks between M and F, M and F and me, and tonight me and F – now a month's suspense!'[56] In a month's time the couple would be interviewed in person before permission was finally granted. The wary pair was invited to Lake Como in May 1903. Mary had her earnest discussion with George, and there was, she told Dorothy, 'a touch of pain in it for me...He is so wholly non-Christian. He looks forward to a civil marriage.'[57] Did Janet realise, she pondered, 'how different his ways of thought are from those in which she has been brought up'? Nevertheless, Mary found George to be a 'dear fellow',[58] and she consented to the marriage. The formalities complete, during an early-morning walk on the flowery hillside behind the Villa Bonaventura, George proposed. 'Jan' happily accepted. George, lover of mountains that he was, told Charles, 'The crown of joys of which only silence can speak, is that she has a mountain foot. We have tried it above Como.'[59]

In March 1904, with their best mountain feet forward, the betrothed were married in the chapel of Manchester College, Oxford. There was much wrangling between the couple and Mary Ward over the nature of the wedding. Mary chose the location, wrote the service herself, and engaged her favourite clergyman, Dr Estlin Carpenter, to perform it. George and Janet had married in a registry office first, and tried to make the chapel experience as secular as possible. The obvious tension between their wishes and those of the bride's mother was evident to all who were present. As Caroline, Lady Trevelyan wrote to Bob, 'There was nothing in the least doctrinal, but it was very high toned and "ethical", all allusions to the Deity being qualified by the words "If Thou existest."'[60] Lytton Strachey was more malicious about the arrangements. 'Bride and bridegroom wanted office, Bride's mother wanted church; compromise arrived at – an Oxford Unitarian chapel with a service drawn up by Bride, Bgroom and B's mother...The happy pair are to lead the Simple Life, and will go to Oxford in a special train.'[61] Strachey quoted Henry James, who also attended the wedding, as saying, 'The ordinary service binds, and makes an impression – it's like a seal; this was nothing more than a wafer.' Strachey's parting shot, in a letter to Leonard Woolf, was to describe the bride and bridegroom as 'almost completely hideous. But I suppose one must let copulation thrive. The service was practically all balls in both senses.'[62]

The happy couple, doubtless relieved to have the ordeal over with, then took the train to Truro. There, according to the account of Bertrand Russell, George leapt off, saying 'he could not face the day without a little walk'.[63] He then walked the forty miles to the Lizard, leaving Janet on the train. Mary Moorman, George's daughter, and Humphrey Trevelyan say that this happened on the second day of the honeymoon not the first – either way, it's not very romantic, but it's certainly true to form. Later on in the honeymoon, after cycling through Umbria and Tuscany, George went off alone for a five-day walk in the snow-clad mountains above Lake Como. Janet was understanding: 'I know what infinite peace and stillness the snows must bring to him – stillness from which he can look out upon our life ahead.'[64] George had much to contemplate as he tramped across the snowy peaks – his next project was already forming in his mind. Among the couple's wedding presents were books from the historian Sir Bernard Pares, including Garibaldi's memoirs and Beluzzi's account of Garibaldi's retreat from Rome in 1849. As George wrote in his autobiography,

Merely because Pares had given me the books, I began one day to turn over the pages, and was suddenly enthralled by the story of the retreat from Rome to the Adriatic, over mountains which I had traversed in my solitary walks: the scene and spirit of that desperate venture, led by that unique man, flashed upon my minds' eye. Here was a subject made to my hand: if ever I could write 'literary history,' this was the golden chance.[65]

J.H. Plumb writes that the choice of Garibaldi as subject matter could not have been more judicious had it been made by a sophisticated journalist in search of a best-seller.[66] George wrote *Garibaldi's Defence of the Roman Republic* in 1906, and it was published in 1907. Plumb also noted that George's timing could not have been better.

These were the years of the greatest liberal victory in English politics for a generation. The intellectual world responded to the optimism of the politicians...The Garibaldi story fitted these moods. The struggles, defeats and ultimate success of Italian Liberalism in the nineteenth century had seemed to many Victorians a demonstration by Providence of the justice of their attitude to life, and of its capacity to save other nations from spiritual and political obscurantism.[67]

George conceived of his Garibaldi trilogy, and set to work, as Janet put it, with 'ardour and fury'.[68] Much of the writing was done at a cottage in the Lake District called Robin Ghyll, one of the most glorious spots in England. George initially rented Robin Ghyll from Dorothy Ward, his sister-in-law, and it remained in the family until the 1970s, when it was sold to the National Trust. I holidayed there as a child, enjoying one of the greatest mountain views in all the Lakes – from the front door of the cottage, you can see the Crinkle Crags, Bow Fell and the Langdale Pikes, or Mummy Pike, Daddy Pike and Baby Pike, as we called them. The garden looks out from the fellside across the Langdale Valley, and close to the house there is a ghyll which provides hours of playtime. George wrote to his sister-in-law Dorothy, 'I have lived in the mountains by sitting on this glorious terrace for the last ten days. I never got through so much work [*Garibaldi's Defence of the Roman Republic*] and at the same time kept so fit and I believe it is largely due to the place, which is not in a hole as most Lake Dwellings are.'[69]

Mary Moorman, who spent many happy times there with her brothers Theo and Humphry (my grandfather), remembers her father returning from his marathon walks.

I have a vision of him now at the end of one of those days, striding along the road through the middle of the valley, his white sweater making him visible nearly a mile away, and finally arriving on the little lawn with his hair standing straight up on his head, as the mountain winds and his scrambles on familiar crags had left it ... [70]

The catalyst for George's purchase of Robin Ghyll from Dorothy, the place where he felt happiest, was his saddest moment, the death of his son Theo in 1911. Of Janet and George's three children, Theodore, born in 1906, was the middle one. Theo was the child George had marked out for greatness, the one to carry the Trevelyan torch in the next generation, and he had been given the revered middle name of Macaulay. By the age of four Theo was showing great promise, able to recite Horatius. But he never lived to achieve all that his father longed for. On holiday in Dorset, Theo developed appendicitis and did not survive. Janet recorded, 'Death called to him with a mastering voice, and as the morning sun, on that 19th day of April, flooded with light the little high-placed room where he lay, Theodore slipped from us, all unknowing, and his little limbs lay still.'[71]

George and Janet were plunged into grief, enveloped with a sense of loss that went beyond the death of a child – George felt he had lost a great man in the making, and grieved accordingly. The family took Theo to Langdale Valley, scene of so much happiness, to be buried. George wrote, 'Now my bravest hopes lie buried here in the fell-side graveyard, beneath the bracken and the rocks, and this is the place of my heart.' George and Janet spent 'a honeymoon of grief and thought'[72] at Robin Ghyll, remembering their lost genius. Unfortunately, neither parent seems to have realised the impact this grieving might have on their remaining children, who were left with the profound impression that their lives were of less value than that of the dead Theo. George poured out his feelings to his parents on the day Theo died:

Dear Mama and Papa,

I cannot bear to write to you about this loss...I shall never be so happy again, as I have been these last five years which have passed the mortal lot for happiness. I hope it makes me better instead. I think he got more joy out of his Horatius than anyone ever did in five years out of any book so he knew the real delights of literature as well as of life. What a happy, and happy making little life.[73]

The entire family was plunged into the deepest depression by the loss of the young prodigy. Mary Ward was devastated by the death of her grandson. On holiday in Italy when she heard the news the distinguished novelist retired to a darkened room, where she took large doses of quinine to calm her nerves. Later, she spent hours designing his headstone. That summer, as she busied herself with the organisation of the London playgrounds for the poorest children, she was haunted by memories of Theo.

Sometimes, when I think of the masses of London children I have been going through I seem to imagine him beside me, his eager little hand in mine, looking at the dockers' children, ragged, half-starved, disfigured, with his grave sweet eyes, eyes so full already of humanity and pity. Is it so that his spirit lives with us – the beloved one – part for ever of all that is best in us, all that is nearest to God, in whom, I must believe, he lives.[74]

While Mary found comfort in God, Charles Philips Trevelyan, Theo's uncle, was brutal about the impact the child's death would have on those left on earth. Charles had been part of the family party in Dorset when Theo died. He wrote this painfully honest letter to his mother on the day of Theo's death:

The truth is that it had better have been any of the other children that are here. For them (George and Janet) it is more doubtful if he can be replaced at all than it would be for us. Of their children, even if Janet had minded losing the others as much, George would have felt it less. He has been building much on Theo's future and it is a very sore blow. He lived just long enough to be clever and have character...It is unfortunately only too obvious that poor little Humphry can never be what Theo was promising to be.[75]

Poor little Humphry indeed, as we shall see in the chapter about my grandfather. George was too wrapped up in his reverie of misery to pay much attention to his surviving children. He upset his daughter Mary by refusing to wear a red tie – now he would only wear black. George was, once more, consumed by a fit of the blue devils, more profound than ever before. From Robin Ghyll, he wrote this letter to his parents ten days after Theo's death.

The passionate, selfish, zest at life that every healthy youth has went from me this week. In fact I am suddenly middle aged … I wish, not rebelliously or passionately, but with a quiet preference, that I were there instead of

'There was to have been another generation – or so at least my fancy had it.' Theo Trevelyan at Wallington in 1910, the year before he died. Courtesy of Tom Trevelyan.

him…for the first thirty five years are the great ones, not the last thirty five, and he was fitted for the great adventure of those first thirty five years as few are fitted.[76]

Neither Janet nor George had God or the promise of the afterlife to comfort them – instead they turned to Theo's memory to sustain them during their mourning. As Janet wrote to her mother from Robin Ghyll, during the grieving honeymoon, 'I know that as we get further from the pain of these last days, the pure joy and beauty of his little life will shine out more and more, and will be like a light in our own hearts to illuminate the rest of our way.'[77]

Janet wrote a book about little Theo's short life, which was published by Longman, just as George and George Otto's works had been. It is a charming account of the life of an Edwardian child, full of tales of soldiers, and early rising in the nursery, dealt with by Nanny not Mummy, and with various examples of Theo's precociousness. But, as others have written,[78] it was perhaps a mistake to make her sorrow so public. The book finishes with a poem by Geoffrey Winthrop Young, George's dear climbing friend, which elaborates on the theme of lost greatness.

> You were made splendid for the great shore game,
> To delve and fashion in the sands of toil;
> Yours the deep thought, the fiery heart, that claim
> Life for a conquest, liberty for spoil;
> And yet you pause, listening open-eyed –
> Perhaps you hear the sea,
> Calling you, child and free,
> Child to remain – and wait no evening tide.[79]

The historian A.L. Rowse found George's grieving for Theo slightly creepy. As he put it, there was 'the extraordinary intensity of his and his wife's cult of their dead son Theo…Never spoken of, but always there in the background – yearly pilgrimages to his grave in the Lake District, uncontrolled grief and lamentations one must not go into, it was so strange.'[80]

Mary Moorman, in her biography of George, makes no mention of how Theo's death affected the rest of her childhood. Yet relatives recall her impatience with the annual trips to Theo's graveside, complete with hysterically weeping parents. Correspondence between mother and daughter in 1939, nearly thirty years after Theo's death, reveals the depth of Mary's feelings of abandonment and inadequacy. Mary tells Janet of her deep-down jealousy not only of Theo, but Humphry – 'brothers dead and living'.[81]

Janet writes back that she has told George of this, and

he thought it most understandable and most pathetic. Poor little creature,
so wounded and yet not knowing how! ... But I suppose that if I had known
more about psychology in those days I should have tried, for your sake, to
put Theo out of our lives much more, or at least only to take with me the
happy side of him. That I did try to do, and with some success I think, while
Daddy just couldn't get over it and was always looking over Humphry's
shoulder for the invisible big brother on the other side. Theo was just
everything that he had ever dreamt of in a son.[82]

Mary had married John Moorman, who was to become the Bishop of
Ripon, although the couple never had any children. She was a Wordsworth
scholar, distinguished in her field, but not a very easy personality. Her marriage
to John encountered sexual difficulties – all of which she suddenly and
unexpectedly revealed to her mother, during this correspondence about
Theo's death. Janet writes,

I really should have sent you to a good woman-doctor before your marriage,
I expect, just as I sent Humphry to a man-doc before he went to school.
Yet the fact that you were frightened at first doesn't excuse John for giving
up the effort to make love to you! He ought to do something big in
reparation – go to a man psychologist at least – and even if it didn't result
in a baby it would obviously make you far happier together. So I'm not
going to give up hope that you still have your share of real happiness in
store, my little Minnie, though you've made such a brave fight without it.[83]

The mystery is how Janet and George, such intelligent and gifted people,
could be so absorbed in their dead child without realising how hurtful it was
to Mary and Humphry. Perhaps the answer is that they belonged to a more
elitist age, one which rated exceptional promise above all else. Theo was to
have been the next Macaulay, and his loss was incalculable. Yet, even those who
valued ability as highly as Janet and George found the couple's behaviour
disturbing. Humphrey, the diplomat cousin, wrote, 'Why did the mother not
realise ... that she could not expect to retain the natural affection of a child
who was brought to ask her whether she thought only of the dead boy? A
degree of estrangement of the son from the father and the daughter from
the mother was the consequence. Time has now healed these wounds, for the
brother – in any case in the difficult position of a son overshadowed by a
famous father of dominating personality – founded his own family and made

his own career at Cambridge...while his sister, blessed with an exceptionally understanding and sensitive husband, had made her name with a study of Wordsworth.'[84] I am not so sure those wounds ever healed.

George was never quite the same after Theo's death – he was forever brooding on what might have been, and became even more depressed by external events than before. Prodigious success was now his, although he didn't care for it as much as he once would have. The Garibaldi trilogy was a triumph. *Garibaldi and the Making of Italy*, published in September 1911, sold 3000 copies in just a few days. He began a life of John Bright, the radical liberal who had entranced the young George Otto. But he could not write while the world was in turmoil – and the First World War was looming into view. He told his parents on Black Bank Holiday, 3 August 1914, 'What I feared has occurred...the system of Alliances and Ententes has, so far from preserving European peace as Grey [then Foreign Secretary] said it would, plunged us all into war, when otherwise Russia, Serbia and Austria would alone be fighting out their Slav question...'[85] Charles resigned from the Liberal Government, a move George supported. The brothers engaged in 'last hour neutrality work',[86] George rushing from Robin Ghyll to London to consult with, among others, E.D. Morel, Ramsay MacDonald and Noel and Charles Buxton on how to prevent the war. Their efforts were sadly futile – George was in London on Tuesday 4 August 1914, the night the war started. It will be the 'shipwreck of civilisation', he wrote to his brother Bob. In another letter he recorded the mood in the capital. 'Attempts to sing the "Marseillaise" by crowds not familiar with the French language made me wonder what Burke, Fox and Pitt would think of a situation to them so paradoxical.'[87]

George returned to Langdale, where, as Julian Huxley recalled, he 'buried his head on his hands on the breakfast table, and looked up weeping. "It will be war, and millions of human beings are going to be killed in this senseless business."'[88] Senseless he thought it was, but George was not a pacifist, unlike his dear brother Charles. The First World War marked a parting of the ways for the two brothers who had been so close. As David Cannadine explains,

> The war changed both of them but in different ways. They were left saddened and worried about the fact that the hopeful and optimistic civilisation to which they felt they belonged had been brought to an end in the mud and gore of Passchendale. Both of them were faced with a new political and social landscape to which their earlier years and liberal views didn't offer much guide.[89]

Charles turned sharply to the left once the war began, while George decided he would reluctantly support it. In a matter of two weeks, the siblings who had been so unified in their purpose became estranged. George explained his position in a letter to Charles written three days after Britain declared war on Germany.

> I wish to see no-one crushed, neither France, Belgium nor Germany, but I should like to see the South Slavs liberated if they want to be, and the people of Alsace-Lorraine free to choose for themselves. I would not have made war for any of these objects, but since war is here that is how I view it. On the whole I think the best chance of stopping militarism in Europe is for the German military party to be defeated in her aggression – but not Germany destroyed. So now that war has come, which I wish we had avoided, I support the war not merely from the point of view of our own survival but because I think German victory will probably be the worst thing for Europe, at any rate her victory in the West.[90]

Aware that Charles disagreed profoundly with this view, George added a PS: 'Whatever happens I am sure you have been right, and I am proud to have been your friend through it. We are certainly bound together by bonds of the most intimate kind possible, and it sweetens life to me so far as it can now be sweet.'

George was full of brotherly advice for Charles on how he should conduct himself now he'd resigned from the Liberal Government in protest against the war. George's overriding concern was that his brother, and his like-minded colleagues, should not become stridently anti-war and place themselves outside the mainstream of public and political opinion, as

> …this is life and death. You will be all the more effective for peace when the time comes if you show patriotism now and don't make yourselves widely unpopular. Until the issue of the war is essentially decided there is and must be the old anti-Napoleonic of 'In Britain is one breath'. I feel that in my bones. For you this course is particularly easy, as you have of all people made your position clear, and sacrificed for it…anything you can now do or say to show you are backing the war, as we are in it, will make you the more effective for peace when the time comes.[91]

There was no chance of Charles coming out in support of a war he regarded as the gravest mistake. Rather, he wanted George to join his group of intellectuals who were publicly opposing the conduct of the war. George shrank away from such a role.

I would rather not join your council. I will give you as much private advice as I am capable of but I am not a politician or a public man and I will not be drawn into it in any responsible manner. Consult me ad lib, needless to say…It has done you great credit and you will occupy a high moral position both with those who agree with you and those who disagree with you, provided you don't butt your head against a stone wall by continuing to argue about the past while we are all watching the North Sea mist and the French frontier. I cannot speak more strongly.[92]

Charles persisted in trying to get George to sign up to his Democratic Policy Council, a forerunner of the Union for Democratic Control. Essentially these groupings of anti-war intellectuals wanted some form of popular control over diplomacy, to prevent future wars. George was not interested, as he repeatedly made clear to his brother.

It grieves me deeply, and indeed makes me actually quite ill, not to be able to help and sympathise in anything that you are doing at this juncture. But frankly I am not going in for any pacific or anti war movements till the war is over to such a degree that I think peace ought to be made. I am very sorry if there has been any misunderstanding about it or if I seem to be failing you and the others we worked with in those nightmare days before war broke out. But when I parted with you at Euston I understood that beyond your resignation and letter (both splendid) you were going to do nothing except try and get administrative work…I certainly did not intend to do anything except try and find some useful function during the war for which I am still looking out.[93]

By 15 August 1914, after a frenetic exchange of letters, George was finding his ideological divorce from Charles both depressing and distressing. As young men across Europe lost their lives, George, feeling oddly remote in the calm of the Lake District, tried to draw a line under the disagreement.

My dearest Charles,

I have written you three letters of argument and now I have done with it. The difference between your policy and my advice may really be very little. And of course in so far as we differ I may be wrong. I never felt more uncertain of things in my life. But my personal instinct says to you 'wait'…At any rate do not fear any real division of sympathy – even political – between us. I am simply doing and saying nothing until I know where we all are. And believe me my affection for you, deep as it was before, has been greatly deepened by the events of the last fortnight. And even politically it is you rather than the official Liberal party I shall be in with in the future – if I am in with anyone. I feel older, and if we survive the war, I shall probably set to writing history and not dabble in politics. But believe me I am far nearer to you in spirit and love than before.[94]

The following day, despite promising to wrap up the correspondence, George felt moved to write again.

Dear Charles,

I am sorry I wrote you such hysterical letters. Please tear them up. The fact is, as I have often told you, I am most unsuited for politics or action because I come to my conclusions (if I ever come to them!) by first feeling one thing strongly, then another and then settling to my final opinion. At present I feel nearer to a final opinion – of not having one at all except for general disgust and misery. I stand, or wobble, halfway between you and those ex-peace Liberals now trying to feel hearty about the war.

Whatever else I said in my letters I never suggested anything half as ridiculous as that you should go and fight! All I said, or meant, was that if I could find nothing else to do I might join the home front or the territorials. I am a fish out of water, for in fact I have nothing in the world that I am any good at except writing history, and until civilisation is partially resumed it is an art useless to anybody.

I have no doubt you will play a very fine and useful part, and of course you must play it in your own way. You are the only person in whose public doings I feel personal interest now. All the rest is much fear and a little hope for the community as a whole.[95]

By March of the following year, with war now raging, George and Charles were still intellectually estranged. George wrote,

I am afraid we are a bad family at discussing things on which we disagree. When you put your views to me I can never debate them for fear of quarrelling, from a knowledge of my own temper. And then I feel I may have let you think I agree more than I do, and write letters in which perhaps I overstate our differences, or at least show temper – which is possibly less harmful on paper than in the flesh. Things will be alright between us on public matters after the war, provided we avoid heated discussions now, for there is no question of anything except difference of opinion. And on all private matters, and on matters connected with

the war provided we keep off argument, we can meanwhile talk as freely as
ever. Propose yourself to breakfast some day next week if you will.

This I feel: that we both want the same sort of world. It is only a question
of the means how to get back to (or on to) that sort of world out of the
present smash, on which we differ. I daresay it takes all sorts to fight a war
– and make a peace.[96]

Feeling helpless in the face of the carnage, alienated from his brother, and
unable to enlist because of his poor eyesight, George was at a loose end. He
lectured in America, but felt his profession was a useless irrelevance because
it provided no answers. He longed for some useful work to distract him from
brooding. Eventually he accepted with relief an invitation masterminded by
his old friends Geoffrey Winthrop Young and Philip Noel-Baker to command
the first British Red Cross ambulance unit in Italy. The unit served the 6th
Army Corps of the Italian Second Army, which was engaged in a mountain
war with the Austrians on Mount Sabotino near Gorizia. George was able to
help the Italy he loved, the Italy he had celebrated in his Garibaldi books,
the Italy his father had romanticised in his encounter with Garibaldi. Now,
under fire, George had found purpose and direction, and was able to mask
his feelings of desolation following Theo's death. In May 1917 he wrote to
his parents,

> We are in the third day and night of the biggest battle we have had yet, and
> likely to be the most prolonged. It is a great pleasure to be in the fullness
> of activity and adventure day after day and night after night. Both in
> Gorizia and also in the high hills such scenes of beauty and romance as
> this big war in the mountains are wonderful indeed. It is a great life for
> me, rushing about from front to front and now and then to the base
> along this thirty miles of mountain battle. No one can have a pleasanter
> part in it.

The job of the Red Cross ambulance unit was to ferry the wounded back
from the perilous front line of Mount Sabotino to the peace and tranquillity
of Villa Trento, the unit's own hospital ten miles from Gorizia. The Italians
and the Austrians were fighting on the great limestone mountain itself – the
Austrians defending the summit, the Italians attacking from below. Rescuing
the wounded in these circumstances was extremely dangerous. Soldiers had
to be carried down the mountainside on stretchers to the nearest point where
an ambulance could collect them – the roads were poor, and it was safest to
travel in pitch darkness, without lights, often under heavy fire. The Red

Cross sign had to be painted out, as it helped the Austrian gunners train their weapons on the ambulances. George described one particularly alarming journey the unit had to undertake, to a village called Plava:

> We cannot go by day or we should be shot for a certainty. Imagine a place with mountains as steep as the fell behind Robin Ghyll, and our car creeping along without lights down that mountain by a winding road at night, with search lights and star shells lighting bits of the ground up at intervals, and then getting to the bottom of the gorge by the rushing river Isonzo, and taking up our wounded within half a mile of the Austrians under cover of night, and creeping up the road again.[97]

Trevy, as George was known to his men, was a fine leader, with a sixth sense for danger. The number of men and ambulances the unit lost was minimal, given the perils of the task. His steadfastness under fire was remarkable. Geoffrey Young, George's lifelong friend who was with him in this adventure too, commanding an ambulance outstation on the mountain spur of Quisca, told George's parents, 'George's nerve and extraordinary endurance stand us in good stead, and he had his usual fortune which is an essential leader quality. He has really mastered the difficult task of leading such a Unit... "Bravissimo" they call him up here.'[98]

The unit's magazine, called *Trento* after the hospital, included a rhyme which fondly celebrates the commander.

> G.M.T. G.M.T.
> He roared from Tolmezzo right down to the sea
> Three blue stripes on his sleeve
> And one on his chest,
> If only you'll believe
> Oh, he never took rest;
> And it's whispered indeed 'twixt the Alps and the Ocean,
> He discovered the means of perpetual motion.[99]

The peripatetic unit commander received official recognition for the sterling work of his men in December 1915, when a surprise visit was paid to Villa Trento by the King of Italy. He awarded George the Silver Medal 'For Valour'. Back in England, George's father wrote to Mary describing this event as 'what is perhaps the most perfectly satisfactory moment of my life... It is a very great enhancement of the pleasure to think what an opportunity for that kind King, and that charming and ideal people, to express their sense of what dear George has otherwise done for Italy.'

George's dog-eared photo albums faithfully record the occasion of the visit of the King, Victor Emmanuel. 'Just like his father,' reads George's note in the margin, approvingly I imagine. The experience of being in the thick of war both appalled and inspired him – he was after all a historian temping as a Red Cross commander. He wrote, 'This is a tremendous drama and painful as it is, the interest of the events and the romance of the setting, seeing it first-hand from doubtful day to day, nullifies if not kills the pain.'

And the war would, he knew, aid his writing if only he could live through it.

> We have been so accustomed for generations to look at the victims of great
> historical catastrophes through a historic telescope from our study chairs
> that to find oneself at the other end of the telescope is disconcerting. But
> I suppose someone has to be here, so why not us? If ever I get back to the
> other end of the telescope, I shall look through it, as Carlyle says, 'with
> other eyes.'

In the quiet periods at Villa Trento, reflecting on the upheaval in Europe, George was mulling over his next work. Green's *Short History of the English People* was getting out of date, he wrote to his father. Here was his chance to write a book that might, as he had hoped in his youth, serve 'the people'.

> In this age of democracy and patriotism, I feel strongly drawn to write the
> history of England as I feel it, for the people... The war has cleared my
> mind of some party prejudices or points of view and I feel as if I have a
> conception of the development of English history, liberal but purely English
> and embracing the other elements. It might be a success as a literary work
> (otherwise I would not touch it). The doubt in my mind is whether it could
> have elbow room to be a literary success without being so long as to prevent
> the wide popularity which would alone justify the choice of it.[100]

From the horrors of the First World War, G.M. Trevelyan's best-selling *History of England* was forged. It was a deliberate attempt to write a book that celebrated what he believed to be the shared values of the English people. Such a project would be fraught with difficulties in our less certain age, but in the aftermath of World War I it seemed more straightforward. As David Cannadine said,

> Trevelyan had a very strong sense of national identity and he wrote his
> books in part because he had that sense of identity but he also wrote his

books to promote that sense of national identity...He believed history had a social and political purpose and on the whole it was to reinforce a sense of identity and belonging rather than to subvert it.[101]

The book was not published until 1926, ten years after he first dreamed of it. While the work gestated, daily life in the mountains continued. The Italian objective in the summer of 1917 was to capture Monte San Gabriele, 'a smoking altar of sacrifice', as George called it, the southernmost peak overlooking Gorizia. Collecting the wounded from here meant travelling across a lethal pass called the Sella di Sol. George's dear companion Geoffrey Young lost his leg from gangrene after being shelled on the Sella. 'Since Theo died I have had no blow like it,' wrote George to Geoffrey's brother Hilton. Geoffrey was cheerful enough, and had a specially designed artificial leg made, which provided him with another forty years of climbing in the Alps. But George was still in shock, as he wrote to his sister-in-law Dorothy.

This must be the last war. And I believe it will be just because of its length and unutterable horror. This month I have seen its very worst shapes and sights absolutely at first hand and I don't know if the worst criticism of war is not one's appalling indifference to them until one's best friend is shot down and he, the dear one, lies before one; one of these statistically calculated wrecks. Then one ceases to be indifferent and gets a glimmering of what the statistics mean.[102]

It was to be a further year before the Austrian Army and Empire finally dissolved. On 2 November 1918, George, in Treviso, became aware of singing and cheering echoing for miles around. He asked a soldier what it was all about – the Austrians have asked for an armistice, he was told. His children Mary and Humphry received this note, written at dawn on 4 November, somewhere between the two great rivers of the Piave and the Tagliamento. 'Now it's fine and anything but misery. I'm so happy. So's everyone. The soldiers sing and carry flowers in their rifle muzzles. The liberated inhabitants cheer us as English. They've had enough of Austrians and Germans! Daddy.'

George's wartime adventures had changed him. The numbing grief of Theo's death had faded, and he had a sense of the history he wanted to write now. He and Janet lived in Berkhamsted, not the academic ghetto of Cambridge, and there he was most productive. In the inter-war years he produced a biography of Lord Grey of the Reform Bill, his long-planned *History of England,* a three-volume study of England under Queen Anne, a memoir of his father George Otto, a biography of Edward Grey and his account of the English Revolution. He became involved in the work of the National Trust, helping to secure the Ashridge estate. He found the Trust a pleasing organisation, which combined his own values of a love of the countryside with a desire to preserve it for future generations. Then, in 1927, Stanley Baldwin, the Conservative Prime Minister, appointed George to the post of Regius Professor of Modern History at Cambridge. Having avoided the cloistered world of the professional academic, George was now to live at the centre of it. Ironically enough, he was succeeding Professor Bury, the man who had so enraged the young George by arguing for scientific history. Professional success was accompanied by personal wealth following the death of his parents in 1928 – George inherited a large chunk of the old Philips fortune from his mother, and control of Macaulay's papers from his father. A fond relative, Florence Cacciola Trevelyan, who lived in Sicily and appreciated George's Italian books, left him a country house and estate of his very own in Northumberland, Hallington Hall. This was only eight miles from the family seat of Wallington, inherited by Charles. The brothers, divided by the war, were neighbours now, and began to regain some of their former intimacy.

George used his considerable new-found wealth to buy up beautiful and historic places in England's threatened landscape. His first big acquisition for the National Trust was Housestead's Farm, next to the Roman camp of Borcovicum along Hadrian's Wall in Northumberland. A more pleasing purchase for a historian it is hard to picture. In the Lake District, to which he remained fiercely devoted, he bought significant properties at the head of the Langdale Valley – the farms of Stool End, Wall End and High Dungeon Ghyll. Determined to preserve the view of Langdale from developers, he later bought the farms of Mill Beck and Harry Place, next to Robin Ghyll. Mary Moorman completed her father's work in 1956 when, with the help of Trinity College, she purchased the last remaining farm in Upper Langdale, Side House. As chairman of the Estates Committee of the National Trust, George joined in the negotiations with the Forestry Commission to persuade them not to plant trees in the Central Lake District. His interest in preserving the countryside was an intelligent and principled one, not mere knee-jerk 'nimbyism'. He wanted to bring down the barriers between the town and the country, and as president of the Youth Hostel Association in the 1930s he loved to travel around opening new hostels, encouraging townies to explore the great outdoors.

Just as H.G. Wells had sarcastically predicted, George became in middle age a walking definition of a pillar of the establishment. The youthful liberal had matured into a Baldwinite Conservative. The son of George Otto, author of 'What Does She Do With It?', the polemic about Queen Victoria's wealth, actually played a part in the 1935 Silver Jubilee of King George V and Queen Mary's reign. Mary Moorman remembers walking along the Mall, decked out with flags, listening to King George's speech to both houses of parliament relayed by loudspeakers from Westminster Hall. She was startled to hear the Monarch quote two lines of verse:

> While thought to wisdom wins the gay,
> While strength upholds the free.[103]

Those are lines from one of Edward Bowen's Harrow songs, 'When Raleigh Rose', familiar to Mary because George, the old Harrovian, often sang it at home, but not widely known. George told Mary a few days later that he had written the King's speech, which reflected upon the historic relationship of Crown and parliament. The rhythm of the words, and the sentiments expressed, are recognisably George's, yet they could equally have been written by his great uncle Lord Macaulay.

> Beneath these rafters of medieval oak, the silent witnesses of historic tragedies and pageants, we celebrate the present under the spell of the past…The complex forms and balanced spirit of our constitution were not the discovery of a single era, still less of a single party or of a single person. They are the slow accretion of centuries, the outcome of patience, tradition and experience, constantly finding channels, old and new, for the impulse towards justice and social improvement inherent in our people down the ages.[104]

Only seven months after the King delivered this speech, he died, and the new Monarch, Edward VIII, created a constitutional crisis due to his desire to marry a divorcee, the American Wallis Simpson. Edward's brother George VI became King. Immediately after Edward abdicated, George wrote to Mary, 'Getting G. instead of the nervous and unstable E. is a great gain in more ways than the marital. My cabinet minister friends, two of them, tell me they had doubted whether he would take on the Kingship at all, he disliked it so. If he had not disliked the office he would not have given it up for Mrs S.'[105]

One of the 'cabinet minister friends' was none other than the Prime Minister, Stanley Baldwin – so George's source for his insight into the government's view of the abdication was impeccable. King George VI and Queen Elizabeth were crowned in Westminster Abbey in 1937, and George, the ardent monarchist, received an invitation. He had by now been awarded the Order of Merit for his services to literature and history – just as his father had before him, a parallel that gave the son tremendous satisfaction. Sitting next to his fellow OM and friend the composer Ralph Vaughan Williams, high above Poet's Corner, George delighted in the occasion.

'I have two doctors, my left foot and my right foot.' Charles and George Trevelyan walking along the Cornish coast, 1905. Courtesy of the Trustees of the Trevelyan family papers.

The scale of beauty was so immense and it was all history. The monuments had all disappeared under the scaffolding and tapestry. It was Henry III's church again for the nonce. No ceremony on earth could equal it for splendour, history, religion and Englishry, all blent into a unique thing...The King in golden robes and a large crown holding the two sceptres was like a mediaeval king. The Queen was the most moving thing in it all, and Queen Mary next – and the King the finest.[106]

While the pomp and the ceremony of the coronation captivated George, outside the confines of Westminster Abbey the world alarmed and depressed him. The slide towards World War II had begun. He felt he did not understand the age in which he lived, and what he did understand he did not like. In a letter to Bob in October 1939, he summed up his state of mind:

The last thing Edward Grey [the Foreign Secretary at the outbreak of World War I] said to me in the few weeks between the Nazi revolution and his death was, 'I see no hope for the world'. There is less now. One half of me suffers horribly, the other half is detached, because the 'world' that is threatened is not my world, which died years ago. I am a mere survivor. Life has been a great gift for which I am grateful, tho' I would gladly give it back now.[107]

As a man of standing and influence, George was pressed into service by the government as part of the megaphone diplomacy aimed at averting war. As his daughter-in-law Molly recorded in a letter to her parents in America, George wasn't entirely happy about all aspects of this, but agreed to do his duty.

Da T. signed a manifesto with other people of note last week to the European nations, or rather to men of good will all over, and to Germany especially, urging them to be friends etc etc. But he wasn't behind it, and while not against it, had to sign it because of orders from above, or at least because of a letter accompanying a request to sign it which was so worded that he felt he must sign it. Mummy T [Janet] felt that it was showing a great fear to broadcast and publish this message, and I think I agree – for there was no reason at the moment to make such an appeal – and besides we know that gentleman's agreements don't appeal to Germany – it only makes them respect us less. But even so, perhaps it did stop something from coming to a head. We certainly can't tell – poor ignorant mortals aren't allowed to know what really goes on.[108]

George also agreed to be part of the public-relations efforts directed at Italy. He found the Italians' role as allies of Nazi Germany most troubling. The German annexation of Austria, and Sudetenland in Czechoslovakia, he regarded as alarming but not without a historical cause. He felt the World War I victors had created an unstable state in Czechoslovakia, and the Czechs had treated their German minority badly. Most upsetting and quite incomprehensible to him was the sight of the Italy he had battled to save a quarter of a century earlier now embracing fascism. In May 1940, at the request of Lord Halifax, the Foreign Secretary, George broadcast to the people of Italy on the radio, in Italian. It was a final appeal for the Italians to choose peace not war. In the broadcast, George recalled his days travelling through Italy, collecting material for the *Life of Garibaldi,* 'following on foot the marches of your national hero, who so greatly loved England and whom England so greatly loved'. He remembered his years on the Italian front in World War One, 'carrying your wounded in ambulances of the Croce Rossa Britannica'. In that war, he reminded the Italians, Italy had fought with England and France to prevent a German domination of Europe. Italy and England, George implored his audience, 'are joint inheritors of a more civilised and noble culture, deriving largely from old Rome and mediaeval Italy, and a more subtle and broad psychology than these Germans who understand nothing but the material might of Germany and her right to crush and trample on everyone else'.[109]

His broadcast was in vain, and George could do nothing more than sit and watch, with a feeling of growing helplessness. He blamed Germany for the war, regarding that country as the Devil, but he always maintained that 'we and France and America in different ways have had our share in raising the Devil from 1919 onwards'.[110] By that he meant the unfairness of Versailles, the failure to rearm, and the sanctions against Germany. As ever, his refuge was literature and history, for 'the past at least cannot be destroyed and it is as real as the present and the future'. He found the world about him baffling, for 'the present nightmare seems to have so little to do with the world in which I was brought up, though actually it is its natural child'. At night his dreams were of evil, and by day 'I maintain a sober interest in all things and a decently cheerful demeanour as we are all most strongly bound to do'.

His outlet in that terrible summer of 1940, as the German advance continued into Holland and the Battle of Britain raged in the skies above, was as ever to busy himself writing letters to the newspapers. This time his subject was the historical importance of the Dutch military record in resisting tyranny.

He wrote to the *Sunday Times,* just as Holland was overwhelmed by Germany. 'This war is full of bitterness. The thought of Norwegian mountains in the power of the dog is scarcely more bitter than the thought of the lovely old brick streets of Holland, full of art, civilization and history, crumbling under bombs. But if freedom died in Europe, what would they any longer be worth?'[111] In July 1940, he wrote an article for the *Sunday Times* placing Britain's trials in historical perspective – his tone was Churchillian. 'Our greatest asset is our national character; it is now to be put to its extreme test, and I believe that it will ring true...That in 1940 the British Empire stood "alone" in the breach, may yet be looked upon in happier days as the proudest service we ever did the world in all our long, historic, testimony for freedom.'[112]

Journalism apart, George was now feeling feeble and useless, as he barely had anyone to teach. The young men of Cambridge were enlisting in their droves, and the colleges were quiet and depressing places. Once more in wartime, the offer of a job was to provide George with the sense of purpose he sought. This time salvation appeared in the unlikely, and initially unwelcome, form of an offer from Winston Churchill, now Prime Minister, and a historical rival of George's in the 1930s. George's *England Under Queen Anne* had come out at almost the same time as Churchill's biography of Marlborough. Because of this, the Blenheim archives were closed to George. The two old Harrovians had disagreed over rearmament in the face of the German threat too – George later conceded that 'we have all been great fools', and that Churchill had been right all along. The old slights laid to one side, Churchill now offered George the Mastership of Trinity College, Cambridge. There are various versions of what happened. It seems the dons of Trinity were influential in persuading a reluctant George to do the right thing. George wrote this letter to his brother Bob in September 1940:

> I want to tell you and Bessie before you see it in the papers, that I am to be Master of Trinity...The Fellows are very anxious I should accept, the more so as they do not know whom Winston would appoint if I refused, and there are some people not without claims whom they don't want. Everyone concerned has been so kind about it that I can't leave them in the lurch. Janet will be the loser, but she is clear that I cannot refuse, and she is being very good about it. I did not want to be Master, and if peace had continued I doubt if anything would have made me accept...That the crash of civilisation should have landed me in the beautiful old Lodge with its peaceful old-world traditions of Montagu Butler and Whewell and Bentley, is a tragic-comic irony.[113]

Hesitant as he was, George felt it would be cowardly and lazy to decline the Mastership of Trinity. He put a good face on it, and wrote a letter of acceptance to Churchill:

> I am touched by your kindness and fortified by your good opinion. In your great way, and my small way, we have been called to unexpected destinies, since the time when, as your junior at Harrow, I admired from a great distance the driving force of your great character, which is now our nation's great support.[114]

And so George and Janet moved into the stately surroundings of the Trinity Master's Lodge. 'Perhaps,' he speculated, 'I shall be "buried in the ruins of my palace" like the Bishop of Bath and Wells in the great storm of 1703.'[115] Trinity escaped the German bombs – and George finished his last major work there, *English Social History*. As he told Mary and Humphry, he wanted to write a history of England 'without any battles in it'.[116] He wanted to imagine the lives of our ancestors in a way that did not depend on 'the well known names of Kings, Parliaments and wars', but instead moved 'like an underground river, obeying its own laws or those of economic change, rather than following the direction of political happenings that move on the surface of life'.[117] He told the story like a play, starting with the age of Chaucer, ending with the reign of Victoria and the railway age. The book couldn't be published in England until 1942, because of wartime paper shortages, but when it finally appeared it was hugely popular. After seven years it sold nearly four hundred thousand copies. J.H. Plumb says that just as with the Garibaldi trilogy, George was exceptionally fortunate in the moment of his publication.

> The war, which we were bringing to a successful end, had jeopardized the traditional pattern of English life, and in some ways destroyed it forever. This created among all classes a deep nostalgia for the way of life which we were losing. Then, again, the war had made conscious to millions that our national attitude to life was historically based, the result of centuries of slow growth, and that it was for the old, tried ways of life for which we were fighting. Winston Churchill, in his great war speeches made us all conscious of our past, as never before. And in this war, too, there were far more highly educated men and women in all ranks of all the services. The twenties and thirties of this century had witnessed a great extension of secondary school education, producing a vast public capable of reading and enjoying a book of profound historical imagination, once the dilemma of their time stirred them to do so.[118]

Criticised by modern social historians for being hopelessly old-fashioned and quaint, the book is George's ultimate homage to the poetic quality of the past. He imagines the contributions to our civilisation made by aristocrats, squires and yeomen, by merchants and craftsmen, by owners of wealth, great and small – in fact, as Plumb points out, by those classes with which George was instinctively familiar and from which he derived his own ancestry. Once again, his work has an elegiac feel.

Each one, gentle and simple, in his commonest goings and comings, was ruled by a complicated and ever-shifting fabric of custom and law, society and politics, events at home and abroad, some of them little known by him and less understood. Our effort is not only to get what glimpses we can of his intimate personality, but to reconstruct the whole fabric of each passing age, and see how it affected him; to get to know more in some respects than the dweller in the past himself knew about the conditions that enveloped and controlled his life.

There is nothing that more divides civilized from semi-savage man than to be conscious of our forefathers as they really were, and bit by bit to reconstruct the mosaic of the long forgotten past. To weigh the stars, or to make the ships sail in the air or below the sea, is not a more astonishing and ennobling performance on the part of the human race in these latter days, than to know the course of events that had been long forgotten, and the true nature of men and women who were here before us.[119]

I owe a debt of gratitude to *English Social History*. From Athens to Delhi, Istanbul to Tokyo, and from Sydney to Beijing, complete strangers have asked if I am related to the man who wrote this book, and fascinating conversations result as they tell me how much they love it, what it taught them about England, and how captivated they are by George's storytelling. Patrician it may be, but the sheer quality of the writing ensures that to this day *English Social History* retains a broad appeal. George's idol Carlyle called the historical researcher 'Dryasdust'. As George pointed out, 'Dryasdust is at bottom a poet.'[120] This book is Dryasdust's swansong.

Trinity provided George with the backdrop for his last best-seller, and the college itself played a part in the history of the war. Trinity was the setting for a crucial part of the preparations for the D-Day landings in 1944. A conference of British officers was held there in the closing days of March 1944, with the Great Court and the front rooms of the Master's Lodge playing the part of the Normandy beaches as the men were coached for their respective roles. General Buckhill, their leader, wrote to George from France on 10 June 1944, saying that he soon hoped to explain to him 'how the plans laid in Trinity helped to mould the course of history'.[121] My father George Macaulay and my uncle Humphry Bennett, George's grandsons, were born in Trinity College on 1 April 1944, just as the D-Day planning reached its climax. My grandmother Molly, an American, was recovering from the birth of the twins when she was told she had some special visitors. As she rushed to make herself presentable, Bernard Montgomery and Dwight Eisenhower were ushered in by a beaming Janet, and the two military strategists who were masterminding D-Day offered their congratulations. My grandmother was poleaxed. Eisenhower was especially delighted to meet a fellow American, but she felt herself unable to rise to the occasion. As the twins wailed, Molly realised that somewhere in Trinity momentous events were being plotted by these warlords.[122]

After the war, George felt altogether happier about the state of the world. His famous laugh returned. As Leonard Woolf wrote, 'When George laughed in the Great Court of Trinity – it sounds like the raucous laughter of a great macaw – I think they could hear it far off in John's on the one side and Clare on the other.'[123] But George could be a bit short on laughs. The craggy figure of the intellectually intimidating Master of Trinity entered into Cambridge legend. The late John Prestwich, an Oxford historian who knew the family, told the tale of Nobby Clark, a modernist historian appointed to Trinity who was very excited about being in the presence of the great man. He sent a letter to George, enclosing a copy of his book. There was no acknowledgement. Arriving at Trinity, there was radio silence for three weeks. Finally Clark plucked up courage and went and sat next to the Master at high table. The soup was served, then the main course, and not a word did George utter. Just before dessert, Clark said rather apologetically, 'Oh Master, I don't know if you ever read my dreary little book which I sent you.' There was no reply. Just as the cheese was coming round, George said, 'Ah Clark, yes, you're right, it was a dreary little book.'[124] Such put-downs were not uncommon. My grandmother Molly, who married George's son Humphry, found her father-in-law a very uncomfortable man. 'He was abrupt,' she told me, 'and people were quite in fear of him. He didn't ever say don't be a fool, but I think he'd often say Bah, rubbish.' Molly was from a wealthy American family, who had inherited their fortune from sales of the Winchester repeating rifle. George would introduce Molly and Humphry to his friends, saying, 'We've gone into business.' That made my grandmother feel awful, and she always wished she'd come back to him and said she was descended from Benjamin Silliman, the first chemistry professor at Yale. Tom Trevelyan remembers his grandfather as 'unemotional, cool, distant, enthusiastic about the classics and history and toy soldiers'. Over lunch at Hallington, George would tell his grandchildren that bread of less than one and a half inches thick was plebeian. His strict code of conduct extended from the thickness of bread to personal morality. He harrumphed loudly about the wrongs of infidelity – a characteristic that was sent up by H.G. Wells in *The New Machiavelli*, in which an MP who has had an affair (much as George's brother Charles did) is ignored by the historian Edward Crampton:

> I still grow warm with amazed indignation when I recall that Edward Crampton, meeting me full on the steps of the Climax Club, cut me dead. 'By God!' I cried, and came near catching him by the throat and wringing out of him what, of all good deeds and bad, could hearten him, a younger man than I and empty beyond comparison, to dare to play the judge to me.[125]

Sanctimonious, upright, lordly – George displayed all these traits. Molly's American mother Mrs Winchester Bennett found her famous relation most intimidating. On a visit to England in the late fifties, Mrs Bennett stayed with George at Hallington, an experience she had been bracing herself for.

> I spent two nights with him and enjoyed his very lovely gardens, and our morning walks around the Dene, and also visiting with him. I had dreaded it a little, as he has no small talk, and conversation is not easy at the best of times, and since Mrs Trevelyan has gone, I thought things might be difficult. We got along however, most of the time, very well in a true companionship of absolute silence. He did seem very glad to see me, and as Humphry was there during most of my visit, that helped at meal times.[126]

Making small talk to relatives was not necessarily George's strong point, but if dining with a like mind he could be expansive. Morgan Philips Price, the Labour MP and cousin of the Trevelyans, lunched with George often at Hallington.

> George was very nice to me, and we had a long talk about history and politics. He has a wonderful brain for the past but admits that he is mystified about the present and future. I wish he would not gloat so much over the past because if he did not I am sure he would be more helpful in present-day problems and perhaps get a better glimpse of the

future from his great knowledge of the past. That, to my mind, is the one weakness of his otherwise marvellous intellect.[127]

My father remembers with pleasure going to tea at the Master's Lodge on Sunday afternoons, where great quantities of Trin Coll Cam Kit Cake were consumed – wedges of Trinity College fruit cake which emerged from the Trinity college kitchens, washed down with gallons of tea. George and Janet delighted in their five grandchildren, and taught them the game of humped-back zebra, an early form of Scrabble. My father recalls his grandfather as 'kindness itself', presiding over 'jokey teas which seemed to go on for ever'. Harriet, another of his grandchildren, also has memories of an encouraging, friendly figure. She found encounters with George gave 'a wonderful introduction to the historical timeframe. He would talk enthusiastically about the first chimney in Northumberland, and tell us about Garibaldi's march through Italy as if he had been there.' The late Lord Blake, the Conservative Party historian, saw the good side of George as well as the gruff. As a guest at Trinity one night, Blake was shown around George's library. 'He had Macaulay's copy of Gibbon's *Decline and Fall of the Roman Empire* with Macaulay's notes in it, which must be a real treasure indeed.'[128]

In his closing days at Trinity, George decided – one can only imagine under protest – to write his autobiography. This he regarded as a 'delicate operation'. A more unrevealing work it would be hard to imagine. But that was just as he intended it – not for him revelatory sensationalism. As he wrote to Bob, 'I think I knew what I was about. After all, one's personal friends and relations are more interested in one, and in one's very mild adventures in life, than the general public can be. I have really said all about myself that I think the public has a right to know or would wish to know.'[129]

George was Master of Trinity until 1951, and then he and Janet retired to their old Cambridge house at Garden Corner. There he pottered around purposefully, returning to the literary loves of his youth, Carlyle and Meredith. He decided to try and interest the younger generation in his heroes, and he edited anthologies of their works. As a young man, George had tramped over the Surrey hills and visited George Meredith at home. Leonard Woolf saw Meredith as 'the prophet, seer, and oracle of the Trevelyans' generation, and one might hear George chanting "Love in the Valley" in a strident singsong as he pounded over the hills of Westmoreland or Surrey'.[130] George found it deplorable that Meredith's works had fallen out of print, and he republished a third of his writings, to enable other lovers of poetry to see if the work could mean anything to them. In 1953 he gave the Clark lectures at Cambridge, choosing 'A Layman's Love of Letters' as his theme. There he defined what he believed to be the essential nature of great literature. 'It is not a set of intellectual conundrums to be solved by certain rules. It is joy, joy in our inmost heart. It is a passion like love or it is nothing.' George appealed to his youthful audience to read as he had done.

When you are young and all the poets are around you waiting to be read, find out what you can love, seeking joy in the springtime, and love it...What an immense and variegated landscape is stretched around you for your delight. It is all free for you to search, of infinite variety in its appeal, from comic prose to the highest poetry, all the ages of England and all the moods of her most remarkable men set down in words inspired. It is your heritage.[131]

Janet died in 1956 after a lengthy and debilitating illness. George had found her later years, when she was paralysed and attended by two nurses, very difficult. A.L. Rowse found his attitude to Janet's illness 'strange – it made him ill. His Cornish nurse told me that no Trevelyan was allowed to be ill. He could not accept the fact of illness.'[132] After Janet's death, George's eyesight, already failing, worsened still further. He took pleasure from being read aloud to. Cambridge academics flocked to perform this task – Jim Butler, Geoffrey Kitson Clark, Noel Annan, George Rylands, Sidney Roberts and J.H. Plumb read everything from Boswell to George's own *History of England*. His daughter Mary would often find him lying on the sofa, reciting the poems he knew by heart. His nurse Elizabeth Thomas spent six years reading from Scott, Dickens, Trollope, Wilkie Collins and John Buchan. She also ploughed through Churchill's *History of the English-speaking Peoples* and the whole of Macaulay's works. His cousin Phil Price saw him the week before his death, and they discussed the last volume of the Cambridge Modern History, entitled *The Age of Violence*. Yes, said George, historian to the last. 'Imperialism was dying but before it died it brought on its death struggles two terrible World Wars. It has indeed been an age of violence.'[133]

The day before he died Elizabeth Thomas read aloud Macaulay's third chapter, just as his mother had at Wallington when he was a little boy, as he lay on the hearth rug in the library. In his final hours he was still drawing inspiration from the famous ancestor who had prompted his life's work. On 21 July 1962 George Macaulay Trevelyan, historian of England, died. His ashes were buried beside Janet and Theo, in the Lake District, 'the place of my heart'.

6

THE EPIGONIC GENERATION

This chapter is about my grandfather Humphry, son of the historian G.M. Trevelyan, and his quest to live a life free from the shadows of the past. He was an epigone – meaning a less distinguished individual than the family members who went before him. That might sound like a harsh judgement, but it is not meant to be. Humphry did not want to be a grand and eminent Trevelyan. That role had already been cast for his elder brother Theo, and after he died at the age of only four the parents mourned their lost genius excessively, making Humphry only too aware of how he was regarded. In any other family, he would have stood out from the crowd. As a German scholar, fellow of King's College, Cambridge, and a translator of the Enigma code at Bletchley Park during World War II he had an impressive CV. But he wasn't particularly impressed by it, or the family, and he strived to define himself differently. Above all, he wanted to be ordinary, but he wasn't really equipped for it. I never met my grandfather – he died at only 55, four years before I was born, of a heart attack. His photograph sits above my desk as I write – craggy and handsome, he also looks rather enigmatic and a little distant, as though it would be hard ever to know what he was thinking. His story marks the end of the Trevelyans as a prominent force in public life – the world changed for ever in the second half of the twentieth century, and with it our cosy place in the established order slipped away. Humphry would have been pleased – the anonymity he craved has been visited upon his descendants.

Charles Humphry Trevelyan was the youngest child of George Macaulay Trevelyan and Janet Ward, born on 6 March 1909. It was a difficult birth.

His mother wrote that he was 'a mid-day baby ushered in by fierce north winds and showers of sleet, and so hardly dealt with in his fight for life, that he all but sighed out his little breath upon the storm'.[1] Theo and Mary, the elder children, were charmed by their baby brother. Mary would carry the basket for his bath up to the nursery, and Theo, not to be outdone, would speak to the baby in approved turn-of-the-century nursery style. 'Isn't he a little sweetie? Did he want a bob bob den?' Janet recorded how the great treat for the children was 'to catch the poor baby giving a crooked yawn – for a slight one-sidedness was now all that was left of poor Humphry's many troubles'.[2] When Humphry was four months old, his nanny went away on her annual holiday, leaving Janet alone with all three of her children. This was something of a shock for the Edwardian lady. As Janet tumbled into bed at night, she felt she had done 'a real day's work. There was a bottle to be given between three and four am, and then another at seven, and then between five and six o'clock Theo would wake up feeling extremely talkative and unless the baby was asleep I hadn't the heart to suppress him.'[3]

The family lived in London, but come high days and holidays they would visit Robin Ghyll, their beloved Lake District cottage, or Wallington, or Stocks, the Hertfordshire home of Janet's mother. At Stocks the infant Humphry was entertained by the novelist Henry James, who observed that a baby's sensations upon waking up must be the most enviable in the world. Janet left Humphry there with her mother and the admiring man of letters, to visit a maiden aunt. 'Poor Humphry baby had been vaccinated, but, nevertheless, I heartlessly left him on the seventh day for Wales and there received bulletins as to his progress.'[4] Baby Humphry was left with his grandmother for nearly two months – Janet writes that 'he came back from Stocks a much fatter, pinker, and more energetic babe than when he went there in December'.[5] Mary Ward, formidable in so many ways, was an adoring and indulgent grandmother. Mary, Theo and Humphry were allowed to pay her a visit every morning, with the breakfast tray. The children would sit on the bed, waiting eagerly for the eminent novelist to execute her egg – then they would eat most of it. When Theo was four and Mary was five, they would pay for their bits of egg by performances of Horatius, or by acting the coming of King Charles into the House of Commons in search of the five members who defied him.[6]

Janet's diaries give the impression that she and George were captivated by Theo and his promise of great ability. Mary and Humphry are praised for their charm and their babyish ways rather than their scholarly aptitude. When in 1911 Theo died of appendicitis while on holiday in Dorset, as I have written

Janet and George were heartbroken, and Charles Philips even suggested that it would have been better if Humphry or Mary had died. The devastated parents derived comfort from memories of their departed prodigy – Janet wrote a story of Theo's life, so 'even the larger world should have a share in him',[7] and became a dedicated campaigner for London children who 'had no Robin Ghyll or Wallington to play in'.[8] Mary and Humphry grew up in a gloomy household where mourning for their dead brother was obligatory. The 12-monthly trek to Theo's graveside was an unpleasant experience for both. My grandmother Molly said that Humphry could never shake off the feeling that he was inadequate compared to his dead brother. Mary was more literary and scholarly than her surviving brother, and became closer to her father. The siblings were not close – Humphry distrusted Mary's interest in religion, which only deepened when she married the future Bishop of Ripon, John Moorman.

Humphry was educated at Berkhamsted School, and in 1928 he went to Trinity College, Cambridge, just as Macaulay, George Otto, Charles Philips and George Macaulay had done before him, and his first cousins George, Julian and Geoffrey were to do. So far, so typical. He read part I of the Classical Tripos, like his grandfather and great-great-uncle. Then he showed signs of breaking free from the family tradition by diverting to modern languages, in which he took a first-class degree, in time-honoured tradition. During this period of study Humphry's passion for the German writer and philosopher Johann Wolfgang Goethe was established. Goethe, author of *Faust*, became Humphry's hero – perhaps he was preferable to the stuffy, self-regarding Trevelyans. Humphry certainly appreciated Goethe's admiration for the grand vision of the Greeks, to which he paid tribute in his only book.

> To sum up Goethe's view of the Greeks, we may say that he saw in them a people that had understood better than any other how to give form to life on a great scale. They had had the urge to strike out recklessly and know life to the limit; but they had also known how to keep this urge within bounds so that it never lost itself in formlessness. Greek form might be at times superhumanly vast, but it remained always form.[9]

The epic sweep of the Greeks combined with the poetry of Goethe certainly made for a change from the dry, establishment life to which Humphry had been raised. After Cambridge, Queens' College approached Humphry with a view to a fellowship, but he was not keen at this stage in his life on becoming an academic like his father. Instead he took off, joining the Grenfell Mission and spending eighteen months in Labrador doing educational and social work among the Eskimos. A spell in the wilderness left him leaning towards academia, despite his reservations about following the same well-trodden path as his father. Humphry published *The Popular Background of Goethe's Hellenism* in 1934, combining his interests of German and the classics. Then, in a further break from the well-trodden Trevelyan path, he went to teach at Yale, in New England, where he met Molly Bennett, who was to become my grandmother.

The young Molly Bennett was charmed by the earnest Briton. He proposed to her in a horse-drawn carriage in Central Park, New York, and she accepted immediately. Her family, owners of the Winchester Repeating Arms company, makers of the eponymous rifle, were thrilled with the match to the son of the famous English historian. For his part, G.M. Trevelyan wrote, 'We know very little about Molly Bennett except that there are five Bennett sisters as in Jane Austen – Humphry's two letters on the subject make me think she's very nice and I have always liked the type and breed.'[10] He was pleased with the idea of a transatlantic family connection, as he made clear in a letter to Molly's father. 'I have so many American friends, particularly New Englanders, and being my father's son am so well up in American history and tradition as seen through English "Whig" eyes, that we need not regard each other as foreigners.'[11]

In June 1936 the pair married at Johnson's Point, the Bennett family summer home near New Haven, Connecticut. It must have been a splendid affair – the wealthy Bennett family knew how to throw a party, Molly's four elder sisters were glamorous and sociable, and the visiting English guests were most impressed by the scene. Johnson's Point is a breathtaking location. The old Bennett family home was an enormous timbered affair, built on a rocky outcrop facing Long Island Sound. Back then it was quite isolated, except for the sound of the sea. The Bennetts had their own beach and did not tolerate trespassers – they would be despatched with a tennis ball, fired from a specially adapted Winchester shotgun. Even today, when the big house is no more and condominiums cloud the once-flawless view, this is still one of the most glorious places. G.M. Trevelyan, three generations earlier, was equally taken with the setting. He wrote to 'Bennett' from the Roosevelt Hotel in New York immediately after the wedding, expressing real tenderness: 'The whole thing has been a dream of happiness to us, and will I think develop into a steady reality of happiness in future, beginning with having Molly with us in July and you two as well in August.'[12]

G.M. approved of his daughter-in-law. 'Molly has great vivacity and initiative as well as charm and sweetness. She will be a great addition to our lives.'[13]

Unfortunately, it was not in the end a particularly happy marriage. G.M.'s dream of happiness was not fulfilled. Humphry was frequently unfaithful to Molly, and was not especially subtle about his affairs. He enjoyed chatting up pretty students, much to her distress. In middle age, he believed, like Goethe, that one could be regenerated by consorting with one's juniors. He took what his King's College obituarist described as an 'honest and unaffected pleasure in the company of youth and beauty'.[14] At my engagement party, my grandmother took me to one side to tell me about her wedding night. She woke up to find that Humphry had gone – and he never really came back to her. They were married, but she had no control over him or his behaviour. Once he died, she was fiercely loyal to his memory, but there was no disguising how much he had upset her.

However, in 1936 there was no hint of the disappointments to come. Humphry was very taken with Molly and her family. Compared to the proper, dutiful Trevelyans, the Bennett family were welcoming and warm, something Humphry responded to instantly. There were similarities between the two families – both had money, social standing, servants, properties aplenty and a love of country pursuits, like shooting. The Bennetts had college connections too – the prestigious Yale University in nearby New Haven was attended by all the male members of the family, and the first chemistry professor at Yale had been a relative. So Humphry would have felt comfortable with the bright Bennetts and at home with their lifestyle. But crucially, the Bennetts exuded enthusiasm, fun and a genuine enjoyment of family life that the more reserved Trevelyans lacked. The optimism and informality of Humphry's New World family contrasted favourably with the worthy, serious atmosphere in which he had grown up. Mr and Mrs Winchester Bennett had five daughters and a son, a noisy collection of children, while G.M. and Janet suffered the loss of Theo and had a more sombre household with only Mary and Humphry. Molly's letters to her family underline how much Humphry enjoyed being with the Bennetts.

> H. feels a strong, silent understanding and friendship…It means a great deal more to him then we realise, being an accepted part of our large tribe – because his own family is so small and although the Wallington T's are large and congenial, still it's only occasionally they see each other, and then it's really only Kitty[15] he has any deep feelings about. So you see, besides having me silently happy at being home with you, you have H drinking you all in most gratefully and feeling happy as he hasn't had much chance to in

just this way before! He does love all the nieces and nephews too – that's an experience totally new to him.[16]

Unlike Molly's, Humphry's letters are usually rather opaque, giving little away about what he really feels. But on the subject of being welcomed into the Bennett fold, he was expansive in a letter to his in-laws. 'It was so good to be with you at Christmas and to feel myself really one of the family. And what a splendid family! I shall never forget the sight of the living-room on Christmas morning. It was a revelation to me of what a family can be.'[17]

G.M., who otherwise had a rather distant relationship with his son, appears from his letters to have appreciated how happy Humphry was following his marriage to Molly, initially at least. In August 1936, when the still-blissful couple are staying with him at Hallington, he tells the soon-to-arrive Mr Bennett that they 'seem very happy, and certainly add immensely to my happiness and to Janet's. Molly is a well-spring of joy. The canoe (a wedding present) had its first voyage yesterday – it was launched with M and H in it and off they paddled. It caused much excitement and fun.'[18]

The letters to Mr Bennett are not just about pleasure – though G.M. tells his new relative he has reserved two days' grouse shooting on the Northumberland moors, and a gun and cartridges are awaiting the American's arrival. There was business to be settled when the Bennetts came to stay with the Trevelyans in England that summer – both children were to be independently wealthy upon their marriage, and the respective parents wanted to discuss the mechanics of the different settlements. Molly's American cash, Winchester 'gun money' as she occasionally called it later in life, was to be left to her via a series of trusts, and Mr Bennett was taking the advice of G.M.'s lawyer. Reading these letters today makes one realise how little had changed between Jane Austen's day and the 1930s. Molly's dowry was the subject of much parental management – how it should be invested in England, whether income tax could be avoided and so on. Ironically enough, after all the time her father spent organising Molly's money, much of it was eventually lost sixty years later through poor management. Molly reflected at the time that the responsibility of the money had always weighed her down – partly with guilt, for she felt badly about inheriting money from the proceeds of the Winchester rifle with its bloody history, and partly because she wanted to live up to her father's expectations. Losing her inheritance was in some ways a relief.

After honeymooning in the Catskills, and visiting both sets of parents in Northumberland, Molly and Humphry went to live in Jena in Germany.

There Humphry undertook the research necessary to turn his earlier work into a book, *Goethe and the Greeks*, which was well received upon publication in 1941. Much care and attention was lavished on this project, which he wanted to be more than a monograph for professionals. His permeation of his hero Goethe with Greek ideals was, he felt, a theme of wider interest.

> Goethe himself indeed looked on the Greek as the ideal type of all mankind, not merely of European man. To him, at the time of his Hellenism, European culture was the only culture that mattered, and it was inevitable that he should regard the Greek, the perfect European, as being identical with the perfect man...Goethe's Hellenism...was an effort to establish the basis of values upon which European civilisation has been built, to purge our culture of the impurities and extravagances which it has acquired in the course of two thousand years, and so to give it a second youth, in which it might conquer new worlds for the human spirit...To live again, an ancient ideal must pass through the living medium of a modern mind. Goethe was this living medium; this is for us the significance and value of his Hellenism.[19]

To explore his theme, Humphry went to study in Goethe's heartland. Jena, in eastern Germany, close to Weimar, has been an important intellectual centre in Germany for centuries – Schiller and Hegel attended the university, and Goethe lived nearby in Weimar. Karl Marx received his doctorate there in 1841. When Humphry and Molly arrived in 1936, to delve into the past, there was no escaping the alarming future. Adolf Hitler was consolidating his hold on power and rearming Germany in preparation for World War II. National Socialism was on the march – and the University of Jena was the cauldron for the more extreme ideas of the Nazi intellectuals. The leading proponents of racial theory and euthanasia set up in Jena – close to the concentration camp of Buchenwald, where their theories became an unspeakable reality. An estimated forty-three thousand prisoners perished there. In the hills above Weimar, horrific acts were performed, in ghastly contrast to the ideals of Goethe and the German Romantics, who had drawn inspiration from the very same landscape only a hundred and fifty years earlier. Just as Humphry and Molly settled into their lodgings in Jena, work was beginning on the concentration camp, which opened in 1937. The newly-weds had no inkling of the sinister plans afoot – one of their favourite pastimes was studying the geology of the Weimar hills, right by the camp itself.

More prosaic concerns were occupying Mr and Mrs Charles Humphry Trevelyan. After the excitements of the courtship, the wedding and the travelling, Molly was glad to have a base at last. As she wrote to her parents, 'T'will be no end good to get settled someplace for a while and to work at something undisturbedly – this going from one place to another, constantly meeting people, and living solely for that purpose is most disturbing – it leaves you feeling shallow, shifting, without any bottom under you, 'cept shifting mud.' Home now was a couple of rooms in the house of Frau Bruller in Jena. The rather basic facilities caused Humphry and Molly much amusement. 'We ring three times in the morning for shaving water, and it appears outside the room in a wee pitcher.'[20] Social life revolved around music – both were to take singing and piano lessons with Herr Volkman, the university music master, and sing Haydn's *Creation* with his choir. 'Such luck as nobody ever had before,' Molly wrote delightedly to Mom and Pops in America. Bicycles were acquired for trundling around town. 'It's a sweet place, set amidst small hills gently sloping down like Alpine arms. The valley is broad and short, and creeps up into smaller valleys…'[21]

New and interesting as life in Jena was, Molly soon missed her parents desperately. While Humphry spent his days in the university library, reading up on Goethe, she filled her time with music lessons and letter-writing. For a 24-year-old who had never left home, to be suddenly deposited thousands of miles from friends and family was hard. She loved Humphry, but hadn't known him for long. Their courtship had been rapid, followed by the social whirl. Now the reality of married life in a foreign place was sinking in. Molly threw herself into Humphry's hobbies. Weekends were spent striding around the countryside, in true Trevelyan style. Just as G.M. had retraced Garibaldi's march in Italy, so Humphry and Molly walked 'where Goethe had hunted with Carl August, the sovereign duke of Saxon Weimar. We tapped at the same outcrops he had investigated, sat where he had sat, writing poetry.'[22] Molly recorded every detail of these trips for her parents. Then at the end of these lengthy letters, she often talked about how she really felt. In October 1936, a month after arriving in Jena, Molly replied to a letter from her mother about the atmosphere in the summer, when the two were about to be parted:

> Oh dear me Mumsie, it wasn't because you showed what you were feeling
> at Hallington that I knew how it was hurting, but just because I was feeling
> it too, and there didn't seem anything to do about it. I began to feel huge
> and clumsy, never able to say anything, either to Mr and Mrs T. or to you

and Dad. Just every now and then we had good talks but then we'd both feel all drawn up inside and couldn't say a word to save ourselves! It's nothing either of us could help, I guess. T'was the situation that made me silent and closed... No, my Mumsie, it's not 'lost'; it's simply you extending a feeler into England – do you see? Look, the way I feel is this: I'm a sort of spider, gone a long distance from the home web, but spinning out a strong thread across that distance... weaving them across the space from here to you more and more thickly all the time. It's a sort of ambassadorish feeling – I'm in touch with you all the time, in a land that isn't, and never will be, my home, among people that never will be my family – I feel really closer to you every minute that I'm here, as things keep cropping up that show how different everything is... It's not, you see, like cutting clean away from you, and becoming totally identified with England and the T's – exactly opposite it is – it's tying up stronger with you, becoming more completely Bennettish than I could possibly be without going away... I haven't changed sides, so to speak, and never will.[23]

The newly-weds' first Christmas together was spent with the in-laws at Hallington, a lonely time for Molly, who pined for the cheery, happy Bennett family gathering in New Haven. The cold, grey Northumbrian skies contrasted unfavourably with the bright crispness of the New England winter, and so did the company. She wrote to her parents, 'If it hadn't been for your gloriously punctual and cheery letters, and monies, I'm sure t'would have been a dreary Christmas indeed!'[24] Molly was successful in hiding her feelings from G.M., who told the Bennetts,

> Nothing but happiness, great happiness to all concerned including Janet and me, seems to have resulted from Molly's marriage. Whether she is a little more home-sick than she lets on I can't say but she seems so happy and she has a gift of spreading happiness around her such I have seldom felt with any other person.[25]

Molly next saw her parents the following Christmas, when she and Humphry sailed across the Atlantic on the *Queen Mary*, in what was to be the last visit to America for ten years. War intervened, yet the letters kept flowing from one side of the Atlantic to the other, as Molly span her web ever more feverishly, determined to hold on to her American home and family.

It wasn't just leaving the United States that was trying for her – she had married into the Trevelyans, who thought rather highly of themselves, yet she had chosen the one member of the family who was ambivalent about it all. Humphry might not have been terribly close to his parents, but he was in their shadow. Molly told her parents,

> He's amazingly tied up with his family, and I don't think he's quite felt on his own two feet. Not that they won't let him, but it's his nature, and he's got quickly to be in his own country, in his own home, with his own job. And the sooner the better. It's different being in another country on a job of your own – you haven't access to your family, so you don't have to contend with the temptations of its ever accommodating sociability...He's no longer a son, he's a man with a wife, he's a German scholar, wishing to make Goethe known to the English that they can appreciate his value – and to do all these things, he must establish himself. Sounds pompous, but one has to be pompous at times. Once established, then we can take vacations.

Humphry applied for several academic jobs in England while studying in Jena. Posts at Exeter and London fell through. He soldiered on with the research for his book. Despite his natural inclination to be a different sort of Trevelyan, his enthusiasm over the purchase of a set of Goethe's works shows him to be very much in the mould of his father. Humphry wrote to his father-in-law about the momentous event.

> There's been great excitement in the family the last few days, all about a 'Weimar-Ausgabe', which is the complete edition of Goethe's works in one hundred and forty three volumes. For two years past I've had my heart set on getting one, but everybody told me they were very rare nowadays, being out of print, and there was clearly no chance of getting one in England or America...the thought of a Weimar-Ausgabe of my own was just too wonderful. At the library here in Jena I'm not allowed to take any volumes of it out, but must read them in the reading-room.[26]

A complete set was located in Berlin, to Humphry's delight. He used Mr Bennett's wedding present of money to pay for this treasure, and collected it in their American station wagon. 'It sounds an unexciting sort of present but to me it's the most exciting purchase I've made in years, and all my life long it will go on being invaluable to me.'[27]

Only when Molly and Humphry returned to England for holidays could they write freely about the political situation in Germany. They seem to have exercised self-censorship when writing from Jena, for they made only the most general references to what was happening there politically. Once back at

Hallington with the in-laws for Christmas 1936, Molly told her parents all about life under Hitler.

> Our last two good newspapers have vanished – the Berliner Tagblatt and the Frankfurter Zeitung – all will now be propaganda and not a word of truth will be printed unless it will condition the minds of the Germans in the right direction – the populace are a bunch of dummies, puppets being made to dance this way and that as it pleases Hitler. I think they don't wish peace broken, it's Hitler who thinks he can read the writing on the wall…Food shortages hadn't affected us before we left…but remember we're in a position to have plenty, not only because Jena is agricultural, but also perhaps because we are foreigners, living in a Nazi family. I can't see anything really bad in Germany right now, because who can say how far Hitler wants to go – he may only want to make the Germans self-sufficient and strong, and stop there…He has more power than anyone living over the Germans, and I do believe they really like it and are glad of it.[28]

Humphry, usually so matter-of-fact in his letters to the Bennetts, was expansive on the subject of German propaganda.

> Life in Germany is almost as different from life in England as life in Kathmandu would be. We in England swim in ease, helped around by all the fruits of the world, the whole world pours its ideas at our feet, and we in turn keenly view the whole world and relate our thought and action to it. We can afford to be individualists and to regard the State as our servant because, internally at least, law and order, property and justice are assured. When you enter Germany a curtain closes behind you, the outside world is shut out. You eat only what Germany can produce. You read in the papers only German news or such as directly affects German interests in the outside world. You talk only of these things, and everywhere the needs and interests of the German people are uppermost in people's minds. A good German must think first how he can serve the state, his own inclinations come second. This is all because their State nearly foundered after the war, sometimes actually lost its power to protect life and property, and had no power at all to protect Germany's rights in the world outside. All this results in a concentration, a narrowing of thought on one object, the reconstruction of a German nation. Spiritual existence becomes as poor and bare as the diet, in so far as it is not concentrated on the one object. It is a good atmosphere to live in if you have work to do, for there

are few distractions available. Coming back to England is like having your helmet taken off after a long spell under water…[29]

Janet and G.M. were worried about Molly and Humphry returning to this strange, new Germany after Christmas 1936, as Janet confided to Mrs Bennett once she had praised her new daughter-in-law.

Certainly she has made a radiant change in this house, for though it was never a dull one with George about, it was getting rather quiet, and now there are such cheerful noises all the time. They sing and they get my Dorothy (Janet's sister) to play for them, and Humphry whistles and Molly shouts aloud, and the noise of their bath-water coming down the new pipe outside the drawing room window reminds us jollily that they are having fun upstairs. They both seem gloriously well, which speaks well for Frau Bruller's feeding of them up to now, but we are feeling a wee bit anxious as to how it will be in this next section of their time out there. I shall certainly try sending them out some extra butter, and hope it will get through! Sometimes one feels anxious about their going there at all just now, with Hitler apparently so mad about his Spanish adventure and not caring how much he provokes the French, but still we don't believe it will actually come to war.[30]

Just 21 months before Hitler's invasion of Poland that was the prevailing view in England's well-connected circles – events in Germany amounted to sabre-rattling rather than anything more sinister. Winston Churchill was a lone voice at that moment in history, warning of the dangers of German re-armament. Back in Germany, Molly and Humphry spent long evenings in Jena with the Bruller family, their hosts, listening to propaganda on the radio. Molly described the scene to her parents:

Humphry was listening intently to the radio while carefully peeling his apple – t'was lovely skin, but underneath t'was riddled with small, deep brown spots – he was totally unaware of it… The solemnity with which he peeled his rotten old apple was too much for me, and I laughed till the tears streamed down my face – nobody else could see that t'was funny. I'm sure you would have if you'd been there – it just seemed to sum everything up so comically – here we were in a funny Nazi family, listening intently to political speeches on the radio, while we politely peeled rotten apples! I shall always laugh when I think of it.[31]

Relief from the tedium of Nazi propaganda was at hand. In the spring of 1937 Molly and Humphry went to Italy with G.M. and Janet Trevelyan, to retrace Goethe's steps. Janet found the couple in good spirits, which she reported to Mrs Bennett.

> We did indeed have a heavenly time with those two young things in Italy. Only eight days, but enough to see how sure and strong is the foundation of their happiness and how each new experience only adds to their bliss. We did a certain amount of sight seeing, but not too much, and then when they had left us and gone on to Rome their letters told us that they were only lazing and drawing in the Forum and Palatine or going for long walks in the Alban Hills. No, I think they did one day of sightseeing in the Vatican! But that was because of Goethe, whose footsteps they did pursue most conscientiously.[32]

The PS to this letter reports that G.M. and Janet have been invited to Westminster Abbey for the Coronation of the new King, George VI. 'I have been faint hearted and am going to our cottage in Westmoreland instead. But G.M.T. is going in black velvet Court dress!'

Molly and Humphry weren't earning any money at this time. Their life in Jena, the trip to Italy, the back and forth to Hallington – all this was paid for by the generous settlements of their parents. Humphry, who in 1937 was aged 28, had never had a job. That summer they bought a house in London, to be close to the British Museum so Humphry could continue his research into Goethe. The advantages of a private income were enormous – one could live as one pleased, within reason. Molly and Humphry were not extravagant, but equally they never had to compromise, to live somewhere they disliked, or take a job just to pay the mortgage. Indeed they never had a mortgage. Finding London life rather cramped, they decided to buy a cottage in the country too. Theirs was a hugely privileged existence, of a kind that has all but died out today. Humphry was able to please himself, to research and write his book in Germany, and return to England at his leisure. He wrote his book without even having a publisher – once it was completed he took it to the Cambridge University Press. Money is a preoccupation in Molly's letters to her parents – she is anxious to spend it wisely. But there was never any question of not having enough of it.

After two years, they returned to England, on the eve of World War II. Molly was expecting her first child. Against a gloomy backdrop of impending conflict, normal life went on. Molly and Humphry continued singing, joining the Bach Cantata Choir. Preparations were made for the baby – cribs and furniture were ordered, and nannies were interviewed for, a terrifying experience for Molly, who didn't like the way the nursery would be out of bounds to her. All the while the menacing news from Europe dominated Molly's letters to her parents. German troops marched into Austria in the spring of 1938, and Hitler declared the two countries had been unified. Molly, who had lived in Germany, was married to a German scholar and had a historian for a father-in-law, tried to explain to her parents that the Austrians might actually be welcoming the Anschluss.

> But one can't help feeling that perhaps we are so prejudiced about Germany that we don't stop to think that the heart of Austria, the peasants, and all the working classes … may be truly happy about it. Even Da T.[33] says that the annexation of Austria by Germany has always been an accepted event which must come true – a perfectly logical development. But it's this beastly show of the military that is so abominable.[34]

Although Molly and Humphry had a happy enough existence in London, Molly was missing her parents more and more. Visits to G.M. and Janet in Cambridge and Hallington were not the same as the chaotic, cheerful Bennett family gatherings in Connecticut. Stilted conversation over the roast beef in Northumberland was no match for bantering over the seafood at Johnson's Point. In June 1938, she wrote wistfully to her parents:

> By now you are at the Shore,[35] enjoying its coolness and quiet! I wish we were with you, not because London is at all bad now, but because the Shore is always such an invigorating, satisfying place after town, even in the hottest weather – and soon you'll be having lobsters on Sundays, and on Thursdays you'll be going, probably all the family together, to the Oasis, or some smaller place, to have Shore dinners. Or having rock-roasts, or all day sails in the Dovelsie – and the tennis court will be ready, so that all of you will be losing pounds as you rush back and forth over the courts, only to put them all back on again at lunch or supper …[36]

Molly was also getting riled by her in-laws, who made no secret of their hopes for a grandson. The desire for a male heir to bear not only the Trevelyan family name but also the tradition was strong. George and his brothers Charles and Robert had at that point no sons, so there was a possibility that the name could die out. The West Country branch of the family was only producing girls too. Molly knew all this but was still irritated.

> I know the T's and Auntie D[37] are expecting it to be a boy, and it annoys me beyond measure – they keep on talking over boys names etc and never

care about choosing a girl's name! It's never what you want it to be anyhow, but people will go on feeding themselves on imaginary hopes – I'm afraid that if it's not a boy they'll all be offended and think I've lied to them![38]

G.M.'s longing for a male grandchild did not diminish – Molly eventually had five children, including three boys, but the first two she produced were girls, much to the great man's not very well concealed disappointment. The Bennetts, who already had ten grandchildren, were rather more relaxed. Mr and Mrs Winchester Bennett missed their youngest daughter very much, and in September 1938 they sailed from New York to London, intending to dock before the birth of their latest grandchild. Baby Jane Winchester Trevelyan arrived early, to the dismay of Mrs Bennett. She found her relatives in a state of quiet apprehension, which she initially believed to be her fault.

> It seemed to me that there was a constraint in the manner of the people we
> met, and self consciously, I laid it to our fiascos in getting over too late.
> It was not until we went to Northumberland for a visit that it dawned on
> me what was really the matter. You know how it is when you are fearfully
> upset about something, and have to make polite conversation with an
> innocent outsider. Only a quarter of your senses seems to focus on the act
> of politeness, while you are tugging away at your problem in the back of
> your mind and saying polite nothings in a perfectly perfunctory manner.
> Those English people were like that. The black cloud of war was hanging
> so low over them then, that they could never get it out of their minds. Even
> the effort they made not to talk about it, only added to the strain. Half the
> time they didn't even hear what you said, and they were so outwardly calm
> and SO polite that it was simply terrifying.[39]

The Bennetts were in London on 12 September 1938 to hear Hitler's speech at the end of the Nazi Congress in Nuremberg broadcast on the BBC. Hitler ominously promised the support of the Reich to the Sudeten Germans – the annexation of the Sudetenland, part of Czechoslovakia, was now all but inevitable. The Bennetts were glued to their wireless set as they heard reports of Neville Chamberlain, the British Prime Minister, flying to see Hitler in an attempt to avert war. Hitler wanted the British to recognise the principle of the Sudetenland's right to self-determination – and in return, he would promise not to wage war. These negotiations would lead ultimately to the Munich Conference and Chamberlain's infamous declaration of peace for our time. To Mrs Bennett, England was grimly preparing for the worst, at some inconvenience to herself. Later she gave this speech to the Thursday Club in New Haven, a New England version of the Women's Institute:

> The first intimation we had of it was when they began digging up Kensington Park, next to our hotel, and they dug up a large area of it, making bomb proofs. It rather spoiled our night's rest, as lorries kept arriving at intervals all night with material, as the work went on day and night. Several times a night we were awakened by the slap of planks being thrown on piles, and the chugging of lorries, and loud conversation on the part of workmen, who had to stay awake and work themselves, and so didn't care whether anyone else slept or not. Every park in London had these bomb proofs, and in the large parks there were two. Every park also had its anti aircraft guns, in the charge of a squad of the Royal Air Force in their natty smoke blue uniforms.[40]

The French and the British started mobilising their troops. Mrs Bennett witnessed the effect at first-hand – the cordon bleu chefs at her Kensington hotel vanished.

> For two days at the hotel things were badly disorganized as we lost two chefs, and it took some time to fill their places satisfactorily. One afternoon when we wanted a taxi, the man at the door was deep in a paper. He apologized profusely, saying, 'I see they have called up the Territorials, and that means me... By the end of that week all pretence of business as usual was flung to the four winds of heaven. Every other person on the streets had a newspaper in their hand. You could get a new one about every four hours. People rushed home from shopping and from luncheons and tea parties to get the latest news over the radio. It was almost impossible to do any business, as all the clerks and so on must talk about the war news. Within a day or two of our sailing we were doing some last minute errands on Regent Street, and I twice saw one quite elderly woman greet another, falling on her neck affectionately and then without any visible reason they both burst into tears. Those women were not very far from the last war. The boy who brought our breakfast in the morning, such a nice apple cheeked young man from Cornwall, always began the day with 'Good Morning Sir. The news is bad (or good) today isn't it Madam? I expect I shall be called out soon Sir.[41]

To the consternation of their American friends, the Bennetts were sailing back to New York in a French boat, the *Ile de France*. It was known in America that German liners had cancelled their passenger bookings and were sailing the Atlantic armed in case of war – what better target than a French boat? Mrs Bennett, who could see gas masks being issued and sandbags everywhere, wanted to leave, but only once she had arranged for her dear daughter Molly, the baby of the family, to be sent somewhere safer. The atmosphere was growing increasingly tense in London as Chamberlain continued his shuttle diplomacy.

> The tension had been frightful, the probability of war, and such a war, was so close. When Chamberlain made his second visit to Germany, and met with Hitler's stubborn resistance to his proposals, the world stood still, not daring to breathe, not daring to hope that life, and happiness, and the pursuit of culture could still go on…On Thursday the 29th of September we sent Molly and the baby and nurse, not to mention her husband, to Northumberland, to get them as far away from the air raids as possible. The night before we had a little farewell supper at an Italian restaurant that Molly and Humphry frequent nearby. There were just the four of us, and it was not very gay. We tried to keep the conversation cheerful and casual, but things would creep in. I think we all deep down in our hearts had the feeling that we might not see each other again. I know my throat ached so that I could hardly swallow, and nothing had any taste. We parted silently after dinner, and went our separate ways, relieved to be alone with our thoughts.[42]

Molly parted sadly from her parents, a separation that was to last nine years, and went north to stay with the Trevelyans at Hallington. There she found that Lord Runciman, Chamberlain's envoy to Czechoslovakia during the Sudetenland crisis, had been a house guest of G.M.'s just days earlier. Hitler, having annexed Austria, wanted the Sudetenland too. German newsreels began showing footage of supposed atrocities committed by the Czechs against the Sudeten Germans. Chamberlain famously decided that this was not one of the 'great issues' that justified war, being 'a quarrel in a faraway country between people of whom we know nothing', and agreed that Hitler could have the Sudetenland. Molly related to her mother this account of Lord Runciman's visit to Hallington:

> Lord Runciman spent a night with them just two or three days ago, and they had good talks – digest of it being that the Sudetans were fired by extremists in their party, that the Czechs are hard to like (his wife truly hates them), that the 'incidents' along the Czech-Sudetan frontier really did take place, but were much exaggerated – not very different from what we all thought.[43]

As Molly was hearing accounts of the behind-the-scenes diplomatic manoeuvrings, the Bennetts actually saw Chamberlain on the day he returned from the Munich Conference. Chamberlain came back having signed a non-aggression pact with Hitler in which the German leader stated his desire never to go to war with Britain again. A year later Hitler derided the agreement as 'just a scrap of paper' and invaded Poland. Britain and France declared war on Germany two days later, and the Second World War began. But in September 1938, Chamberlain was feted as a hero by many of the British people, anxious to avoid another bloody and prolonged war. Others, most notably Churchill, believed the Conservative leader was mistakenly appeasing Germany. On 30 September 1938 Chamberlain stood in front of 10 Downing Street and declared, 'My good friends, for the second time in our history, a British Prime Minister has returned from Germany bringing peace with honour. I believe it is peace for our time … go home and get a nice quiet sleep.'

Mrs Bennett, about to sail for New York, recorded the mood on the streets of London that very afternoon.

> It was like the sun breaking through clouds. Everyone went about with broad grins on their faces, and I felt like skipping myself. I am not ashamed of the fact that tears of joy were in my eyes most of that day, foreigner that I was. Everybody threw aside their usual reserve and talked to everybody else in their overwhelming joy and relief. We went to pay some parting calls that afternoon, and so it happened that we found ourselves standing in the rain on Cromwell Road, waiting to see Chamberlain come by on his way back from Heston airport. The road was jammed with people waiting patiently, hardly conscious of the steady drizzle. He was a long time coming for the police could not control the crowds. All at once there was a roar of cheering, hats flew in the air, and handkerchiefs were waved and the car bearing the hero of the hour came slowly along. The crowd closed in front of the car trying to open the door in order to shake Chamberlain by the hand, but failing that they patted the car with their hands, some even kissing the fenders. Nothing was too good for the man who by his courage and clear vision had turned aside the grim horror of a war too terrible to think about. Then the car having passed people stood there still with tears streaming down their faces. The more exuberant ones, usually men, grabbed the hand of the nearest person and shook it violently.[44]

Mrs Winchester Bennett delivered this speech to her New Haven Thursday Club of genteel ladies in October 1938, eleven months before Hitler made a mockery of his promise to Chamberlain. Mrs Bennett, like so many who could not bear the thought of another war, was convinced at the time that Chamberlain had chosen the right path.

> You can imagine my surprise and indignation to find everybody over here criticizing Chamberlain, I felt without the smallest right, as our stand off policy gives us no right to judge the nations who must bear the consequences of what may come. I cannot bear even now to hear Chamberlain criticized, and heavily blamed for 'selling out' as they put it, Czechoslovakia…Again and again I shall go on saying it, as long as I have breath left to say it with, Chamberlain without the shadow of a doubt, saved the world from chaos.[45]

Molly agreed. She, like millions of others, was relieved.

> Thank Heavens it's all over, and I don't have to try not to think about what would happen to Humpin in a war, and what would become of our cosy life, perhaps for ever! My throat felt permanently swollen and tight from continually swallowing back imagined misery – but the poor Czechs! Though as Da T[46] says, they really deserve what's come, because they have treated their minorities badly, though propaganda here and over on your side had formerly been to the effect that Czechoslovakia was a model state – and wasn't that natural since England and the States were responsible for its making?[47]

Molly's letters to her parents reveal something of Humphry's thinking on Germany's position in the months leading up to war. As a man of German letters, he seems to have had some empathy with Hitler's actions.

> One can't help being dismayed at the possible truth of Humpin's feeling that the taking of Czechoslovakia was a frightened move in answer to our pushing of armaments in spite of Munich – you see, if Hitler took our great armament programme after Munich as a breaking of faith, as a sign that we weren't sincere, then he felt of course that he must have extra strength as quickly as possible – and isn't it truly logical to realise that Hitler and Musso think of England and France as great war-mongerers as we think of them? They fear us as we fear them – they think we want to dominate them, just as we are certain they want to dominate us – oh it is senseless and lamentable, because it is really all avoidable if only we would trust each other!

Before twelve months had elapsed, the world was plunged into chaos. Hitler defied Chamberlain, who resigned, a broken man. Humphry, scholar of German literature and personal friend of many Germans, was conflicted when the war finally began. He joined the Auxiliary Fire Service in London, and during the bombing of the docks saw more active service than most of the armed forces at that period. Molly, and her baby daughter Jane, lived in Rose Cottage near Henley-on-Thames, and saw Humphry one day in every three, when his shifts allowed. Days after war broke out, Molly wrote to her parents, 'I am afraid my letters will have to be brief, because of censorship – "Brief and clear" they said to make them! That's hard for me.'[48] Pregnant with her second child, with a husband doing dangerous war work in London, this was an anxious time for Molly. Humphry's first letter to Molly's parents once war had been declared was full of reassurance – just what the censor ordered.

> Don't worry for us. There's been a lot of hair raising stuff written about what this war is going to be like, but it's mostly exaggerated. This country is well able to defend itself now and we three have made our arrangements so that we shall be as happy and comfortable as any people are in the present circumstances.[49]

London moved onto a wartime footing in September 1939, making it an eerie place, as the capital waited for Hitler's bombs to fall. Dorothy Ward, Humphry's aunt, explained to the Bennetts how much the atmosphere had changed:

> You would be amazed by the sight of London nowadays – sandbags by the thousand protecting lower walls and windows, trailer pumps attached to taxi-cabs at frequent intervals, silvery balloons 4500 feet above us, floating in a lovely blue sky – special police, and air-raid wardens everywhere, night and day; windows covered with cellophane or criss crossed with strips and gummed paper to prevent splintering – and by night complete blackness over everything. Troops in all the parks, shelter trenches not only in all the parks and many squares but dug in the asphalt yards in between blocks of flats. By the end of this week, petrol rationing will have begun and a severe rationing it is going to be – how I hope Humphry will be able to get enough for his journeys to the cottage![50]

For the Bennett family in Connecticut, worried about their youngest daughter, September 1939 was an alarming time. Molly and Humphry had been due to visit in July, but the trip was cancelled due to the worsening international situation. America was staying out of the war for the time being,

'The smoke billowed up, livid yellow and green in the failing light.' Humphry Trevelyan in his Auxiliary Fire Service uniform, circa 1940. He was a fireman during the Blitz. Courtesy of Tom Trevelyan.

and the Bennetts were waiting nervously for news from the other side of the pond. Mr Bennett wrote to Molly,

> I am dreadfully afraid that that the Allies need help in the shape of man power, which apparently we are not going to offer, for the present at any rate…I am at a loss to see how France and Britain can really get at Germany effectually. Certainly I have never spent so much time at the end of a radio as I have in the last few days.[51]

Later, his letters combined emotions with high politics:

> I hope that you will bear it in mind to write to us frequently even though you cannot write at length. I wonder if you understand how anxious we are to hear from you, and really how little information we are getting…Congress meets today to consider an amendment to the present 'Neutrality Act', and no man knoweth what they may do. There is a very strong sentiment against opening our markets for the sale of munitions, and it is surprising to me to see how many apparently stable people are adverse to any sales. Roosevelt would be glad to make them, but Hoover, Lindbergh, and many others, besides Senators and politicians, are firmly convinced that we should not do so…On the other hand, there is a very general conviction that we will ultimately appear as combatants. Bets at even amount are offered this point in New York, that we will be engaged in hostilities in six months, but at the present moment, it looks as though we were very far away from any active part in the hostilities.[52]

Mr Bennett was correct in his analysis of American intentions – not until after Pearl Harbor in 1941 did the United States formally enter the war. This was an odd period on Molly's side of the Atlantic – the phoney war, as it became known. The nation was poised for conflict but there was no sign of the Germans. Humphry, all ready to put out fires in London, told the Bennetts he was having a quiet time.

> We have had very little to do so far in the Fire Service. I use the leisure time to do a lot of reading of a more varied kind than I have had time for these last three years. Publication of my book[53] is postponed indefinitely. That is a big disappointment but of course this would be the worst possible time to publish a book of that sort.[54]

Anti-German sentiment was running high, and not even an academic book about Germany's Shakespeare, as Goethe was known, could be risked. So it was on with the waiting for fireman Humphry. Dorothy Ward tried to give the anxious Bennetts as much detail as she could about Humphry's work.

> I wish you could see Humphry in his A.F.S. uniform, he looks so nice! It is dark blue, with red fixings. They wear a peaked cap but have a steel helmet strung at the waist, also a lantern and an axe! Gas mask etc in a small, strong haversack over their shoulder. But the poor dear, and all his comrades, are very much bored, as after the morning's P.T. (physical training) and drill and seeing to their pumps etc they hardly have anything to do, in the absence of air-raids so far, and yet they are kept very strictly to their quarters all day and all night and may never go out except on their regular days off. Well, I expect they will have enough serious work to do some day! Meanwhile I go every couple of days and pay H. a little visit in the afternoon and am allowed to sit upstairs with him in an upstairs sort of 'lounge' and we steal a little conversation while the other young men play the piano, or table tennis! So I always get the latest news of Molly that way.[55]

Humphry told Mr Bennett more about the rhythm of his days:

> Here in London, especially confined all day to our fire station, we see nothing of the war but the underside of barrage balloons. In spite of our inactivity, life is tolerable for me at least, as I have a certain amount of work and responsibility in running the station; and the one day's leave in three enables me to live a family life alongside my fireman's existence. Every leave day I take the train to Henley and have from 1pm to 8 o'clock next morning actually at the cottage. It is heavenly there now, with spring, as we understand it, in full swing.[56]

In December 1939, Molly gave birth to Mary Harriet, or Heidi as she was to be known. G.M. wrote to 'Dear Bennett' to mark the occasion:

> So you and I have got another grandchild in common – isn't that fine? And she came so well and easily too which is a great thing. And Janet reports on her dark hair which will be a lovely contrast to the exquisite Jane's light hair. They will be a lovely couple and I am sure a great delight and consolation to Molly. It's very sad that we can't look forward to you and Mrs Bennett coming over to see them and us yet…speculation about the future is perfectly idle, and any prophecy one makes will probably be wrong.[57]

G.M., who had badly wanted Molly's first child to be a boy, was disappointed by the appearance of yet another girl. Janet had to write to the Bennetts and smooth things over.

And first of all, George wants me to assure you that he really didn't mind about its being another girl! Of course he hopes that some day there may be a boy – or even two – and for that reason rejoices that this one came so much more easily than Jane, but he too realises how perfectly sweet two jolly little girls can be, and looks forward to watching their growth and childhood.[58]

Girls could be perfectly sweet and jolly, then, but not standard-bearers for the family. G.M, whose much-adored Theo died young, was already looking for the next achiever in the family. The Bennetts meanwhile had more practical concerns about the family across the water. Molly's parents were hatching a plan to bring their daughter and grandchildren to safety in America. Mr Bennett lobbied his senator to contact the Department of State in Washington. The State Department sent a telegram to the American Embassy in London stating that Mr Bennett suggested that Molly and the two children return to the United States on the *President Roosevelt*. From Grosvenor Square came this telegraphed reply: 'Mrs Mary Trevelyan and children all well and intend remaining in England. They will move to Westmoreland safe area if necessary.'[59]

Molly feared she would not be allowed to return to England once she had delivered the children to America. Humphry telegraphed the Bennetts: 'Fear your information incorrect impossible Molly return here with either British or American passport have decided keep children here danger not great don't worry Trevelyan.'[60] In a letter he explained the situation more fully:

The chief reason was that Molly could not have got back to this country, after taking them over, for at least six months… By the time we had tried all the alternatives and had found out the exact regulations governing the case (…my father got at a friend in the Foreign Office who got a ruling from the head of the Passport Office), it was beginning to look more and more risky to send them across the Atlantic. The torpedoings of the last few days have made us very glad we did not try… as the crossing is getting more dangerous, it is best they stay where they are. The risks are really very small – very little more than none at all, unless this country is actually invaded and overrun and that will not happen.[61]

By 1940 the phoney war was over. Having overrun Belgium, the Netherlands and northern France in May 1940 with *Blitzkrieg*,[62] the Nazis' focus shifted to Britain. In the summer of 1940, the Luftwaffe attempted to win the skies over southern Britain and the English Channel by destroying the Royal Air Force and the British aircraft industry. The Battle of Britain had begun. In the midst of this epic air battle, Churchill gave his famous speech to parliament on 20 August, when he said, 'Never in the field of human conflict has so much been owed by so many to so few.' The RAF held off the Luftwaffe and so ultimately changed the course of the war. Without air superiority the Germans could not risk a land invasion. In September 1940 the Germans began sustained bombing of London and the major cities. This was an attempt to destroy British morale. The newspapers nicknamed the bombings 'the Blitz', after the German word for lightning. Humphry, having twiddled his thumbs with the other firemen for months, was now in the thick of it. Over 24 nights in September, the Luftwaffe dropped 5300 tons of high explosives on London. In the midst of the Blitz, Humphry wrote to the Bennetts, deploying the famous British stiff upper lip, and downplaying the impact of the unremitting bombs:

> The German air attack has completely failed to achieve any decisive result. In spite of nightly raids and daily attempts (always foiled) on a huge scale London is still practically unscathed. You could travel through and about it for a week and never see a damaged house. As for the nine tenths of the country that are outside the range of fighter escorts, they never hear a German plane except at night, and the Germans cannot cripple us by night bombing.[63]

Molly, writing to her parents on 13 September, was less gung ho.

> As you can imagine, Humpin has been very busy – when the first air raid started last Saturday, he'd just got back from leave down here. They went out on a call to the docks at six on Saturday evening and stayed out until 3pm on Sunday! Then Sunday evening…they went on a call at midnight, getting back about six o'clock in the morning. So Monday, when he came down, he was dead tired…He just wasn't himself. His hair and his clothes reeked burned smell, and his chin was bruised from falling too quickly onto his face when a bomb fell very near – bombs scream all about them as they work, and as long as they aren't holding too strong a stream (of water), they fall flat when they hear bomb warnings. It is a business.[64]

In a diary written some time after the event, Humphry vividly described the events of that Saturday night, 7 September 1940. After months of inactivity, he was to be tested to his very limits. Humphry looked up into a cloudless blue sky, and his war began.

> Everybody was (out) in the mews, gazing intently at the eastern sky. We looked too, and presently saw silver flashes high up in the blue, like the

flash of minnows in a stream. The sun caught the planes just as they swung
around and turned for home. And all the while there was this booming
and thudding such as we had not heard before. 'The East End's catching
it,' somebody said. But even then I did not realise that this was the moment
for which we had waited so long and that we should soon be in action.[65]

Humphry and his crew got the call to join the procession of fire engines
heading for the devastated East End. The sirens were wailing – after all the
drills, this was it.

The streets were full of people, staring and anxious. Then we saw a private
car with children in the back with bandaged heads and arms; soon after
that a bus, burnt out and half wrecked, in the middle of the road. We
reached Homerton before seven, and while Willis went in to report, I
bought a couple of buns. If I had any sense I would have bought dozens.[66]

Humphry and his crew were not keen on Willis – he had a stripe on his
uniform, so he was senior to Humphry, who resented being under his
command on this eventful evening.

Soon Willis came back, and said we were ordered on to No 24 Brunswick
Road. Nobody had much idea where that was, except that it was down
towards the docks. As we turned South, we saw what gave us the first hint
of what we were in for. A vast curtain of smoke, already turning pink in
the evening light, hung across the southern sky. As we came nearer we
could see some of the separate conflagrations that fed the curtain. The
smoke billowed up, livid yellow and green in the failing light, and beneath
the flames leapt. In our search for Brunswick Road (which we did not find
until well after dark) we passed several of these blazes, and not once did
we see a pump at work on one of them. In particular I remember a big
timber yard well alight, and a row of houses beside it just catching. We were
one of a train of pumps that passed it by, and not one could stop for all
had orders to go elsewhere. The streets were crammed with pumps, all
struggling amid the smoke and sparks to get to more distant fires.[67]

At last the crew reached their destination, a blazing fire in the docks next
to the Isle of Dogs.

We hitched up, and drove round, by a tortuous route, over a swing bridge,
through a great warehouse and out onto another dock beside a smaller
basin. Some fifty railway trucks were on the dock, and beyond them there
was, or had been, another warehouse. It was a mass of roaring, leaping

flames, the most majestic and terrible sight I had ever seen. It was long past saving. All we could do was to stop the fire spreading to the dock and the trucks. In the basin was a score or so of barges and on the other side was another great warehouse, it too blazing from end to end. Pettitt and I found ourselves standing on the rim of a small bomb crater.[68]

At long last Humphry and his crew had got to see the fun, as they called it. The busy period didn't last long. By November 1940, Humphry told the Bennetts, 'I haven't been to a fire for five weeks now. There have been a few busy nights but always when I have been on leave. Most nights are very quiet.'[69]

The imminent threat of a German invasion had subsided, but wartime life continued. Humphry got the welcome news that his book, *Goethe and the Greeks*, was to be published after all, despite the war. Cambridge University Press, and not Longman, publisher of two generations of Trevelyans, was to produce the book. The choice of publishing house shows Humphry's independence of spirit. He had written a book, like his relatives before him, but he was going to do so in a manner of his choosing. Longman had even published Janet's recollections of Theo – they would probably have found room in their list for the son of the eminent historian. But Humphry, typically, was disdainful of such connections. Molly explained the situation to her parents:

> We go to Cambridge this weekend – the first in a long time. Rather amusing, 'cause Humpin will be seeing the Cambridge Press about his book, and the Longmans, Da T's[70] publishers will be at Garden Corner too for the week end – they are bad in paying Da T. his share, so we think we'll try Cambridge; besides, I think it's bad to go to the same people that published your great-grandfather, grandfather and father's books – perhaps later, but not for our first book – But Humpin felt so before I did, so that's alright. It's rather a strain being a great man's son, not to speak of a great man's grandson. That's why he went to Labrador, and why he came to Yale – and a good thing too.

Molly, apart from the odd visit to Cambridge, was otherwise confined to Rose Cottage. She was finding wartime living a trial. She had guests constantly, from German refugees to evacuees from London. Day-to-day life, as she explained to her parents, was a series of petty irritations:

> I think this is one of the most important aspects of the war; that almost everyone has had to give up their private lives, and join in communal

life. I haven't taken to it any too kindly, though I hope I haven't shown it too clearly. Just try for a minute to imagine what it's like to have your kitchen manhandled by careless people, your fat, carefully saved from roasts, used up on a leg of lamb which has in itself a good bowlful of natural fat; to have your nice pram mattresses, and cots ditto, and blankets all messed up with other children's big jobs; your carpets sharing the same fate! To have everything treasured poked over, used and grabbed by other people before you yourself have a chance of enjoying them as you have planned to in your rare leisure moments. You may be interested to know that all the New Yorkers that come so kindly from you to me are never opened by me, and rarely read by me. Whenever I have a minute to spare, too short to start a big project in, I lick my lips and look about for a New Yorker, only to find that Diana has taken them all up to her cottage for Jim to look at... This may amuse you, as I expect it does, and it will me in a minute or two. The upshot of all this is that I have become very uncommunicative, and not very warm and friendly. Compared to the things most people are having to bear in this war, my complaints are shameful; I'm ashamed now to have told you about it. Mostly I don't mind because really it's a sort of war job, and it's really only when I'm awfully tired that I feel so horrid about it.[71]

While Molly struggled, Humphry painted a more positive picture for the Bennetts of life at Rose Cottage, with its assortment of people and animals:

It's a wonderful sight to see the living room at meal times – all the babies eating, or some refusing to and hollering, some of the grown-ups eating and some feeding babies, two grown-ups trying to converse above the din and maybe the one o'clock news turned on to add to the pandemonium, and the goat bleating outside because her dinner's been forgotten, and the hen clucking because she's laid an egg, and a great smell of crab apples coming from the kitchen where some are stewing for jelly. It's a great life really, and I only wish you could see it.[72]

In 1941 Humphry was recruited to join an obscure department of the Foreign Office. At least, that was what he told everyone. Actually, he was involved in the famous code-cracking operation at Bletchley Park, where the Enigma cipher used by the Germans for their high-level communications was decoded. Ultra was the Allied codename for the Enigma decodes. It is hard to overstate the importance of this breakthrough. As Ralph Bennett, who would have worked alongside Humphry, put it,

When Enigma was broken in 1940 nobody really knew what it was going to do. It is important to understand that up until then intelligence was not rated very highly by the ordinary army chap. It is difficult now to remember but before May 1940 when Enigma was first broken, military intelligence of all kinds was in the same state it had been at the Battle of Hastings. If you wanted to know what the enemy was going to do, the only way you could find out was by getting an agent to disguise himself with a beard and spectacles and tell him to go and have a look, come back across the lines, which he might not do, he might be caught, and anyway he would be a bit late because it would take him a long time to do this. The intelligence world changed completely in May 1940.[73]

Thanks to the intelligence from Ultra, the war was shortened and lives were saved. The lethal threat posed by the German U-boats to British ships in the Atlantic was lessened. The Allied victory in North Africa also owed much to the work done at Bletchley. In the assessment of the late Harry Hinsley, one of the brainy youngsters at Bletchley who played a key role and then became an academic historian, the 1944 invasion of Normandy would have been impracticable – or failed – without the precise and reliable intelligence provided by Ultra about German troop strengths.[74] The Official Secrets Act kept the extraordinary achievement of Bletchley Park under wraps until the 1970s. When government officials were searching for a suitable location for their gifted, eccentric code-breakers, they carried out a reconnaissance at Bletchley, beginning the tradition of secrecy by describing themselves as members of Captain Ridley's shooting party. In Churchill's famous phrase, the ten thousand men and women who subsequently worked at the Elizabethan mansion were 'the geese who laid the golden eggs and never cackled'.[75]

As a fluent German speaker and scholar, and a Cambridge man, Humphry was just what the Bletchley talent-spotters were looking for. His cousin Mary Trevelyan felt he was wasting his talents as a fireman – and suggested he work at Bletchley. Sciatica was anyway making his firefighting work more and more difficult, and he was on sick leave, so Humphry responded to Mary's prodding. In September 1941, while the family was staying with G.M. at the Master's Lodge, Trinity, the recruitment process got under way. Molly told her parents,

> Ever since we came Humpin has been meeting different people who are now employed by the Government, but used to be Humpin's tutors etc. They all want him to join them in their present work. He is thinking it over, and in time he may see if he can; for I believe there would be a lot

more to it than their invitation to join them – in many ways I hope he will, as one can't help feeling he's more needed in this line, with his special qualifications – that it would be the nearest thing to opposing Hitler face to face. I should love to be able to be closely connected with those elements that make up the frustrating net in which one enemy tries to entangle the other.[76]

The censor was usually diligent in cutting huge holes out of Molly's letters to America, much to the annoyance of Mrs Bennett. Somehow this passage escaped the censor's scissors. Perhaps the reference to intelligence work was too obscure, even though it clearly identifies Trinity College as a source of some interesting networking, at the very least. In October 1941 Molly told her parents Humphry had successfully applied for a new job, in 'another department of the war machine which badly needs men with Humpin's linguistic bents'.[77] He was to take up the post once his back had been operated on. Janet wrote, 'It is something in the German branch of the F.O., as I expect he has already told you, and it is NOT in London. But I hear that it is very arduous, so he must get quite well before he undertakes it.'[78]

Humphry joined Hut 3 at Bletchley Park, which was full of professor-type academic German scholars,[79] as Ralph Bennett, the duty officer, put it. Once the Enigma code had been cracked by those great mathematical brains toiling away in Hut 6, the job of Hut 3 was to translate the material from German to English, work out what went in the inevitable gaps, and make sure the intelligence went to the right place in the military command structure. This was an extraordinary responsibility for the dons. As Ralph Bennett explained, 'Not foreseeing what they were letting escape from their control, it is to be presumed, the War Office and the Air Ministry allowed a Secret Service operation, hitherto staffed mainly by civilians, to handle operational intelligence.'[80]

The huts were a most unremarkable setting. Ramshackle and dilapidated, Ralph Bennett found Hut 3 'nauseating at night when the black-out imprisoned the fumes from leaky coke-burning stoves'.[81] F.L. Lucas, one of the original heads of Hut 3, described the atmosphere inside the bleak wooden building on a snowy morning in January 1940 when the first Enigma decodes arrived:

> The four of us who then constituted Hut 3 had no idea what they were about to disclose. Something fairly straightforward like German police, or something more diplomatic – neat and explicit documents straight from the office tables of the Fuhrer and the Wehrmacht that would simply need translating and forwarding to ministries?[82]

Those initial decodes were, Lucas recalled, disappointingly mundane:

In the afteryears, even the Fuhrer's orders were duly to appear. But meanwhile here lay a pile of dull, disjointed, and enigmatic scraps, all about the weather, or the petty affairs of a Luftwaffe headquarters no one had heard of, or trifles of Wehrkreise[83] business; the whole sprinkled with terms no dictionary knew, and abbreviations of which our only guide, a small War Office list, proved often completely innocent. Very small beer, in fact, and full of foreign bodies.[84]

Hut 3, where the translating was done, was right next to Hut 6, where Enigma was deciphered. Ralph Bennett explained how the two huts corresponded in the most low-tech way imaginable: 'They were linked by a small square wooden tunnel through which a pile of currently available decodes were pushed, so I remember by a broom handle, in a cardboard box, so primitive were things in those days.'[85]

Michael Smith in *Station X* described how the work of Hut 3 was organised:

The messages arrived from Hut 6 in batches of between fifteen and twenty and were immediately sorted into different degrees of urgency by the Watch number 1...The rest of the watch dealt with piles in order of priority. They first attempted to 'emend' them, filling in any gaps left because of radio interference or garbled letters, a process that, like much of the code-breaking was not unlike solving a crossword puzzle. They then wrote out chits containing intelligence reports, always working from the original German rather than translating it first, in order to guard against the introduction of errors.[86]

John Prestwich, historian, friend and colleague of Humphry's inside Hut 3, related how the six or seven members of each watch would work eight-hour shifts. The watch would sit in a half-circle round a horseshoe-shaped table, with the watch leader, known as Number One, in the middle. Messages came round on trays, like old-fashioned telegrams. Once they had finished working on their translations, they were placed in a basket. Number One would pass the translations on to the military or the Air Adviser, who sat at the next table in the crowded watch-room. The adviser would decide who needed to be notified about the intelligence received. At the start of the war, those who received the translations were not supposed to know they had come from internal British intelligence. To keep the number of people who knew Enigma had been broken to a minimum, the translated messages were presented as

MI6 field agents' reports.[87] As Ron Gray, another Hut 3 veteran and a friend of Humphry's, explained, he and the others had to write the messages to give the impression they had come from an imaginary British spy within Germany. 'We would put "source interrupted" on the translations,' Gray said. 'It was very important that those who received the messages didn't know where they had really come from.'[88] If anyone ever asked what he was doing as he sat on the bus on the way into Bletchley, Ron Gray was told to say he was looking after ration books. 'If the Germans had any spies in Buckinghamshire, they would have known something was up – all those buses going into Bletchley at one time,' Ron told me. Large numbers of staff were billeted in villages outside Bletchley – the place was run on a rota system with three eight-hour shifts a day, so the influx of buses at the point the shifts changed would have given a clue to anyone watching for signs of unusual activity. But the Germans had no idea that Bletchley existed, and believed Engima was unbreakable.

Number One on Humphry's watch was his friend Bob Marshall, a *wunderkind* German scholar from Corpus Christi College, Cambridge, who started at Bletchley aged only 21. Humphry was a relatively old man at 32. Bob Marshall's entry in *Who Was Who* has a low-key description of his war years: '1939–1945, Foreign Office temp. appointment'. In fact he was in the Hut 3 hot seat, deciding on the significance of the translations. In September 1942, Molly wrote to her parents about Humphry's work.

> He's been doing Number One man's job for this week, while Number One was away, which meant that instead of getting to bed by quarter to one a.m. as usual, he didn't get to bed until an hour later, and one night not until two hours later. There seems to have been a terrific lot of extra work, as well as someone high up who's been experimenting with methods of work. They apparently aren't all as sensible, those in command, as one would wish. But that's what happens when sheer intellect is necessary, I expect.[89]

The 'terrific lot of extra work' was the preparation for the Battle of El Alamein. When that letter was written, on 26 September 1942, the North Africa campaign was entering its decisive stage. In the sands of Egypt, General Bernard Montgomery and the 8th Army were ranged against the Afrika Corp of Erwin Rommel, the tactician known as the 'Desert Fox'. North Africa was an important theatre in the war. As Professor Richard Holmes says, 'After the fall of France in 1940, there was nowhere else British and Commonwealth troops could engage the Germans and Italians on land. Egypt sat at the centre of a crucial strategic network that included the Eastern Mediterranean,

Abyssinia, the Middle East and the Suez Canal – there was even talk of an Axis offensive through Egypt linking up with a German drive down from Russia. A German mounted infantryman declared that the objective of the German thrust in South Russia in 1942 was simple: "Down the Caucasus, round the corner, slice the British through the ear, and say to Rommel, Hello General, here we are."'[90]

Montgomery's troops, with the assistance of Bletchley Park, defeated Rommel at the battle of Alam Halfa, triumphing on 7 September. Hut 3 had worked round the clock to translate the wealth of material from Rommel's camp picked up by Ultra. On 23 October, Montgomery would launch the Battle of El Alamein, knowing, thanks to Huts 6 and 3, that Rommel was faced with chronic shortages of food and supplies. No wonder Humphry was late getting to bed. Throughout El Alamein, Humphry was in the Number One chair inside Hut 3, thrown into pole position by the exhaustion of one of his gifted young friends. Molly could see his workload was increasing, as she told the Bennetts:

> Bob Marshall, No 1 man on Humpin's shift, has been ordered three weeks leave by his doctor so as to rest up, and that means Humpin must be No 1 while he is away, a rather bleak outlook, as No 1 is always kept on very late – an hour or so overtime is the usual thing – so it's just as well Humpin has had a good rest. Bob has been so enthusiastic over the job, you see, that being 21 only and a bachelor, he has thrown himself into it so vehemently that he has often given up leave days when not necessary, or gone off hiking when he should have used his next day to catch up on sleep.[91]

The North Africa campaign of 1941–42, which Humphry felt he had observed at first-hand, was the high point for Hut 3. Rommel's battle plans, which he was transmitting to Hitler, were intercepted and translated, enabling Montgomery to know just what the Desert Fox was plotting next. Montgomery knew how many tanks Rommel had, even where they were to be positioned. Hut 3 translated the message from Rommel to Hitler in November 1941 that said 'Panzerarmee ist erschopft'. The Panzer Army was exhausted, and Rommel wanted Hitler's permission to withdraw. Back from Berlin came the response that Rommel should stand his ground. He was to 'show no other road to his troops than the road leading to death or victory'. Yet the hut felt Montgomery didn't use their work as effectively as he could have. There was dismay inside Hut 3 at what Ralph Bennett called Montgomery's painfully slow advance from Alamein to Tripoli, incomprehensible in the light of the mass of Ultra intelligence showing that throughout his retreat Rommel was too weak to withstand serious pressure. He had only eleven tanks on 9 November and still no more than 54 a month later...so that Montgomery might have annihilated him...His delay seemed to cast doubt on the whole point of our work.[92]

Such debates were part of the intensity that was life in Hut 3. Humphry, though, took it all in a collected way, recalled John Prestwich, sitting silently while the others were consumed by the drama of the moment.[93] The Battle of El Alamein secured Egypt and the Middle East, and was a major defeat of the German–Italian Axis. British self-confidence, battered by defeat in France in 1940, and by the collapse in the Far East that was to culminate in the loss of Singapore, was boosted. As Churchill said, Alamein was 'the end of the beginning'. Dorothy Ward wrote to the Bennetts, 'What a wonderful piece of organisation was our combined sweep on North Africa! I am sure both our countries are legitimately proud of it. How I should like to talk more about the War but I gather the censor does not approve!'[94] Not even after the war could Dorothy know of the part her own nephew played in that episode – she died before the wraps came off Bletchley in the seventies.

Almost everyone at Bletchley felt what they were doing was of such importance and excitement that they became completely caught up in it. For John Prestwich, Ron Gray and the others, this was a cause. Ron Gray felt at last he could play a part in defeating Hitler; not Humphry, whose ambivalence to the war extended to the work of Bletchley. He was a detached observer, without the sense of mission that drove the others. Prestwich described him as a reassuring, calm presence in the otherwise excitable and stressful atmosphere of Hut 3. While the others were biting their nails, waiting for the latest intercept from Rommel's camp, Humphry would get out his sketch pad and pass the time drawing his colleagues. Even at critical times, he never got excited. After a day's leave, John Prestwich would avidly read all the translations of the intercepts to see what had been happening. Humphry treated Bletchley as a necessary day job that he carried out as a professional German academic rather than a committed partisan. As the other German scholars gathered round and scratched their heads, working out how to phrase the material the code-crackers had intercepted, Humphry would observe, 'That's not how Goethe would have put it.'[95] Gray recalls that Humphry very quiet, noticeable only because he was a stickler for detail, frequently getting up to check a card index of German military technical terms. He was expert at picking up on the literary references in the Germans' messages and codes. The exact flavour of a German word was always important. As William Millward wrote in *Life in and out of Hut 3*,

> Strength and stock returns, especially from North Africa, often finished with the statement that the situation was *untragbar*. Literally the word meant 'unbearable'; we translated it as 'intolerable.' Both renderings are too strong. The weight of this German word is probably best caught by 'unacceptable', but of course this changes the metaphor.[96]

Carefully choosing the precise meaning of a German word was Humphry's forte.

Life at Bletchley had its compensations. There were plenty of attractive young women in Hut 3, working assiduously at keeping an index of all the translations. John Prestwich described them as 'a charming, debby lot, supposed to be secure because they were the daughters of admirals. They knew German because of ski-ing in Austria.'[97] Hut 3 sang carols at Christmas, and invited the index girls along to the party afterwards. Edward Thomas, in *Codebreakers*, says the indexers were

> a talented group of loyal and lovely ladies. Mostly Wrens and WAAFs, they were always on duty, keeping a record of every detail that might be needed for reference in solving some future conundrum. Often, with a gentle word, they would guide the harassed watchkeeper to the solution that had been eluding him.[98]

During the Bletchley years, Humphry and Molly moved from Oxfordshire to a Buckinghamshire house called The Haven, in Bow Brickhill, near to Humphry's new 'office'. John Prestwich and his wife boarded with them for a while. John enjoyed the contrast between the boarding-school atmosphere of Bletchley and scenes of family life with the Trevelyans. Molly, whom John admiringly described as a frontierswoman, would bathe the children in a canvas bath on the lawn, which she rigged up even when it was snowing. All the windows at The Haven were flung open all the time, as Molly believed in masses of fresh air. When her mother-in-law Janet was staying one time, snow came in through the open window and settled on her hair – rather than close the window, Humphry draped a shawl round his mother's shoulders.[99]

Molly was told little about the work at Bletchley – Humphry and John didn't give her many clues. She was in the dark, just like all the other Bletchley spouses. When Harry Hinsley addressed a reunion of Bletchley veterans and their partners shortly before the publication of his official history of British intelligence during WW2, the husbands of a number of Wrens told him, 'She never breathed a word to me.'[100] John Prestwich said that what they were doing was so significant that it was too great a responsibility for anyone else to carry – he never told his own wife until long after it was all over. Molly knew they were in intelligence – that much was clear from the way Humphry had been recruited at Cambridge. She found it hard not being able to discuss what was going on: 'Humphry would come home and be a family man, and then he'd go off again to work more shifts. I felt really like a war widow.'[101] Even after the war, although she knew more about what he had been doing at Bletchley, it was still classified and so they didn't talk about it in detail.

While Humphry was translating Rommel's battle plans, laughing occasionally as the Desert Fox's quartermaster complained about the quality of his supplies, Molly's descent into depression was accelerating. In 1942 she became pregnant with her third child. The monotony of caring for toddlers, combined with cleaning, cooking and sharing her house with wartime guests against a backdrop of war and a largely absent husband, all became too much. A move from one cramped cottage in Oxfordshire to another flea-infested one did nothing to help. The strain of a prolonged absence from her family was also taking its toll – she hadn't seen her parents for five years. First her foot and then her finger became poisoned, and she was sent to a nursing home. She wrote to her parents

> It's been quite a year now that I've felt myself getting more and more frayed – so I haven't always been as fair and as patient as I should have been. However, if we just hold on for a bit, I'll soon get on my feet again. Everyone is so kind and eager to help … I've only been in bed for a day and a half, but already I feel calmer, and my finger is beginning to do the things it should.[102]

After the nursing home, Molly went to recuperate with her in-laws at the Master's Lodge. No cooking, no cleaning – and Janet was there to help with the children. From these peaceful surroundings she wrote,

> Not much to say at present. Hope some day to have some other interest than house and children – when I see so many women being very important in war work, I find it very difficult to be content. But then I realise that I've no special knowledge of anything, and what I could do would be very little use unless I could give full-time to it. I guess I'd better try to knit or

sew...It's disheartening to have as untrained a mind as mine is, and I'm always ashamed to discover how little I've exercised it.[103]

From Trinity, the family moved into a new house close to Bletchley, during the April of 1942. Immediately Molly began to feel better. Rose Cottage in Oxfordshire had been isolated, cramped, dingy, and only deepened her depression. There she found it difficult to find reliable domestic help, and had to do all the chores herself. Now help was at hand, in the form of a teenager. 'The nice little girl, Doris West, who is working here, is proving a jewel! She does all the cleaning and washing up, and well too, though she's only fourteen years old. She loves children, and is very good with Jane and Maymay.[104] I expect before long she will take them out for walks in the afternoon.'[105]

At the same time, G.M. was writing to 'Dear Bennett' with his analysis of Molly's depression:

> I think soon you may feel comfortable about Molly and her children. She had overdone herself in trying to run the establishment without a servant. But since then both she and the babies have had some very happy and quiet weeks here, properly looked after, and she got, I believe, quite well again. Now she is resuming life again under much more satisfactory conditions, in a nice home near H's new work, with a little servant girl who (so far) proves satisfactory...[106]

Dorothy Ward also attributed Molly's bleak period to the lack of proper help. As she wrote to Mrs Bennett,

> Of course between you and me, I never cease regretting that she had not had, all the last two years, one adult resident maid, either a nurse, who would undertake the children entirely, or a 'cook-general', whichever she preferred, but at any rate one full-time person so that Molly herself could be much more free: but somehow she has never wanted to do this...It seems almost as if she were frightened of English servants – I'm so sorry about this as really you can still get very nice ones! Altho' just now, in the middle of the War, of course it is very difficult to get servants.[107]

After the war, Humphry, the reluctant academic, returned to Cambridge, where he taught German for a year at King's before his election to a fellowship in August 1947. This achievement could well have owed something to the status of Humphry's father. G.M. Trevelyan, Master of Trinity as well as historian of England, loomed large over the Cambridge scene in those days.

Connections spoke volumes in that era, and Humphry belonged to a family with a fine history and tradition of involvement with Cambridge. Unlike his ancestors, he only ever wrote one book, *Goethe and the Greeks*. In his King's obituary, Humphry was described as

> a competent University Lecturer and Director of Studies in the College. He taught individuals sympathetically, but in many ways he was a most undonnish academic. He had little belief in the value of examinations and consistently questioned the existence of any connection between intellectual ability and personality and character. Music apart, he remained by choice outside the closed and rather parochial circle of University life.

Off to tea with the Master. Humphry Trevelyan, his wife Molly, and their children Tom, Harriet, George and Humphry Junior, Trinity College, Cambridge, 1948. Courtesy of George Trevelyan.

He would not have thanked anyone who labelled him an intellectual, nor did he at any time in his life confine his acquaintanceship to them: and anything which savoured of intellectual arrogance he viewed with profound distaste.[108]

Ron Gray, who admired Humphry's gifts greatly, nevertheless concluded that he lacked ambition. Yet he was a considerable talent. In the Goethe year, 1949, he contributed an important study of 'Goethe as thinker' to a volume of essays. Verse translation interested him enormously. His rendering of Schubert's *opera buffa The Conspirators* was admired. 'What he could have done in this field,' wrote Professor L.W. Forster,

> can be seen from his verse rendering of Kleist's *Penthesilea*, which appeared in 1957 in an American collection...This very difficult and disquieting play is a hard task for any translator, but Trevelyan surmounted it with great verve and produced an admirable rendering – the first in English. The play raises in extreme form the problems of the relation between the Greek and the modern spirit which had occupied him throughout his professional life.[109]

Just as at Bletchley, in college Humphry rarely spoke. He spent his time at meetings making careful pencil drawings of his colleagues, and did the same during Cambridge University Musical Society rehearsals. Godfrey Curtis, a fellow tenor, found Humphry had an unassuming wit and made droll doodlings in the flyleaves of music scores. He loved to sing, enjoying madrigals and rounds with his five children. He and George Barker founded the Cambridge Opera da Camera, financed partly by the East of England Arts and underwritten by Humphry. This worked on the principle that a worthy company including artists such as Eric Shilling and Miles Malleson could work with amateur talents to raise money for charity. Operas such as *Il Seraglio* and plays including Vanbrough's *The Relapse* were performed at stately homes from Blenheim Palace to Audley End, raising thousands of pounds for cancer research.

Humphry's enthusiasms were wide-ranging – music and parlour games, mountains and sailing, woodcarving and watercolours. He was interested in the fun to be had out of life, rather than the activities that would bring him status. He was also very generous with his wealth. He and Molly helped Jewish refugees from Germany who stayed at their Cambridge home, Gazeley, and supported struggling artists. Godfrey Curtis recalls the couple's informal philanthropy:

> Together with Molly, and sometimes independently, they supported to a greater or lesser extent several 'lame ducks' who had the good fortune

to be befriended by them, setting them up in cottages and other accommodation, often at nominal rents, and ignoring in several cases the stigma which was at that time attached to single parents. Many of these people were artists who went on to produce significant work.

On Sundays, Molly and Humphry had an open house, and cooked lunch for whoever might turn up. Many Cambridge students and friends remember these meals with warmth. Ron Gray and his family came to lunch Sunday after Sunday, and enjoyed many a madrigal evening. Ron, who had a difficult time in the immediate post-war years, felt he owed much to Molly and Humphry's kindness and generosity.

Friends recall Humphry as a gracious, if eccentric, host. During the Christmas of 1962, when a bigger-than-expected party at Hallington caused a run on the wineglasses, he provided jam jars and flower vases instead. That was a severe and snowy winter, and the guests were snowed in for days. Humphry, according to Godfrey Curtis, remained unflappable, coping 'with a dreadfully ancient and potentially disastrous heating system (held together predominantly with clay) with all the patience and manner of a doctor, as well as arranging the collection of milk from the farm by sleigh and ski and organising hunting parties to shoot for the pot'.[110] Humphry was extremely patient. On one occasion, he returned from a holiday to find his three teenage sons had been go-carting round the garden at Gazeley. The result was a wide and deeply rutted track around the lawn – a sight which was truly devastating. 'Ah well,' said Humphry mildly, after several long moments of silent contemplation, 'let's go and make some tea.'[111]

Managing tenants and estates was another aspect of Trevelyan life that Humphry eschewed. The role of lord of the manor was not one that interested him, despite his enjoyment of country life. He sold Hallington after G.M. died, transferring his allegiance to Molly's collection of country houses, particularly on the island of Arran. Molly had decided on a whim to purchase a row of cottages at Lochranza. Humphry immersed himself in the local island scene, sailing throughout the southern Western Isles in his ten-ton yacht *Jancis* and driving all over Arran in his 1930s banger enjoying the scenery. Godfrey Curtis sailed with him, finding him 'almost unrecognisable then; disciplined and safety conscious and in my memory a seriously professional sailor'.

Consorting with youth and beauty, just like Goethe, was Humphry's private pursuit. He continued to have plenty of female friends, sketching them in Molly's retreats from Wales to Scotland. He doesn't appear to have had a conscience about this – Ron Gray, a dear friend of Molly's as well as

Humphry's who valued the couple's friendship tremendously, wrote a letter telling Humphry he was misbehaving and making Molly unhappy. 'It was a good letter, Ron, but not to worry,'[112] came the reply. Godfrey Curtis remembers the rather crumpled shirts that became Humphry's hallmark: 'He explained to us one day that what with one thing and another Molly had felt he should be responsible for his own laundry!'[113]

Humphry spent much of life absorbed by trying to make sense of an insoluble task – how to be a common man when you have been born into the intellectual aristocracy. He wanted to be ordinary rather than Olympian. His oldest son Tom remembers Humphry asking if he would like to be apprenticed to a garage, instead of going to university to learn Latin or Greek. Tom thought life must surely offer some other choices – he opted to become a doctor. My father, George, was encouraged to go to sea in the merchant navy, rather than study at Oxford, no doubt for the same reasons. He became a civil servant, and was awarded the honour of Companion of the Bath upon his retirement.

After a severe heart attack in 1957, Humphry was supposed to slow up a little. He embraced sailing, exploring the west coast of Scotland in his fleet of boats. After a second heart attack in 1964, he died. Although Humphry benefited from being a Trevelyan, inheriting the lifestyle and the smoothed path into academic life, it seems he never enjoyed it as his ancestors had done. He did not wish to have his path in life set out, and appears to have rejected the values of his father, grandfather and great-grandfather completely. Although very able, he never wanted to make an impression on the wider world. Instead, whether at Bletchley or King's, he was a diffident observer. Gentle, contemplative and modest, he was most unlike previous generations. He rejected the strict morals of his father, preferring Goethe as a role model. Others were impressed by his family heritage – Ron Gray said he had never met anyone quite like Humphry before, surrounded by ancient books, exuding a low-key but unmistakable charisma. But Humphry was not impressed by his lineage, seeing it as a burden that left him struggling to relate to more ordinary people.

EPILOGUE

With the death of George Macaulay Trevelyan in 1962, the family began to slip gently back into relative obscurity. The tradition of excellence and hyper-achievement petered out, as the Trevelyans became as ordinary as most others in late-twentieth-century middle-class Britain. They had mortgages and credit cards, not allowances, got divorced rather than suffering in silence, and holidayed in Majorca not Northumberland. A terraced Victorian house, not a stately home, was the abode of necessity. Outdoor pursuits were still popular with Trevelyans, but not those, like shooting, which required a private estate. Humphry would have been pleased, although Macaulay, Charles Edward, George Otto and George Macaulay would have mourned the family's lost status. Charles Philips, the socialist, could only have been sanguine about the end of elitism, although I'm sure he would have minded terribly about his descendants losing their shooting rights at Wallington. After the Second World War, the rise of the meritocracy in Britain challenged the position of established families. The Butler Education Act created opportunities for those who previously had none. Even the gates of Trinity creaked open somewhat to allow in a slightly wider intake. And the family money ran out.

This combination of quiet social revolution and lack of funds meant the Trevelyans had to fend for themselves in the world, deprived of the cushions of connections and cash. Whereas once Charles Edward could take George Otto off to India with him for a year, no questions asked, and in turn George Otto could write letters demanding to know why Charles Philips was not in government, now nepotism and string-pulling were less effective. The playing field levelled a little. While G.M. Trevelyan's work was the result of what G.M. Young called 'the fruit of leisure, of freedom, of independence', the money that supported such a fortunate lifestyle had run dry by the sixties. G.M. left only a modest £157,000 to his two children, while his brother

Charles only had £95,000 to go round six of his offspring. Compare that to the £500,000 George Otto left his three sons in 1928. Future generations of Trevelyans were going to have to go out and earn a living on their merits, without the prop of a substantial private income.

As the privileges of the Trevelyans and so many others slipped away, so did the assumptions that had underpinned England's ruling class. The social assurance that led George Otto and his sons to believe one was born to rule, or at least play an important part, was undermined. David Cannadine wrote that G.M. Trevelyan 'never applied for a job he did not get: indeed, with the exception of his Trinity fellowship, he never applied for a job at all'.[1] Not so for his descendants. Noel Annan's portrait of English intellectuals between the world wars and their common values could never be written now. Annan asked rhetorically, 'How did one get accepted as a member of Our Age? In the same way that most people have always got accepted – by ability, by family connections and knowing someone.'[2] That cohesive, cosy world has vanished.

The homes that provided the setting for the Trevelyans' leisured lifestyle of writing, shooting and public affairs have gone too: Wallington to the National Trust, Welcombe to hotel owners, while Hallington is now a bed and breakfast. Modern historians, not to mention family descendants, have less gracious settings. As Stefan Collini wrote after a visit to Wallington,

> It is a pretty safe bet that the National Trust will never attempt to acquire the graceless 1950s bungalow on the edge of the Shirley Hills beyond Croydon where I grew up. Nor can I believe that some latter-day Pevsner will ever feel obliged to catalogue its few distinctive features (large 'lounge' giving on to pretentiously balustraded 'terrace').[3]

Both the means and the bricks and mortar that had sustained the old ways disappeared after the Second World War. The grammar schools created a new class of achievers, and so the intellectual elite of yesteryear had to adapt. The aristocracy of talent became a meritocracy of talent. Virtually all the families listed by Noel Annan in his essay on the intellectual aristocracy suffered a similar decline in their standing and influence. The Wedgwoods, the Darwins and so on also faded from the scene. Noel Annan wrote, 'Aristocracies which seem to be secure can vanish overnight if society rejects the credentials by which they have established themselves or if they lose self confidence; and in the 1960s some of their children who might have been expected to excel abandoned the goal of a fellowship and with a sigh of relief dropped out.'[4]

Some did drop out in the next generation. This tendency towards non-conformism had begun with Robert Calverley Trevelyan, brother of Charles Philips and George Macaulay. Described by one relative as 'a child of nature',[5] Bob was a Georgian poet and Greek scholar on the fringes of the Bloomsbury group. A friend of E.M. Forster, their joint explorations inspired *A Passage to India*. Intelligent, but with an untidy mind, Bob was scruffy and eccentric, given to bathing in the nude in full view of passers-by. Leonard Woolf described how in conversation Bob's tongue would suddenly break loose and soar away into an argument or description, slightly absurd, irrelevant, fantastic, not entirely under his control, but extraordinarily funny.[6] Bob's friends saw him as unworldly, and devoted to nature and poetry. Virginia Woolf, after receiving a Horatian ode from Bob, wrote back, 'I wish you would sometimes write about Monday and Tuesday.'[7] Max Beerbohm wrote that Bob reminded him of the scholar gipsy. 'Even among the books in his fine and beloved library, he seemed to be a man of the woodland; and out among the hills and the dales he was yet unmistakenly a bookman.'[8] Bob was part of the American art critic Bernard Berenson's circle, and was a regular at Berenson's splendid Italian villa I Tatti, a mecca for European and American intellectuals. After Bob's death, Berenson wrote, 'Trevy played a great part in our lives for fully fifty years. How often I recall his ways, his almost romantic devotion to literature, his whims, his rages, his tender affectionateness. No other man counted so much and emerges in my recollections as he does.'[9]

Bob's only surviving child, Julian, was a modernist painter and printmaker, one of the first British surrealists. Tall, long-faced and handsome, Julian's sweetness of manner disguised a mercurial temperament.[10] He studied printmaking in Paris under Stanley William Haytner, working alongside Joan Miro, Max Ernst, and Pablo Picasso. Julian's paintings, often inspired by the Thames – which he could see from the Hammersmith home he shared with his second wife, the artist Mary Fedden – were judged to be distinguished. He adopted 'a deliberately gauche painterly manner and a vehement colourism … his work was distinguished always by an authentic innocence of eye, and a spirit by turns passionate, ironic and humorous. A brilliantly inventive etcher, his linear technique and imaginative texturing … established him as one of the finest printmakers of his generation.'[11]

The more unconventional traits represented by Julian's father Bob were writ large in two of Charles Philip's children, Kitty and George Lowthian. Kitty's life was dominated by spiritual experiences. She was interested in the teachings of Rudolf Steiner, and eventually became a member of a movement known as Subud, which taught its followers about spiritual death and rebirth. George Lowthian, deprived of Wallington, found a home in the eighteenth-century mansion of Attingham Park, where he was warden of the Shropshire adult college. Some students got the impression that Attingham was George's ancestral home. He was an inspired appointment – Attingham became a centre for music-making, drama and film appreciation, and proved influential in the development of social history, industrial archaeology and garden history.[12] However, George's courses, such as 'Man know thyself', and 'Towards light and love', embarrassed the governing body. When George retired, he became a prophet among 'New Age' thinkers. He set up the Wrekin Trust to further his ideas on spiritual regeneration, and published a succession of books, including a trilogy entitled *The Aquarian Redemption*.

So, while some Trevelyans embraced alternative lifestyles, surely a reaction against their eminent ancestors, there was one more member of what could be described as the ruling class. Sir Humphrey, later Lord Trevelyan, was exceptional in the approved G.M. style, regarded as the most outstanding diplomat of his generation. He joined the Indian civil service in 1929, eventually becoming ambassador to Moscow, and on his eventual retirement, Chairman of the Trustees of the British Museum. The Labour Foreign Secretary George Brown thought so highly of Humphrey, who was ambassador to Egypt at the time of the Suez Crisis, that he persuaded him to come out of retirement to handle the British withdrawal from Aden. Humphrey agreed, although 'I had no illusions that it would be an ungrateful and prickly task'.[13] Humphrey's sister Mary was the founder of the International Student's House in London and a devoted friend of T.S. Eliot's. Their brother John was the film censor in the 1970s.

Humphrey was the last star turn to date. But the tradition of public service and authorship still survives. My cousin Raleigh Trevelyan has written widely about the family and his own wartime experience at Anzio. My father's generation of Trevelyans includes doctors, civil servants, architects, academics and film-makers. Those I knew in that group distanced their own lives from the supposed Trevelyan legacy. As a child growing up in the 1970s, I knew next to nothing about the family history. No one mentioned it, or not that I noticed. No reciting Macaulay's *Lays of Ancient Rome* for my siblings and me. We never went to Wallington. As a child of Camden Town in London, I didn't even know where Northumberland was. I was 26 before I even saw Wallington. We did holiday at Robin Ghyll when I was young, but then that was sold to the National Trust too. There was no bust of Macaulay sitting on my non-existent desk – I did all my homework on my bed. All that history and elitism and privilege must have seemed stuffy, unfashionable and irrelevant to the sixties generation. My maternal grandmother was thrilled when her daughter married the grandson of the great historian. But Mum lived in the present, teaching in Ghana, then marching against nuclear weapons and camping at Greenham Common. Despite that, it was my mother's family rather than my father's who impressed upon me the significance of the family name. 'Darling, never forget you have the brains of a Trevelyan,' said my maternal great-aunt frequently. I wondered what she meant. My parents divorced when I was eight, and my father remarried. My stepmother did talk about the Trevelyans, usually in an attempt to keep her end up. She was always promising to put up a collage of her Yorkshire relatives on the beach next to the statue of Garibaldi on the mantelpiece, to show that her family had a history too. I still didn't know who Garibaldi was, let alone that a relative had written about him. Only when I was studying A-level history at school did the penny drop.

As I got older, it all began to fall into place. Working as a BBC correspondent, people that I met expected me to know about the family history. MPs and peers would ask where I fitted in. So I had to mug up, in order to save face. Then I became genuinely interested. Journalism is the first draft of history, as Philip Graham memorably said, so now I like to think that my interest in public affairs and in writing is in some way consistent with the family's past. Rather like Macaulay, George Otto and George Macaulay, I have indulgently written about my relatives. But, unlike my forefathers, I have come to this book as an outsider, despite my blood relationship to those inside the covers.

So my cast of characters has vanished, like George Macaulay's ghosts at cockcrow. Their trace can still be seen – Wallington stands as a memorial to Charles Philips's vision of socialism, Charles Edward's values inform the civil service even now, and George Macaulay is still remembered for his style of literary history. They were the product of their altruistic times, and their aspirations were noble even if they didn't always quite live up to them. George Macaulay, as usual, expressed the family's modus vivendi best: 'We are all moles – though of course we must all go on driving our little tunnels as straight as we can and with all our strength, until the mole-catcher come. But if we are moles in vision, the best of us become Gods in spirit.'[14]

'Are they a sect, these Trevelyans, like the Wesleyans?' The three brothers, Charles, Robert and George, on a shoot at Wallington after the Second World War. Courtesy of the Trustees of the Trevelyan family papers.

NOTES

Introduction

1 Leonard Woolf, Foreword to Charles Philips Trevelyan's *Letters from North America and the Pacific.*
2 Broadcast by the author, *People and Politics,* BBC World Service Radio, 22 February 2002.
3 Humphrey Trevelyan, *Public and Private,* p. 128.
4 Leonard Woolf, Foreword to Charles Philips Trevelyan's *Letters from North America and the Pacific.*
5 Virginia Woolf, *Night and Day,* p. 33.
6 *Times Literary Supplement,* 23 August 1928.
7 Trevelyan Family Papers, Newcastle University, CPT 237 (3), letter from GMT to CPT 23 December 1905.

Chapter 1

1 A.N. Wilson, *The Victorians,* p. 1.
2 Tailfeathers.
3 Henry VI.
4 G.M. Trevelyan, *Sir George Otto Trevelyan, A Memoir,* p. 2.
5 Humphrey Trevelyan, *Public and Private.*
6 G.M. Trevelyan, *Sir George Otto Trevelyan, A Memoir,* p. 2.
7 Humphrey Trevelyan, *Public and Private,* p. 110.
8 James Lees-Milne, *People and Places,* p. 150.
9 As related in a letter from George Otto Trevelyan to Theodore Roosevelt, 8 December 1904, Joseph Bishop, *Theodore Roosevelt And His Time,* vol. II, p. 145.
10 James Lees-Milne, *People and Places,* p. 151.
11 Fenwick.
12 Raleigh Trevelyan, *Wallington,* p. 9.
13 Edward Keith, *Memories of Wallington,* p. 48.
14 Raleigh Trevelyan, *Wallington,* p. 10.
15 Edward Keith, *Memories of Wallington,* p. 49.
16 Raleigh Trevelyan, *Wallington,* p. 18.
17 Humphrey Trevelyan, *Public and Private,* p. 110.
18 Humphrey Trevelyan, *Public and Private,* p. 111.

19   Humphrey Trevelyan, *Public and Private*, p.110.
20   James Lees-Milne, *People and Places*, p.152.
21   Raleigh Trevelyan, *A Pre-Raphaelite Circle*, p.14.
22   James Lees-Milne, *People and Places*, p.152.
23   Raleigh Trevelyan, *Wallington*, p.25.
24   James Lees-Milne, *People and Places*, p.154.
25   Edward Keith, *Memories of Wallington*, p.80.
26   Raleigh Trevelyan, *Wallington*, p.25.
27   Raleigh Trevelyan, *Wallington*, p.29.
28   David Cannadine, *G.M. Trevelyan: A Life in History*, p.11.
29   Robin Ironside, 'Pre-Raphaelite painters at Wallington', *Architectural Review*, December 1942.
30   Raleigh Trevelyan, *Wallington*, p.26.
31   Raleigh Trevelyan, *A Pre-Raphaelite Circle*, p.206.
32   Edward Keith, *Memories of Wallington*, p.41.
33   David Cannadine, *The Decline and Fall of the British Aristocracy.*
34   The Bequest of Wallington to the National Trust, broadcast by Sir Charles Trevelyan, 23 March 1937.
35   Noel Annan, *The Dons*, p.11.
36   David Cannadine, *G.M. Trevelyan: A Life in History*, p.8.
37   H.G. Wells, *The New Machiavelli*, p.40.
38   A.N. Wilson, *The Victorians*, p.1.

CHAPTER 2

1   G.M. Trevelyan, *Sir George Otto Trevelyan, A Memoir*, p.4.
2   Anthony Trollope, *The Three Clerks*, p.58.
3   Broadcast by the author, *People and Politics*, BBC World Service Radio, 22 February 2002.
4   Simon Schama, *A History of Britain*, vol.III, p.210.
5   Simon Schama, *A History of Britain*, vol.III, p.210.
6   Robin Haines, *Charles Trevelyan and the Great Irish Famine*, p.34.
7   Humphrey Trevelyan, *Public and Private*, p.113.
8   Trevelyan family papers, Newcastle University, CET 89.
9   Trevelyan family papers, Newcastle University, CET 89.
10   Humphrey Trevelyan, *The India We Left*, p.39.
11   George Otto Trevelyan, *Life and Letters of Lord Macaulay*, p.278.
12   John Clive, 'Macaulay, the Shaping of the Historian', p.317.
13   Trevelyan family papers, Newcastle University, CET 89.
14   Humphrey Trevelyan, *Public and Private*, p.114.
15   George Otto Trevelyan, *Life and Letters of Lord Macaulay*, p.278.
16   Simon Schama, *A History of Britain*, vol.III, p.201.
17   John Clive, 'Macaulay, the Shaping of the Historian', p.319.
18   John Clive, 'Macaulay, the Shaping of the Historian', p.361.
19   John Clive, 'Macaulay, the Shaping of the Historian', p.361.
20   Thomas Babington Macaulay, *Indian Education*, 1835. Also John Clive, 'Macaulay, the Shaping of the Historian', p.372.
21   Thomas Babington Macaulay, *Indian Education*, 1835. Also John Clive, 'Macaulay, the Shaping of the Historian', p.372.

22   Letter to Macaulay, 30 September 1834, Trevelyan family papers, Newcastle University, CET 8.
23   'A Treatise on the means of communicating the learning and civilisation of India to Europe', Trevelyan family papers, Newcastle University, CET 93.
24   Simon Schama, *A History of Britain*, vol. III, p. 214.
25   John Clive, 'Macaulay, the Shaping of the Historian', p. 260.
26   Lady Hannah Trevelyan, *Reminiscences*, Trinity MSS 59. John Clive, 'Macaulay, the Shaping of the Historian', p. 279.
27   Macaulay to Hannah, 21 August 1833, Trinity College correspondence. John Clive, 'Macaulay, the Shaping of the Historian', p. 279.
28   Hannah to Fanny Macaulay, February 1834, Huntington MSS. John Clive, 'Macaulay, the Shaping of the Historian', p. 284.
29   Margaret to Hannah, 28 May 1834, Huntington MSS. John Clive. 'Macaulay, the Shaping of the Historian', p. 282.
30   Hannah to Fanny Macaulay, 1834, Huntington MSS. John Clive, 'Macaulay, the Shaping of the Historian', p. 284.
31   George Otto Trevelyan, *Life and Letters of Lord Macaulay*, p. 278.
32   George Otto Trevelyan, *Life and Letters of Lord Macaulay*, vol. I, p. 357.
33   Nancy was Macaulay's nickname for Hannah.
34   G.M. Trevelyan, *Sir George Otto Trevelyan, A Memoir*, p. 9.
35   Humphrey Trevelyan, *The India We Left*, p. 47.
36   G.M. Trevelyan, *Sir George Otto Trevelyan, A Memoir*, p. 10.
37   Letter from G.M.T. to his brother Robert Calverley Trevelyan, 20 November 1928, from RCT papers, held at Trinity College Library, Cambridge. Peter Raina, *G.M. Trevelyan: A Portrait in Letters*, p. 110.
38   S.C. Roberts, *Adventures with Authors*, p. 121.
39   John Clive, 'Macaulay, the Shaping of the Historian', p. 286.
40   Lady Hannah Trevelyan, 'Reminiscences', 63, Trinity MSS. John Clive, 'Macaulay, the Shaping of the Historian', p. 287.
41   John Clive, 'Macaulay, the Shaping of the Historian', p. 288.
42   Macaulay to Frances Macaulay, 6 July 1844, Pinney, *Letters of Thomas Babington Macaulay*, vol. IV, p. 204.
43   G.M. Trevelyan, *Sir George Otto Trevelyan, A Memoir*, p. 11.
44   Jennifer Hart, 'Sir Charles Trevelyan at the Treasury', *English Historical Review*, vol. 75, 1960.
45   Cecil Woodham-Smith, *The Great Hunger: Ireland 1845–1849*, p. 410.
46   Robert Kee, *Ireland, A History*, p. 8.
47   Robin Haines, *Charles Trevelyan and the Great Irish Famine*, p. 2.
48   Robert Peel to Sir James Graham, Home Secretary, 15 October 1843, from the Graham Papers. Cecil Woodham-Smith, *The Great Hunger: Ireland 1845–1849*, p. 60.
49   Peter Hennessy, *Whitehall*, p. 33.
50   Chapman and Greenway, *The Dynamics of Administrative Reform*, p. 23. Peter Hennessy, *Whitehall*, p. 32.
51   Charles Trevelyan to Routh, 23 June 1846. Cecil Woodham-Smith, *The Great Hunger: Ireland 1845–1849*, p. 86.
52   Charles Trevelyan to Routh, 6 July 1846. Cecil Woodham-Smith, *The Great Hunger: Ireland 1845–1849*, p. 87.
53   Cecil Woodham-Smith, *The Great Hunger: Ireland 1845–1849*, p. 87.
54   CET to Routh. Cecil Woodham-Smith, *The Great Hunger: Ireland 1845–1849*, p. 89.
55   CET to Routh. Cecil Woodham-Smith, *The Great Hunger: Ireland 1845–1849*, p. 89.

56   CET to Jones, 21 September 1846. Robin Haines, *Charles Trevelyan and the Great Irish Famine*, p.249.
57   Cecil Woodham-Smith, *The Great Hunger: Ireland 1845–1849*, p.142.
58   CET to Sir C.Wade, 10 October 1846. Robin Haines, *Charles Trevelyan and the Great Irish Famine*, p.253.
59   CET to Labouchere 15 December 1846. Robin Haines, *Charles Trevelyan and the Great Irish Famine*, p.266.
60   Cecil Woodham-Smith, *The Great Hunger: Ireland 1845–1849*, p.171.
61   CET to Routh, 18 January 1847. Cecil Woodham-Smith, *The Great Hunger: Ireland 1845–1849*, p.171.
62   CET to Colonel Douglas, Relief Inspector, 1 February 1847. Cecil Woodham-Smith, *The Great Hunger: Ireland 1845–1849*, p.177.
63   CET to Monteagle, 9 October 1846, CET 18. Robin Haines, *Charles Trevelyan and the Great Irish Famine*, p.5.
64   CET to Monteagle, 9 October 1846, CET 18. Robin Haines, *Charles Trevelyan and the Great Irish Famine*, p.6.
65   CET to Dr Horne, 20 September 1846, CET to Routh, 29 April 1846, CET 18. Robin Haines, *Charles Trevelyan and the Great Irish Famine*, p.4.
66   Cecil Woodham-Smith, *The Great Hunger: Ireland 1845–1849*, p.177.
67   Earl of Clarendon to Lord John Russell, 9 February 1849. Clarendon told Russell he was unable 'to shake Charles Wood and Trevelyan, that the right course was to do nothing for Ireland, and to leave things to the operation of natural causes'. Cecil Woodham-Smith, *The Great Hunger: Ireland 1845–1849*, p.375.
68   Robin Haines, *Charles Trevelyan and the Great Irish Famine*, p.1.
69   Simon Schama, *A History of Britain*, vol.III, p.231.
70   Simon Schama, *A History of Britain*, vol.III, p.232.
71   Robin Haines, *Charles Trevelyan and the Great Irish Famine*, p.544.
72   Treasury Minute, 14 September 1847, Trevelyan family papers, Newcastle University.
73   CET letter to Lord John Russell, 15 August 1848, Trevelyan family papers, Newcastle University.
74   Peter Hennessy, *Whitehall*, p.33.
75   Peter Hennessy, *Whitehall*, p.35.
76   Dr Roseveare, *The Treasury*, pp.165–166. Peter Hennessy, *Whitehall*, p.37.
77   Dr Roseveare, *The Treasury*, pp.168–169. Peter Hennessy, *Whitehall*, p.38.
78   Peter Hennessy, *Whitehall*, p.38.
79   Northcote–Trevelyan report 1854.
80   Peter Hennessy, *Whitehall*, p.42.
81   CET 48, Press cutting, Trevelyan family papers, Newcastle University.
82   *Morning Post*, 26 September 1854, CET 35. Trevelyan family papers, Newcastle University.
83   Lord John Russell to Gladstone, 20 January 1854. Peter Hennessy, *Whitehall*, p.44.
84   Anthony Trollope, *The Three Clerks*, p.59.
85   Raleigh Trevelyan, *The Golden Oriole*, pp.286–287.
86   John Morley, *The Life of William Ewart Gladstone*, vol.1, p.649. Peter Hennessy, *Whitehall*, p.44.
87   Peter Hennessy, *Whitehall*, p.45.
88   Peter Hennessy, *Whitehall*, p.45.
89   CET to Raglan, 13 February 1854. Jennifer Hart, *Trevelyan at the Treasury*, p.103. Peter Hennessy, *Whitehall*, p.45.

90 Jennifer Hart, *Trevelyan at the Treasury*. Peter Hennessy, *Whitehall*, p.45.
91 Peter Hennessy, *Whitehall*, p.46.
92 CET to Gladstone 19 June 1858, CET 80. Trevelyan family papers, Newcastle University.
93 John Clive, 'Macaulay, the Shaping of the Historian', p.409.
94 Raleigh Trevelyan, *The Golden Oriole*, p.319.
95 John Clive, 'Macaulay, the Shaping of the Historian', p.409.
96 Humphrey Trevelyan, *The India We Left*, p.70.
97 G.M. Trevelyan, *Sir George Otto Trevelyan, A Memoir*, p.51 fn.
98 Raleigh Trevelyan, *The Golden Oriole*, p.329.
99 Raleigh Trevelyan, *The Golden Oriole*, p.333.
100 Raleigh Trevelyan, *The Golden Oriole*, p.337.
101 Raleigh Trevelyan, *The Golden Oriole*, p.381.
102 Raleigh Trevelyan, *The Golden Oriole*, p.393.
103 Hansard 3, 11 May 1860, vols 1130–1161. *Dictionary of National Biography*, Sir Charles Edward Trevelyan entry.
104 Raleigh Trevelyan, *The Golden Oriole*, p.394.
105 Raleigh Trevelyan, *The Golden Oriole*, p.395.
106 Raleigh Trevelyan, *The Golden Oriole*, p.395.
107 Raleigh Trevelyan, *The Golden Oriole*, p.396.
108 Raleigh Trevelyan, *The Golden Oriole*, p.409.
109 Raleigh Trevelyan, *The Golden Oriole*, p.411.
110 Raleigh Trevelyan, *The Golden Oriole*, p.431.
111 Raleigh Trevelyan, *The Golden Oriole*, p.436.
112 Raleigh Trevelyan, *The Golden Oriole*, p.438.
113 Raleigh Trevelyan, *The Golden Oriole*, p.439.
114 G.M. Trevelyan, *Sir George Otto Trevelyan, A Memoir*, p.7.
115 Edward Keith, *Memories of Wallington*, p.13.
116 Edward Keith, *Memories of Wallington*, p.21.
117 Humphrey Trevelyan, *Public and Private*, p.120.

CHAPTER 3

1 George Otto Trevelyan, *Life and Letters of Lord Macaulay*.
2 George Otto Trevelyan, *Life and Letters of Lord Macaulay*, p.485.
3 George Otto Trevelyan, *Life and Letters of Lord Macaulay*, p.485.
4 George Otto Trevelyan, *Life and Letters of Lord Macaulay*, p.492.
5 George Otto Trevelyan, *Life and Letters of Lord Macaulay*, p.492.
6 Charley Cropper, a family friend.
7 George Otto Trevelyan, *Life and Letters of Lord Macaulay*, p.493.
8 G.M. Trevelyan, *Sir George Otto Trevelyan, A Memoir*, p.15.
9 Edward Keith, *Memories of Wallington*.
10 G.M. Trevelyan, *Sir George Otto Trevelyan, A Memoir*, p.30.
11 G.M. Trevelyan, *Sir George Otto Trevelyan, A Memoir*, p.20.
12 G.M. Trevelyan, *Sir George Otto Trevelyan, A Memoir*, p.21.
13 G.M. Trevelyan, *Sir George Otto Trevelyan, A Memoir*, p.27.
14 G.M. Trevelyan, *Sir George Otto Trevelyan, A Memoir*, p.31.
15 G.M. Trevelyan, *Sir George Otto Trevelyan, A Memoir*, p.33.
16 G.M. Trevelyan, *Sir George Otto Trevelyan, A Memoir*, p.36.

17 G.M. Trevelyan, *Sir George Otto Trevelyan, A Memoir*, p. 37.
18 G.M. Trevelyan, *Sir George Otto Trevelyan, A Memoir*, p. 39.
19 Letter from Thomas Babington Macaulay to George Otto, 24 October 1859. G.M. Trevelyan, *Sir George Otto Trevelyan, A Memoir*, p. 43.
20 G.M. Trevelyan, *Sir George Otto Trevelyan, A Memoir*, p. 46.
21 George Otto Trevelyan, *Life and Letters of Lord Macaulay*, p. 686.
22 George Otto Trevelyan, *Life and Letters of Lord Macaulay*, p. 687.
23 G.M. Trevelyan, *Sir George Otto Trevelyan, A Memoir*, p. 39.
24 H.A.L. Fisher, Raleigh Lecture on History, 1928. Humphrey Trevelyan, *Public and Private*, p. 126.
25 G.M. Trevelyan, *Sir George Otto Trevelyan, A Memoir*, p. 52.
26 G.M. Trevelyan, *Sir George Otto Trevelyan, A Memoir*, p. 53.
27 G.M. Trevelyan, *Sir George Otto Trevelyan, A Memoir*, p. 56.
28 G.M. Trevelyan, *Sir George Otto Trevelyan, A Memoir*, p. 62.
29 Raleigh Trevelyan, *The Golden Oriole*, p. 411.
30 Sir William Denison.
31 Raleigh Trevelyan, *The Golden Oriole*, p. 410.
32 George Otto Trevelyan, *The Competition Wallah*.
33 George Otto Trevelyan, *The Competition Wallah*.
34 George Otto Trevelyan, *The Competition Wallah*.
35 GOT to Pauline Trevelyan 16 February 1863. Raleigh Trevelyan, *The Golden Oriole*, p. 413.
36 George Otto Trevelyan, *The Competition Wallah*.
37 George Otto Trevelyan, *The Competition Wallah*.
38 George Otto Trevelyan, *The Competition Wallah*.
39 Preface to George Otto Trevelyan, *The Competition Wallah*, by Martin Bulmer, unpublished.
40 John Clive, 'Peter and the Wallah: from kinsfolk to competition', in John Clive, *Not By Fact Alone: Essays on the Writing and Reading of History*.
41 Introduction to George Otto Trevelyan, *The Competition Wallah*, by Edward Shils: edition never published.
42 G.M. Trevelyan, *Sir George Otto Trevelyan, A Memoir*, p. 66.
43 Raleigh Trevelyan, *The Golden Oriole*, p. 431.
44 *Times Literary Supplement*, 23 August 1928.
45 Raleigh Trevelyan, *A Pre-Raphaelite Circle*, p. 214.
46 Raleigh Trevelyan, *A Pre-Raphaelite Circle*, p. 215.
47 Raleigh Trevelyan, *A Pre-Raphaelite Circle*, p. 215.
48 Broadcast by the author, *People and Politics*, BBC World Service Radio, 22 February 2002.
49 G.M. Trevelyan, *Sir George Otto Trevelyan, A Memoir*, p. 66.
50 George Otto Trevelyan, *Ladies in Parliament*.
51 G.M. Trevelyan, *Sir George Otto Trevelyan, A Memoir*, p. 69.
52 Raleigh Trevelyan, *A Pre-Raphaelite Circle*, p. 210.
53 G.M. Trevelyan, *Sir George Otto Trevelyan, A Memoir*, p. 72.
54 Raleigh Trevelyan, *A Pre-Raphaelite Circle*, p. 211.
55 G.M. Trevelyan, *Sir George Otto Trevelyan, A Memoir*, p. 72.
56 G.M. Trevelyan, *Sir George Otto Trevelyan, A Memoir*, p. 69.
57 George Otto Trevelyan, 'Recollections of Disraeli', *Saturday Review*. G.M. Trevelyan, *Sir George Otto Trevelyan, A Memoir*, p. 76.
58 George Otto Trevelyan, 'Recollections of Disraeli', *Saturday Review*. G.M. Trevelyan, *Sir George Otto Trevelyan, A Memoir*, p. 77.

59 GOT to Lady Desborough, 24 June 1924, published in *The Times.* G.M. Trevelyan, *Sir George Otto Trevelyan, A Memoir,* pp. 80–85.
60 G.M. Trevelyan, *Sir George Otto Trevelyan, A Memoir,* p. 85.
61 G.M. Trevelyan, *Sir George Otto Trevelyan, A Memoir,* p. 86.
62 *Clarissa* is an eighteenth-century novel by Samuel Richardson – the heroine, Clarissa Harlowe, is an heiress whose parents try to force her into a marriage she does not want.
63 G.M. Trevelyan, *Sir George Otto Trevelyan, A Memoir,* p. 86.
64 G.M. Trevelyan, *Sir George Otto Trevelyan, A Memoir,* p. 86.
65 G.M. Trevelyan, *Sir George Otto Trevelyan, A Memoir,* p. 87.
66 G.M. Trevelyan, *An Autobiography and Other Essays,* p. 6.
67 Edward Keith, *Memories of Wallington,* p. 67.
68 Edward Keith, *Memories of Wallington,* p. 67.
69 *Vanity Fair,* 2 August 1873.
70 GOT to Wilson, 29 June 1870. G.M. Trevelyan, *Sir George Otto Trevelyan, A Memoir,* p. 91.
71 GOT to Gladstone, 21 June 1870. Trevelyan family papers, Newcastle University.
72 G.M. Trevelyan, *Sir George Otto Trevelyan, A Memoir,* p. 92.
73 G.M. Trevelyan, *Sir George Otto Trevelyan, A Memoir,* p. 92.
74 Hansard 3, vol. 225, 7 July 1875, column 1096. *Dictionary of National Biography,* Sir George Otto Trevelyan entry.
75 G.M. Trevelyan, *Sir George Otto Trevelyan, A Memoir,* p. 92.
76 G.M. Trevelyan, *Sir George Otto Trevelyan, A Memoir,* p. 92.
77 G.M. Trevelyan, *Sir George Otto Trevelyan, A Memoir,* p. 97.
78 G.M. Trevelyan, *Sir George Otto Trevelyan, A Memoir,* pp. 96–97.
79 G.M. Trevelyan, *Sir George Otto Trevelyan, A Memoir,* p. 101.
80 G.M. Trevelyan, *Sir George Otto Trevelyan, A Memoir,* p. 102.
81 *Times Literary Supplement,* 23 August 1928.
82 Broadcast by the author, *People and Politics,* BBC World Service Radio, 22 February 2002.
83 Gladstone to GOT, 28 November 1880. Trevelyan family papers, Newcastle University.
84 GOT to Gladstone, 29 November 1880. Trevelyan family papers, Newcastle University.
85 GOT to CET, 29 November 1880. Trevelyan family papers, Newcastle University.
86 G.M. Trevelyan, *Sir George Otto Trevelyan, A Memoir,* p. 104.
87 G.M. Trevelyan, *Sir George Otto Trevelyan, A Memoir,* p. 110.
88 *Dictionary of National Biography,* Sir George Otto Trevelyan entry.
89 G.M. Trevelyan, *Sir George Otto Trevelyan, A Memoir,* p. 110.
90 G.M. Trevelyan, *Sir George Otto Trevelyan, A Memoir,* p. 110.
91 G.M. Trevelyan, *Sir George Otto Trevelyan, A Memoir,* p. 112.
92 G.M. Trevelyan, *Sir George Otto Trevelyan, A Memoir,* p. 113.
93 G.M. Trevelyan, *Sir George Otto Trevelyan, A Memoir,* p. 115.
94 Edward Keith, *Memories of Wallington,* p. 37.
95 *Dictionary of National Biography,* Sir George Otto Trevelyan entry.
96 Buckle, *Queen's Letters,* series III, pp. 561, 565.
97 L. Harcourt, journal, 17 November 1884, Harcourt MSS. *Dictionary of National Biography,* Sir George Otto Trevelyan entry.
98 G.M. Trevelyan, *Sir George Otto Trevelyan, A Memoir,* p. 122.
99 G.M. Trevelyan, *Sir George Otto Trevelyan, A Memoir,* p. 122.
100 G.M. Trevelyan, *Sir George Otto Trevelyan, A Memoir,* p. 123.

101   G.M. Trevelyan, *Sir George Otto Trevelyan, A Memoir*, p.136.
102   *Dictionary of National Biography*, Sir George Otto Trevelyan entry.
103   Roosevelt to Trevelyan, 24 November 1904. Joseph Bishop, *Theodore Roosevelt And His Time*, vol.II, p.144.
104   Henry James to George Otto Trevelyan, 25 November 1903. G.M. Trevelyan, *Sir George Otto Trevelyan, A Memoir*, p.141.
105   G.M. Trevelyan, *Sir George Otto Trevelyan, A Memoir*, p.140.
106   *Dictionary of National Biography*, Sir George Otto Trevelyan entry.
107   Joseph Bishop, *Theodore Roosevelt And His Time*, vol.II, p.137.
108   G.M. Trevelyan.
109   H.W. Brands (ed.), *The Selected Letters of Theodore Roosevelt*, p.358.
110   Joseph Bishop, *Theodore Roosevelt And His Time*, vol.II, p.141.
111   H.W. Brands (ed.), *The Selected Letters of Theodore Roosevelt*, p.494.
112   H.W. Brands (ed.), *The Selected Letters of Theodore Roosevelt*, pp.505–6.
113   Joseph Bishop, *Theodore Roosevelt And His Time*, vol.II, p.183.
114   G.M. Trevelyan, *Sir George Otto Trevelyan, A Memoir*, p.144.
115   Charles Philips Trevelyan to Jennie Lee, 23 February 1949. Jennie Lee papers, Open University.
116   Katharine Trevelyan, *Fool In Love*, p.45.
117   Katharine Trevelyan, *Fool In Love*, p.44.
118   H.G. Wells, *The New Machiavelli*, p.212.
119   Humphrey Trevelyan, *Public and Private*, p.127.
120   Edward Keith, *Memories of Wallington*, pp.13–14.
121   Edward Keith, *Memories of Wallington*, p.40.
122   Charles Philips Trevelyan to Jennie Lee, 23 February 1949. Jennie Lee papers, Open University.
123   G.M. Trevelyan, *Sir George Otto Trevelyan, A Memoir*, p.148.
124   Edward Keith, *Memories of Wallington*, p.66.
125   Katharine Trevelyan, *Fool In Love*, p.63.
126   Charles Philips Trevelyan to Jennie Lee, 23 February 1949. Jennie Lee papers, Open University.
127   *Dictionary of National Biography*, Sir George Otto Trevelyan entry.
128   G.M. Trevelyan, *Sir George Otto Trevelyan, A Memoir*, p.152.

CHAPTER 4

1   Humphrey Trevelyan, *Public and Private*, p.128.
2   *The Diary of Beatrice Webb*, vol. IV, *The Wheel of Life, 1924–1943*, p.350. David Cannadine, *G.M. Trevelyan: A Life in History*, p.11.
3   Leonard Woolf, Foreword to Charles Philips Trevelyan's *Letters from North America and the Pacific*, p.ix.
4   A.J.A. Morris, *C.P. Trevelyan, Portrait of a Radical*, p.2.
5   Reverend C.G. Chittenden to GOT, 31 August 1880. GOT 133, Trevelyan family papers, Newcastle University. A.J.A. Morris, *C.P. Trevelyan, Portrait of a Radical*, p.4.
6   Reverend C.G. Chittenden to GOT, 27 December 1880 and 3 January 1881. GOT 133, Trevelyan family papers, Newcastle University. A.J.A. Morris, *C.P. Trevelyan, Portrait of a Radical*, p.5.
7   Charles Philips Trevelyan to Jennie Lee, 23 February 1949. Jennie Lee papers, Open University Archive.

8   CPT to GOT, 8 November 1885. GOT 37. Trevelyan family papers, Newcastle University. A.J.A. Morris, *C.P. Trevelyan, Portrait of a Radical*, p. 8.
9   CPT to GOT, GOT 36 and GOT 39. Trevelyan family papers, Newcastle University. A.J.A. Morris, *C.P. Trevelyan, Portrait of a Radical*, p. 7.
10   CPT to GOT, 22 May 1892. GOT 45. Trevelyan family papers, Newcastle University. A.J.A. Morris, *C.P. Trevelyan, Portrait of a Radical*, p. 11.
11   CPT to Caroline, Lady Trevelyan, 15 June 1892. GOT 45, Trevelyan family papers, Newcastle University.
12   A.J.A. Morris, *C.P. Trevelyan, Portrait of a Radical*, p. 10.
13   A.J.A. Morris, *C.P. Trevelyan, Portrait of a Radical*, p. 10.
14   A.J.A. Morris, *C.P. Trevelyan, Portrait of a Radical*, p. 14.
15   CPT to Caroline, Lady Trevelyan, 6 February 1893. GOT 46, Trevelyan family papers, Newcastle University. A.J.A. Morris, *C.P. Trevelyan, Portrait of a Radical*, p. 13.
16   CPT to Caroline, Lady Trevelyan, 22 February 1893. GOT 46, Trevelyan family papers, Newcastle University. A.J.A. Morris, *C.P. Trevelyan, Portrait of a Radical*, p. 15.
17   CPT to GOT, 28 July 1893. Trevelyan family papers. A.J.A. Morris, *C.P. Trevelyan, Portrait of a Radical*, p. 17
18   CPT to Caroline, Lady Trevelyan, 30 November 1893, GOT 46. Trevelyan family papers, Newcastle University. A.J.A. Morris, *C.P. Trevelyan, Portrait of a Radical*, p. 18.
19   H.G. Wells, *The New Machiavelli.*
20   CPT to Caroline, Lady Trevelyan, 12 April 1895. Trevelyan family papers, Newcastle University. A.J.A. Morris, *C.P. Trevelyan, Portrait of a Radical*, p. 22.
21   CPT to Caroline, Lady Trevelyan, 5 October 1895. Trevelyan family papers. A.J.A. Morris, *C.P. Trevelyan, Portrait of a Radical*, p. 23.
22   CPT to Caroline, Lady Trevelyan, 5 December 1895. GOT 48. A.J.A. Morris, *C.P. Trevelyan, Portrait of a Radical*, p. 25.
23   Boston Speech, CPT 52, Trevelyan family papers. A.J.A. Morris, *C.P. Trevelyan, Portrait of a Radical*, p. 24.
24   Leonard Woolf, Foreword to Charles Philips Trevelyan's *Letters from North America and the Pacific*, p. xv.
25   Leonard Woolf, Foreword to Charles Philips Trevelyan's *Letters from North America and the Pacific*, p. xvi.
26   Charles Philips Trevelyan, *Letters from North America and the Pacific, 1898*, p. 3.
27   Charles Philips Trevelyan, *Letters from North America and the Pacific, 1898*, p. 21.
28   Charles Philips Trevelyan, *Letters from North America and the Pacific, 1898*, p. 20.
29   Charles Philips Trevelyan, *Letters from North America and the Pacific, 1898*, p. 15.
30   Charles Philips Trevelyan, *Letters from North America and the Pacific, 1898*, p. 25.
31   Charles Philips Trevelyan, *Letters from North America and the Pacific, 1898*, p. 14.
32   Charles Philips Trevelyan, *Letters from North America and the Pacific, 1898*, p. 35.
33   Charles Philips Trevelyan, *Letters from North America and the Pacific, 1898*, p. 46.
34   Foreword by Leonard Woolf to Charles Philips Trevelyan, *Letters from North America and the Pacific, 1898*, p. xvii.
35   CPT to the family, 8 May 1898, CPT 3. Trevelyan family papers, Newcastle University. A.J.A. Morris, *C.P. Trevelyan, Portrait of a Radical*, p. 30.
36   Charles Philips Trevelyan, *Letters from North America and the Pacific, 1898*, p. 117.
37   Charles Philips Trevelyan, *Letters from North America and the Pacific, 1898*, p. 128.
38   Charles Philips Trevelyan, *Letters from North America and the Pacific, 1898*, p. 133.
39   Charles Philips Trevelyan, *Letters from North America and the Pacific, 1898*, pp. 138–39.

40   Charles Philips Trevelyan, *Letters from North America and the Pacific, 1898*, p. 140.
41   CPT to Herbert Samuel, 2 October 1898, CPT 2. Trevelyan family papers. A.J.A. Morris, *C.P. Trevelyan, Portrait of a Radical*, p. 31.
42   Letter from Charles Philips Trevelyan to Claud Bicknell, 9 November 1950.
43   Philip Staveley Foster, the Tory candidate in Elland.
44   *Manchester Examiner*, February 1899, CPT 51. Trevelyan family papers. A.J.A. Morris, *C.P. Trevelyan, Portrait of a Radical*, p. 32.
45   A.J.A. Morris, *C.P. Trevelyan, Portrait of a Radical*, p. 34.
46   CPT to his constituents, 7 February 1900. A.J.A. Morris, *C.P. Trevelyan, Portrait of a Radical*, p. 37.
47   Humphrey Trevelyan, *Public and Private*, p. 129.
48   CPT to Caroline, Lady Trevelyan, 17 July 1901. CPT. Trevelyan family papers. A.J.A. Morris, *C.P. Trevelyan, Portrait of a Radical*, p. 63.
49   A.J.A. Morris, *C.P. Trevelyan, Portrait of a Radical*, p. 64.
50   Mary, Lady Trevelyan, 'The Number of My Days', published privately, 1963.
51   Pat Jalland, *Women, Marriage and Politics 1860–1914*, p. 73.
52   CPT to Molly Trevelyan, 20 December 1903. CPT. Trevelyan family papers. A.J.A. Morris, *C.P. Trevelyan, Portrait of a Radical*, p. 66.
53   Mary, Lady Trevelyan, 'The Number of My Days', published privately, 1963.
54   Jennie Lee, *My Life With Nye*, p. 67.
55   Humphrey Trevelyan, *Public and Private*, p. 139.
56   Katherine Trevelyan, *Fool In Love*, p. 16.
57   Pat Jalland, *Women, Marriage and Politics 1860–1914*, p. 249.
58   Pat Jalland, *Women, Marriage and Politics 1860–1914*, pp. 243–44.
59   Molly Trevelyan's diary, 4 January 1906. Pat Jalland, *Women, Marriage and Politics 1860–1914*, p. 244.
60   Molly Trevelyan to CPT, 15 December 1906. Trevelyan family papers. Pat Jalland, *Women, Marriage and Politics 1860–1914*, p. 245.
61   GOT to H.H. Asquith, 15 April 1908. A.J.A. Morris, *C.P. Trevelyan, Portrait of a Radical*, p. 74.
62   A.J.A. Morris, *C.P. Trevelyan, Portrait of a Radical*, p. 117.
63   CPT to MKT, 4 August 1914. A.J.A. Morris, *C.P. Trevelyan, Portrait of a Radical*, p. 117.
64   CPT to Elland constituents, 5 August 1914.
65   CPT to Molly Trevelyan, 14 September 1914. Trevelyan family papers. A.J.A. Morris, *C.P. Trevelyan, Portrait of a Radical*, p. 127.
66   CPT to Molly Trevelyan, 26 December 1914. Trevelyan family papers.
67   *Brighouse Echo*, 8 October 1915. CPT 42 Trevelyan family papers.
68   CPT's parliamentary constituency.
69   *Daily Sketch*, CPT 42 Trevelyan family papers.
70   C.P. Scott to CPT, 5 September 1914, CPT 73 Trevelyan family papers.
71   A.J.P. Taylor, *The Trouble Makers*, p. 132.
72   GBS to CPT, 28 February 1918, Trevelyan family papers.
73   Charles Philips Trevelyan, 'Can Socialism and Radicalism Unite?', *The Nation*, 1917.
74   J.B. Pollok McCale to CPT, 3 February 1918, CPT 83 Trevelyan family papers.
75   Molly Trevelyan to CPT, Humphrey Trevelyan, *Public and Private*, p. 131.
76   CPT to Molly Trevelyan, Humphrey Trevelyan, *Public and Private*, p. 132.
77   CPT to Jennie Lee, 23 February 1949. Jennie Lee papers, Open University archive.

78   A.J.P. Taylor, *The Trouble Makers*, p.166
79   A.J.A. Morris, *C.P. Trevelyan, Portrait of a Radical*, p.155.
80   GOT to CPT, 23 January 1924, CPT 108, Trevelyan family papers.
81   CPT to Bernard Russell, May 1929. CPT 138, Trevelyan family papers.
82   Draft to CPT letter to Ramsay MacDonald, 19 February 1931.
83   Notes for CPT speech to PLP, CPT 142 Trevelyan family papers.
84   CPT to RCT, February 1931.
85   Autobiographical notes kept by Morgan Philips Price, given to the author by Martin Bulmer, son of CPT.
86   Mrs Winchester Bennett, 'Roaming around England in a Land Rover', talk given to the New Haven Thursday Club, 1957.
87   CPT speech to tenants, April 1929, Trevelyan family papers.
88   Lord Lothian's speech at the National Trust Conference, 19 July 1935.
89   'The Bequest of Wallington to the National Trust', BBC Radio broadcast by Sir Charles Trevelyan, ex Newcastle, 23 March 1937.
90   As told by Robin Dower to the author, August 2005.
91   Marjorie, Lady Weaver, interview with the author, 2002.
92   Geoffrey Trevelyan, *From Wallington: Sir Charles Trevelyan and the National Trust.*
93   Frances Farrer, *Sir George Trevelyan and the New Spiritual Awakening*, p.35.
94   GMT to Robert Calverley Trevelyan, 8 April 1941, RCT papers, Trinity College, Cambridge. Peter Raina, *G.M. Trevelyan: A Portrait in Letters*, pp.138–39.
95   Letter from Sir Charles Trevelyan to George Macaulay Trevelyan, 21 October 1941.
96   Source: National Trust.
97   Source: National Trust.
98   Letter from James Lees-Milne to Bruce Thompson, National Trust. James Lees-Milne, *People and Places*, p.163.
99   Macaulay shaved while reading, hence the soap and blood on his books.
100 Harriet Trevelyan, as told to the author.
101 Letter to Claud Bicknell, 9 November 1950.
102 Harriet Trevelyan, as told to the author.
103 Katharine Trevelyan, *Fool In Love*.
104 MacLeod Matheson, National Trust secretary.
105 James Lees-Milne, *People and Places*, p.162.
106 James Lees-Milne, *People and Places*, p.162.
107 Tom Trevelyan, as told to the author.
108 Harriet Trevelyan, as told to the author.
109 Katharine Trevelyan, *Fool In Love*, pp.73–74.
110 Janet Trevelyan to Mary Moorman, 8 June 1939. MM 2/4/18/13, Trevelyan family papers, Newcastle University.
111 Janet Trevelyan to Mary Moorman. MM 2/4/18/13, Trevelyan family papers, Newcastle University.
112 George Lowthian Trevelyan, Molly's son.
113 Katharine (Kitty) Trevelyan to Ann Gillie, 6 September 1941.
114 Molly Trevelyan to Ann Gillie, around the time of Martin Bulmer's birth, 1943.
115 Molly Trevelyan to Ann Gillie, 10 September 1943.
116 Molly Trevelyan to Ann Gillie, 10 October 1943.
117 Edith Bulmer to CPT, 3 September. CPT 154–156, Trevelyan family papers, Newcastle University.
118 Janet Trevelyan to Mary Moorman, 17 August 1939. MM 2/4/18/19, Trevelyan family papers, Newcastle University.

119 Tom Trevelyan, as told to the author.
120 Michael Foot, interviewed by the author for *People and Politics*, BBC World Service Radio, 22 February 2002.
121 Jennie Lee to Frank Wise, 8 March 1933, Jennie Lee papers, Open University archive.
122 Jennie Lee, *My Life With Nye*, p.54.
123 Broadcast by the author for *People and Politics*, BBC World Service Radio, 22 February 2002.
124 George Macaulay Trevelyan to Mary Moorman, 20 September 1938. David Cannadine, *G.M. Trevelyan: A Life in History*, p.134.
125 CPT to Joseph Stalin, 19 January 1939, CPT 264, Trevelyan family papers.
126 CPT to Nehru, 16 October 1954, CPT 264, Trevelyan family papers.
127 Nehru to CPT, 21 November 1954, CPT 264, Trevelyan family papers.
128 CPT to Jennie Lee, 23 February 1949. Jennie Lee papers, Open University.
129 CPT to Claud (Bicknell?), 9 November 1950.
130 Humphrey Trevelyan, *Public and Private*, p.140.

CHAPTER 5

1   G.M. Trevelyan, *Clio: A Muse*.
2   J.H. Plumb, *G.M. Trevelyan*.
3   Broadcast by the author for *People and Politics*, BBC World Service Radio, 22 February 2002.
4   *The Diary of Beatrice Webb*, vol.II, p.183.
5   G.M. Trevelyan, *An Autobiography and Other Essays*, p.7.
6   G.M. Trevelyan, *An Autobiography and Other Essays*, p.7.
7   G.M. Trevelyan, *Sir George Otto Trevelyan, A Memoir*, p.114.
8   Robert Calverley Trevelyan, *Windfalls*, 1944.
9   Jennie Lee, *My Life With Nye*, p.60.
10 G.M. Trevelyan, *Sir George Otto Trevelyan, A Memoir*, p.134.
11 Mary Moorman, *George Macaulay Trevelyan*, p.9.
12 GMT to Mary Moorman, 16 July 1917. Mary Moorman, *George Macaulay Trevelyan*, p.11.
13 G.M. Trevelyan, *An Autobiography and Other Essays*, p.9.
14 Mary Moorman, *George Macaulay Trevelyan*, p.19.
15 G.M. Trevelyan, *An Autobiography and Other Essays*, p.23.
16 G.M. Trevelyan, *An Autobiography and Other Essays*, p.3.
17 G.M. Trevelyan, *An Autobiography and Other Essays*, p.3.
18 Mary Moorman, *George Macaulay Trevelyan*, p.24.
19 George Otto Trevelyan, *Life and Letters of Lord Macaulay*, p.54.
20 George Otto Trevelyan, *Life and Letters of Lord Macaulay*, p.55.
21 Mary Moorman, *George Macaulay Trevelyan*, p.43.
22 *The Diary of Beatrice Webb*, vol. II, pp.85–86.
23 Paul Levy (ed.), *The Letters of Lytton Strachey*, p.66.
24 George Macaulay Trevelyan, *England Under the Stuarts*, 1904.
25 Lytton Strachey to Leonard Woolf, 2 December 1904. Paul Levy (ed.), *The Letters of Lytton Strachey*, p.39.
26 GMT to CPT. Mary Moorman, *George Macaulay Trevelyan*, p.46.
27 GMT to CPT. Mary Moorman, *George Macaulay Trevelyan*, p.45.
28 GMT to CPT. Mary Moorman, *George Macaulay Trevelyan*, p.45.

29   GMT to CPT. Mary Moorman, *George Macaulay Trevelyan*, p.45.
30   H.G. Wells, *The New Machiavelli*, p.193.
31   H.G. Wells, *The New Machiavelli*, p.193.
32   H.G. Wells, *The New Machiavelli*, p.222.
33   Mary Moorman, *George Macaulay Trevelyan*, p.52.
34   David Cannadine, *G.M. Trevelyan: A Life in History*, p.183.
35   Mary Moorman, *George Macaulay Trevelyan*, p.48.
36   Mary Moorman, *George Macaulay Trevelyan*, p.75.
37   Mary Moorman, *George Macaulay Trevelyan*, p.79.
38   J.B. Bury, 'The Science of History', in J.B. Bury, *Selected Essays*.
39   David Cannadine, *G.M. Trevelyan: A Life in History*, p.214.
40   George Macaulay Trevelyan, *Clio, A Muse*, 1913.
41   J.H. Plumb, *G.M. Trevelyan*, p.9.
42   G.R. Elton, 'George Macaulay Trevelyan', in G. Smith, *1000 Makers of the Twentieth Century*. G.R. Elton and R.W. Fogel, *Which Road to the Past? Two Views of History*. David Cannadine, *G.M. Trevelyan: A Life in History*, p.218.
43   J.P. Kenyon, *The History Men*, pp.227, 231.
44   J.C.D. Clark, *Revolution and Rebellion*, pp.18–19. David Cannadine, *G.M. Trevelyan: A Life in History*, p.219.
45   Stefan Collini, *English Pasts: Writing the 'National History'*, p.25.
46   Richard Evans, *In Defence of History*, p.251.
47   David Cannadine, *G.M. Trevelyan: A Life in History*, p.227.
48   Mary Moorman, *George Macaulay Trevelyan*, p.90.
49   Joseph Bishop, *Theodore Roosevelt And His Time*, vol.II, pp.141–142.
50   Humphrey Trevelyan, *Public and Private*, p.159.
51   Humphrey Trevelyan, *Public and Private*, p.160.
52   John Sutherland, *Mrs Humphry Ward, Eminent Victorian, Pre-Eminent Edwardian*, p.177.
53   John Sutherland, *Mrs Humphry Ward, Eminent Victorian, Pre-Eminent Edwardian*, p.178.
54   Mary Moorman, *George Macaulay Trevelyan*, p.90.
55   G.M. Trevelyan, *An Autobiography and Other Essays*, p.29.
56   Dorothy Ward's diary, 20 April 1903, UCL. John Sutherland, *Mrs Humphry Ward, Eminent Victorian, Pre-Eminent Edwardian*, p.250.
57   Mrs Humphry Ward to Dorothy Ward, 20 May 1903. John Sutherland, *Mrs Humphry Ward, Eminent Victorian, Pre-Eminent Edwardian*, p.250.
58   John Sutherland, *Mrs Humphry Ward, Eminent Victorian, Pre-Eminent Edwardian*, p.250.
59   Mary Moorman, *George Macaulay Trevelyan*, p.91.
60   Caroline, Lady Trevelyan to RCT and his wife Bessie Trevelyan, 20 March 1904. David Cannadine, *G.M. Trevelyan: A Life in History*, p.36.
61   Lytton Strachey, 1904.
62   Michael Holroyd, *Lytton Strachey*, vol.I, pp.189–190.
63   Humphrey Trevelyan, *Public and Private*, p.160.
64   Mary Moorman, *George Macaulay Trevelyan*, p.93.
65   G.M. Trevelyan, *An Autobiography and Other Essays*, p.31.
66   J.H. Plumb, *G.M. Trevelyan*, p.18.
67   J.H. Plumb, *G.M. Trevelyan*, p.18.
68   Mary Moorman, *George Macaulay Trevelyan*, p.102.
69   Mary Moorman, *George Macaulay Trevelyan*, p.95.
70   Mary Moorman, *George Macaulay Trevelyan*, p.95.

A Very British Family

71 Janet Trevelyan, *Two Stories*, p.129.
72 GMT to GOT/Lady Trevelyan, 21 April 1911. Trevelyan family papers, Newcastle University.
73 GMT to GOT/Lady Trevelyan, 19 April 1911. Trevelyan family papers, Newcastle University.
74 Mrs G.M. Trevelyan, *The Life of Mrs Humphry Ward*, p.255.
75 CPT to Caroline, Lady Trevelyan, 19 April 1911, Trevelyan family papers, Newcastle University.
76 GMT to GOT/Lady Trevelyan, 21 April 1911. Trevelyan family papers, Newcastle University.
77 Janet Trevelyan to Mrs Humphry Ward, 23 April 1911. Trevelyan family papers, Newcastle University.
78 Humphrey Trevelyan.
79 Geoffrey Winthrop Young, *Oliver's Man: Two Stories by Janet Trevelyan*, p.130.
80 A.L. Rowse, *Memories of Men and Women*, p.107.
81 Quoted by Janet Trevelyan, letter to Mary Moorman, 8 June 1939. Mary Moorman papers, Newcastle University.
82 Janet Trevelyan to Mary Moorman, 8 June 1939. Mary Moorman papers, Newcastle University.
83 Janet Trevelyan to Mary Moorman, 8 June 1939. Mary Moorman papers, Newcastle University.
84 Humphrey Trevelyan, *Public and Private*, p.161.
85 Mary Moorman, *George Macaulay Trevelyan*, p.126.
86 Mary Moorman, *George Macaulay Trevelyan*, p.126.
87 Mary Moorman, *George Macaulay Trevelyan*, p.126.
88 Julian Huxley, *Memories*, p.101.
89 Broadcast by the author, *People and Politics*, BBC World Service Radio, 22 February 2002.
90 GMT to CPT, 7 August 1914. Trevelyan family papers, Newcastle University.
91 GMT to CPT, 14 August 1914. Trevelyan family papers, Newcastle University.
92 GMT to CPT, 14 August 1914, Trevelyan family papers, Newcastle University.
93 GMT to CPT, 13 August 1914, Trevelyan family papers, Newcastle University.
94 GMT to CPT, 15 August 1914. Trevelyan family papers, Newcastle University.
95 GMT to CPT, 16 August 1914, Trevelyan family papers, Newcastle University.
96 GMT to CPT, 15 March 1915, Trevelyan family papers, Newcastle University.
97 Mary Moorman, *George Macaulay Trevelyan*, p.156.
98 Mary Moorman, *George Macaulay Trevelyan*, p.155.
99 Mary Moorman, *George Macaulay Trevelyan*, p.147.
100 Mary Moorman, *George Macaulay Trevelyan*, p.165.
101 Broadcast by the author, *People and Politics*, BBC World Service Radio, 22 February 2002.
102 Mary Moorman, *George Macaulay Trevelyan*, p.169.
103 Mary Moorman, *George Macaulay Trevelyan*, p.223.
104 King George V's Silver Jubilee speech, Westminster Hall, 9 May 1935.
105 GMT to Mary Moorman, 15 November 1936. Mary Moorman, *George Macaulay Trevelyan*, p.224.
106 Mary Moorman, *George Macaulay Trevelyan*, p.225.
107 GMT to Robert Calverley Trevelyan, 4 October 1939. RCT papers, Trinity College. Peter Raina, *G.M. Trevelyan: A Portrait in Letters*, p.126.
108 Molly Trevelyan to Mr and Mrs Winchester Bennett, 10 February 1939. Private correspondence, Trevelyan family.

109 Foreign Office 371/24, 951, file 60, paper 6, 173 ff 40–54. Includes text of GMT's broadcast. Mary Moorman, *George Macaulay Trevelyan*, p.229.
110 GMT to Mary Moorman, 7 March 1940. David Cannadine, *G.M. Trevelyan: A Life in History*, p.134.
111 Letter by GMT to *Sunday Times*, 11 May 1940.
112 George Macaulay Trevelyan, 'All In The Front Line Now: Are We Ready Heart and Soul?', *Sunday Times*, 7 July 1940.
113 GMT to Robert Calverley Trevelyan, 27 September 1940. RCT papers, Trinity College. Peter Raina, *G.M. Trevelyan: A Portrait in Letters*, p.130.
114 J.R. Colville, *The Fringes of Power: 10 Downing St Diaries 1939–1955*, p.253. David Cannadine, *G.M. Trevelyan: A Life in History*, p.135.
115 Mary Moorman, *George Macaulay Trevelyan*, p.231.
116 Mary Moorman, *George Macaulay Trevelyan*, p.232.
117 G.M. Trevelyan, *English Social History*, Introduction.
118 J.H. Plumb, *G.M. Trevelyan*, p.31.
119 G.M. Trevelyan, *English Social History*.
120 G.M. Trevelyan, *English Social History*, Introduction to post-war editions.
121 Mary Moorman, *George Macaulay Trevelyan*, p.236.
122 Molly Trevelyan interviewed by the author, 2002.
123 Leonard Woolf, Foreword to Charles Philips Trevelyan's *Letters from North America and the Pacific*, p.x.
124 John Prestwich, interviewed by the author, 2002.
125 H.G. Wells, *The New Machiavelli*.
126 Mrs Winchester Bennett, 'Roaming around England in a Land Rover', talk given to the New Haven Thursday Club, 1957.
127 Morgan Philips Price, autobiographical notes 1931.
128 Broadcast by the author, *People and Politics*, BBC World Service Radio, 22 February 2002.
129 GMT to Robert Calverley Trevelyan, 20 May 1949. RCT papers, Trinity College, Cambridge. Peter Raina, *G.M. Trevelyan: A Portrait in Letters*, p.154.
130 Leonard Woolf, Foreword to Charles Philips Trevelyan's *Letters from North America and the Pacific*, p.x.
131 George Macaulay Trevelyan, 'A Layman's Love of Letters', Clark Lectures, Cambridge University 1953.
132 A.L. Rowse, *Memories of Men and Women*, p.109.
133 Mary Moorman, *George Macaulay Trevelyan*, p.245.

CHAPTER 6

1 Janet Trevelyan, *Two Stories*, p.24.
2 Janet Trevelyan, *Two Stories*, p.24.
3 Janet Trevelyan, *Two Stories*, p.27.
4 Janet Trevelyan, *Two Stories*, p.37.
5 Janet Trevelyan, *Two Stories*, p.50.
6 Janet Trevelyan, *The Life of Mrs Humphry Ward*, p.254.
7 Janet Trevelyan, *Two Stories*, p.133.
8 Janet Trevelyan, *Two Stories*, p.133.
9 Humphry Trevelyan, *Goethe and the Greeks*.
10 George Macaulay Trevelyan to George Otto Trevelyan, 8 June 1936, Trevelyan family papers, Newcastle University.

11   George Macaulay Trevelyan to Mr Winchester Bennett, 27 March 1936. Private correspondence, Trevelyan family.

12   George Macaulay Trevelyan to Mr Winchester Bennett, 20 June 1936. Private correspondence, Trevelyan family.

13   George Macaulay Trevelyan to Mary Moorman, March 1936. Trevelyan family papers, Newcastle University.

14   King's College annual report, November 1964.

15   Kitty Trevelyan, daughter of Charles Philips Trevelyan.

16   Molly Trevelyan to Mrs Winchester Bennett, 19 January 1938. Private correspondence, Trevelyan family.

17   Humphry Trevelyan to Mr and Mrs Winchester Bennett, 21 February 1938. Private correspondence, Trevelyan family.

18   George Macaulay Trevelyan to Mr Winchester Bennett, 6 August 1936. Private correspondence, Trevelyan family.

19   Humphry Trevelyan, *Goethe and the Greeks.*

20   Molly Trevelyan to Mr and Mrs Winchester Bennett, 18 September 1936. Private correspondence, Trevelyan family.

21   Molly Trevelyan to Mr and Mrs Winchester Bennett, 18 September 1936. Private correspondence, Trevelyan family.

22   Molly Trevelyan to Mr and Mrs Winchester Bennett, 4 October 1936. Private correspondence, Trevelyan family.

23   Molly Trevelyan to Mr and Mrs Winchester Bennett, 4 October 1936. Private correspondence, Trevelyan family.

24   Molly Trevelyan to Mr and Mrs Winchester Bennett, 27 December 1936. Private correspondence, Trevelyan family.

25   George Macaulay Trevelyan to Mr Winchester Bennett, 31 July 1937. Private correspondence, Trevelyan family.

26   Humphry Trevelyan to Mr Winchester Bennett, 9 October 1936. Private correspondence, Trevelyan family.

27   Humphry Trevelyan to Mr Winchester Bennett, 9 October 1936. Private correspondence, Trevelyan family.

28   Molly Trevelyan to Mr and Mrs Winchester Bennett, 27 December 1936. Private correspondence, Trevelyan family.

29   Humphry Trevelyan to Mr and Mrs Winchester Bennett, 27 December 1936. Private correspondence, Trevelyan family.

30   Janet Trevelyan to Mrs Winchester Bennett, 2 January 1937. Private correspondence, Trevelyan family.

31   Molly Trevelyan to Mr and Mrs Winchester Bennett. Private correspondence, Trevelyan family.

32   Janet Trevelyan to Mrs Winchester Bennett, 20 April 1937. Private correspondence, Trevelyan family.

33   G.M. Trevelyan.

34   Molly Trevelyan to Mr and Mrs Winchester Bennett, 29 March 1938. Private correspondence, Trevelyan family.

35   Johnson's Point, the Bennett family summer home, near Branford, Connecticut.

36   Molly Trevelyan to Mr and Mrs Winchester Bennett, 14 June 1938. Private correspondence, Trevelyan family.

37   Dorothy Ward, Janet Trevelyan's sister.

38   Molly Trevelyan to Mr and Mrs Winchester Bennett, 28 June 1938. Private correspondence, Trevelyan family.

39 Mrs Winchester Bennett, 'England During the Crisis', talk given to the New Haven Thursday Club, October 1938.
40 Mrs Winchester Bennett, 'England During the Crisis', talk given to the New Haven Thursday Club, October 1938.
41 Mrs Winchester Bennett, 'England During the Crisis', talk given to the New Haven Thursday Club, October 1938.
42 Mrs Winchester Bennett, 'England During the Crisis', talk given to the New Haven Thursday Club, October 1938.
43 Molly Trevelyan to Mr and Mrs Winchester Bennett, 30 September 1938. Private correspondence, Trevelyan family.
44 Mrs Winchester Bennett, 'England During the Crisis', talk given to the New Haven Thursday Club, October 1938.
45 Mrs Winchester Bennett, 'England During the Crisis', talk given to the New Haven Thursday Club, October 1938.
46 G.M. Trevelyan.
47 Molly Trevelyan to Mr and Mrs Winchester Bennett, 4 October 1938. Private correspondence, Trevelyan family.
48 Molly Trevelyan to Mr and Mrs Winchester Bennett, 7 September 1939. Private correspondence, Trevelyan family.
49 Humphry Trevelyan to Mr and Mrs Winchester Bennett, 12 September 1939. Private correspondence, Trevelyan family.
50 Dorothy Ward to Mr and Mrs Winchester Bennett, 18 September 1939. Private correspondence, Trevelyan family.
51 Mr Winchester Bennett to Molly Trevelyan, 2 September 1939. Private correspondence, Trevelyan family.
52 Mr Winchester Bennett to Molly Trevelyan, 21 September 1939. Private correspondence, Trevelyan family.
53 *Goethe and the Greeks*, published in 1941.
54 Humphry Trevelyan to Mr and Mrs Winchester Bennett, 22 October 1939. Private correspondence, Trevelyan family.
55 Dorothy Ward to Mrs Winchester Bennett, 3 December 1939. Private correspondence, Trevelyan family.
56 Humphry Trevelyan to Mr Winchester Bennett, 14 April 1940. Private correspondence, Trevelyan family.
57 G.M. Trevelyan to Mr Winchester Bennett, 17 December 1939. Private correspondence, Trevelyan family.
58 Janet Trevelyan to Mrs Winchester Bennett, 29 January 1940. Private correspondence, Trevelyan family.
59 US Embassy London to State Department, Washington, 29 May 1940.
60 2 July 1940, telegram from Humphry Trevelyan to the Bennett family.
61 Humphry Trevelyan to Mr Winchester Bennett, 6 July 1940. Private correspondence, Trevelyan family.
62 'Lightning war'.
63 Humphry Trevelyan to Mr Winchester Bennett, 9 September 1940. Private correspondence, Trevelyan family.
64 Molly Trevelyan to Mr and Mrs Winchester Bennett, 13 September 1940. Private correspondence, Trevelyan family.
65 Humphry Trevelyan's wartime diary, Trevelyan family.
66 Humphry Trevelyan's wartime diary, Trevelyan family.
67 Humphry Trevelyan's wartime diary, Trevelyan family.
68 Humphry Trevelyan's wartime diary, Trevelyan family.

69   Humphry Trevelyan to Mr and Mrs Winchester Bennett, 24 November 1940. Private correspondence, Trevelyan family.

70   G.M. Trevelyan.

71   Molly Trevelyan to the Bennett family, 1 December 1940. Private correspondence, Trevelyan family.

72   Humphry Trevelyan to Mr and Mrs Winchester Bennett, 24 November 1940. Private correspondence, Trevelyan family

73   Michael Smith, *Station X*, p. 91.

74   F.H. Hinsley and Alan Stripp, *Codebreakers: The Inside Story of Bletchley Park*, p. 12.

75   Christopher Andrew, 'From Bletchley in Pre-War Perspective', in Michael Smith and Ralph Erskine (eds), *Action This Day*, p. 1.

76   Molly Trevelyan to Mr and Mrs Winchester Bennett, 14 September 1941. Private correspondence, Trevelyan family.

77   Molly Trevelyan to Mr and Mrs Winchester Bennett, 13 October 1941. Private correspondence, Trevelyan family.

78   Janet Trevelyan to Mrs Winchester Bennett, 31 October 1941. Private correspondence, Trevelyan family.

79   The Duty Officer, Hut 3, by Ralph Bennett. From Hinsley and Stripp, *Codebreakers*, p. 30. Alastair Denniston originally called for the recruitment of 'men of the professor type' to Government Code and Cipher School.

80   Ralph Bennett, 'The Duty Officer, Hut 3', in F.H. Hinsley and Alan Stripp, *Codebreakers: The Inside Story of Bletchley Park*, p. 31.

81   Ralph Bennett, 'The Duty Officer, Hut 3', in F.H. Hinsley and Alan Stripp, *Codebreakers: The Inside Story of Bletchley Park*, p. 30.

82   Michael Smith, *Station X*, p. 35.

83   Could be 'Weltreise'.

84   Michael Smith, *Station X*, p. 35.

85   Michael Smith, *Station X*, p. 39.

86   Michael Smith, *Station X*, p. 40.

87   John Prestwich, interviewed by the author, 18 June 2002.

88   Ron Gray, interviewed by the author, 13 August 2002.

89   Molly Trevelyan to Mr and Mrs Winchester Bennett, 26 September 1942. Private correspondence, Trevelyan family.

90   Professor Richard Holmes, BBC History website.

91   Molly Trevelyan to Mr and Mrs Winchester Bennett, 19 October 1942. Private correspondence, Trevelyan family.

92   Ralph Bennett, 'The Duty Officer, Hut 3', in F.H. Hinsley and Alan Stripp, *Codebreakers: The Inside Story of Bletchley Park*, p. 37.

93   John Prestwich, interviewed by the author, 18 June 2002.

94   Dorothy Ward to Mrs Winchester Bennett, 9 December 1942. Private correspondence, Trevelyan family.

95   John Prestwich, interviewed by the author, 18 June 2002.

96   William Millward, 'Life In and Out of Hut 3', in F.H. Hinsley and Alan Stripp, *Codebreakers: The Inside Story of Bletchley Park*, p. 21.

97   John Prestwich, interviewed by the author, 18 June 2002.

98   Edward Thomas, 'A Naval Officer in Hut 3', in F.H. Hinsley and Alan Stripp, *Codebreakers: The Inside Story of Bletchley Park*, p. 49.

99   John Prestwich, interviewed by the author, 18 June 2002.

100   Michael Smith and Ralph Erskine (eds), *Action This Day*, p. 2.

101   Molly Trevelyan, interviewed by the author, 11 August 2002.

102 Molly Trevelyan to Mr and Mrs Winchester Bennett, 24 January 1942. Private correspondence, Trevelyan family
103 Molly Trevelyan to Mr and Mrs Winchester Bennett, 22 February 1942. Private correspondence, Trevelyan family.
104 Mary Harriet Trevelyan, Molly and Humphry's younger daughter.
105 Molly Trevelyan to Mr and Mrs Winchester Bennett, 6 April 1942. Private correspondence, Trevelyan family.
106 George Macaulay Trevelyan to Mr Winchester Bennett, 20 April 1942. Private correspondence, Trevelyan family.
107 Dorothy Ward to Mrs Winchester Bennett, 9 December 1942. Private correspondence, Trevelyan family.
108 King's College annual report, November 1964.
109 King's College annual report, November 1964.
110 Godfrey Curtis, note for the author, August 2005.
111 Godfrey Curtis, note for the author, August 2005.
112 Ron Gray, interviewed by the author, 13 August 2002.
113 Godfrey Curtis, August 2005.

Epilogue

1 David Cannadine, *G.M. Trevelyan: A Life in History*, p. 18.
2 Noel Annan, *Our Age*, p. 7.
3 Stefan Collini, *English Pasts: Writing the 'National History'*, p. 24.
4 Noel Annan, 'The Intellectual Aristocracy', in Noel Annan, *The Dons*, p. 340.
5 Humphrey Trevelyan, *Public and Private*, p. 141.
6 Leonard Woolf, Foreword to Charles Philips Trevelyan's *Letters from North America and the Pacific*.
7 Humphrey Trevelyan, *Public and Private*, p. 145.
8 Humphrey Trevelyan, *Public and Private*, p. 145.
9 Humphrey Trevelyan, *Public and Private*, p. 144.
10 *Dictionary of National Biography*, Julian Otto Trevelyan entry.
11 *Dictionary of National Biography*, Julian Otto Trevelyan entry.
12 *Dictionary of National Biography*, George Lowthian Trevelyan entry.
13 Humphrey Trevelyan, *Public and Private*, p. 60.
14 G.M. Trevelyan to Sir George Otto Trevelyan, 25 December 1898.

BIBLIOGRAPHY

Annan, Noel, *Our Age*, 1990
Annan, Noel, *The Dons*, 1999
Brands, H.W. (ed.), *The Selected Letters of Theodore Roosevelt*, 2001
Briggs, Asa, *Victorian People*, 1955
Bucklin Bishop, Joseph, *Theodore Roosevelt and His Time*, vol. II, 1920
Butterfield, Herbert, *The Whig Interpretation of History*, 1965
Cannadine, David, *G.M. Trevelyan, A Life In History*, 1992
Cannadine, David, *The Decline and Fall of the British Aristocracy*, 1999
Cannadine, David, *The Rise and Fall of Class in Britain*, 1999
Clive, John, *Macaulay, The Shaping of the Historian*, 1973
Collini, Stefan, *English Pasts*, 1999
Collini, Stefan, *Public Moralists*, 1991
Dangerfield, George, *The Strange Death of Liberal England*, 1935
Dower, Pauline, *Living at Wallington*, 1984
Edwards, R. Dudley and Williams T. Desmond (eds), *The Great Famine: Studies in Irish History 1845–1852*, 1956
Evans, Richard J., *In Defence of History*, 1997
Farrer, Frances, *Sir George Trevelyan and the New Spiritual Awakening*, 2002
Haines, Robin, *Charles Trevelyan and the Great Irish Famine*, 2004
Hennessy, Peter, *Whitehall*, 1989
Hinsley, F.H. and Alan Stripp, *Codebreakers: The Inside Story of Bletchley Park*, 1993
Hobsbawm, Eric, *Age of Extremes: The Short Twentieth Century, 1914–1991*, 1994
Hollis, Patricia, *Jennie Lee, A Life*, 1997
Huws Jones, Enid, *Mrs Humphry Ward*, 1973
Jalland, Pat, *Women, Marriage and Politics, 1860–1914*, 1986
Kee, Robert, *Ireland, A History*, 1980
Keith, Edward, *Memories of Wallington*, 1939
Lees-Milne, James, *People and Places: Country House Donors and the National Trust*, 1992
Levy, Paul (ed.), *The Letters of Lytton Strachey*, 2005
Macaulay, Lord, *The History of England, 1848–1861*,
Mandler, Peter, *History and National Life*, 2002
Moorman, Mary, *George Macaulay Trevelyan: A Memoir*, 1980
Morris, A.J.A., *C.P. Trevelyan, Portrait of a Radical*, 1977
Ó'Gráda, Cormac, *The Great Irish Famine*, 1989
Plumb, J.H., *G.M. Trevelyan*, 1951
Price, M. Philips, *My Three Revolutions: Russia, Germany, Britain 1917–1969*, 1969
Raina, Peter (ed.), *George Macaulay Trevelyan: A Portrait of Letters*, 2001

Rowse, A.L. *Memories of Men and Women,* 1980
Schama, Simon, *A History of Britain,* vol. III, *1776–2000: The Fate of Empire,* 2002
Sebag-Montefiore, Hugh, *Enigma, the Battle for the Code,* 2000
Siraut, Mary (ed.), *The Trevelyan Letters to 1840,* 1990
Smith, Michael, *Station X: The Codebreakers of Bletchley Park,* 1998
Smith, Michael and Ralph Erskine (eds), *Action This Day,* 2002
Surtees, Virginia (ed.), *Reflections of a Friendship: John Ruskin's letters to Pauline Trevelyan 1848–1866,* 1979
Sutherland, John, *Mrs Humphry Ward: Eminent Victorian, Pre-Eminent Edwardian,* 1990
Taylor, A.J.P., *English History 1914–1945,* 1965
Taylor, A.J.P., *The Trouble Makers: Dissent over Foreign Policy 1792–1939,* 1957
Trevelyan, Charles Philips, *Letters from North America and the Pacific,* 1969
Trevelyan, George Macaulay, *English Social History,* 1942
Trevelyan, George Macaulay, *An Autobiography and Other Essays,* 1949
Trevelyan, George Macaulay, *Garibaldi and the Thousand,* 1909
Trevelyan, George Macaulay, *History of England,* 1926
Trevelyan, George Macaulay, *Poetry and Philosophy of George Meredith,* 1912
Trevelyan, George Macaulay, *Sir George Otto Trevelyan O.M.: A Memoir,* 1932
Trevelyan, George Otto, *The Early History of Charles James Fox,* 1880
Trevelyan, George Otto, *The Life and Letters of Lord Macaulay,* 1881
Trevelyan, George Otto, *The American Revolution,* part II, 1903
Trevelyan, George Otto, *The Competition Wallah,* 1866
Trevelyan, Humphrey, *Public and Private,* 1980
Trevelyan, Humphrey, *The India We Left,* 1972
Trevelyan, Humphry, *Goethe and the Greeks,* 1941
Trevelyan, Janet, *The Life of Mrs Humphry Ward,* 1923
Trevelyan, Janet, *Two Stories,* 1954
Trevelyan, Katharine, *Fool In Love,* 1962
Trevelyan, R.C., *Selected Poems,* 1953
Trevelyan, Raleigh, *A Pre-Raphaelite Circle,* 1978
Trevelyan, Raleigh, *The Golden Oriole: Childhood, Family and Friends in India,* 1987
Trevelyan, Raleigh, *Wallington, Northumberland,* 1994
Trollope, Anthony, *The Three Clerks,* 1858
Vincent, John, *The Formation of the British Liberal Party,* 1966
Waterson, Merlin, *The National Trust, The First Hundred Years,* 1994
Wells, H.G., *The New Machiavelli,* 1911
Wilson, A.N., *The Victorians,* 2002
Woodham-Smith, Cecil, *The Great Hunger: Ireland 1845–1849,* 1962
Young, G.M., *Victorian England: Portrait of an Age,* 1936

INDEX